Solaris™ System Management

New
Riders

New Riders Professional Library

Solaris™ System Management

New Riders

201 West 103rd Street,
Indianapolis, Indiana 46290

John Philcox

Solaris System Management

Trademarks

Warning and Disclaimer

Publisher
David Dwyer

Associate Publisher
Al Valvano

Executive Editor
Stephanie Wall

Managing Editor
Gina Brown

Product Marketing Manager
Stephanie Layton

Publicity Manager
Susan Petro Nixon

Acquisitions Editor
Ann Quinn

Development Editor
Thomas Cirtin

Project Editors
Elise Walter
Sean Monkhouse

Copy Editor
Krista Hansing

Indexer
Chris Morris

Book Designer
Louisa Klucznik

Cover Designer
Aren Howell

Proofreader
Sarah Cisco

Composition
Jeff Bredensteiner
Amy Parker

Contents

About the Author

John Philcox is the owner and director of Mobile Ventures Limited, a computer consultancy based in Cheltenham, Gloucestershire, in the United Kingdom, that provides technical support and management for UNIX systems and networks. He has more than 20 years of experience in IT in a variety of multivendor environments. His first 17 years were spent working for central government, and the last 4 he spent as a consultant in both the public and private sectors.

Sun, SunOS, and Solaris have been John's major computing interest for the last 14 years. He is a certified Solaris system administrator as well as a member of the Institution of Analysts and Programmers and the Institute of Management of Information Systems.

John was the technical editor on the *Solaris 2.6 Administrator Certification Guide, Part II* and the *Solaris 7 Administrator Certification Guide*.

About the Technical Reviewers

These reviewers contributed their considerable hands-on expertise to the entire development process for *Solaris System Management*. As the book was being written, these dedicated professionals reviewed all the material for technical content, organization, and flow. Their feedback was critical to ensuring that *Solaris System Management* fits our readers' need for the highest quality technical information.

Phil Kostenbader is currently employed by Johnson & Johnson network computing services on the Internet Development team. Previously, he worked for Rutgers University as the lone security analyst and firewall consultant. He also worked for IBM Global Services as the team lead for an eight-person system admin group at the Lucent Microelectronics account. With more than 20 years of experience in the UNIX operating system, he represented IBM during Xerox outsourcing contract negotiations as a UNIX/Sun Enterprise 1000 consultant. He also worked at Lafayette College as the networking and systems coordinator and, while there, was involved in the installation of the campus network and the initial configuration and connection to the Internet in 1990. Phil resides on the East Coast with his wife, Karen.

Mary Morris' background includes 19 years in various computer/MIS roles with a wide variety of companies. Her writing in the UNIX world includes authoring *Solaris Implementation: A Guide for System Administrators* and co-authoring a couple of Web-related books and Cybercareers. Mary has taught courses for the ACM, Sun Education, San Jose State University Professional Development Center, the Stanford Alumni Association, ZDU, SmartPlanet, and Element K, and she has spoken at several conferences. She also has worked for or consulted with Sun Microsystems, Cisco Systems, the U.S. Navy, Auspex, Legato, and Bay Networks.

This book is dedicated to my wife, Tracey, and our boys, Nathan and Lewis, for being so patient and for just being there.

Acknowledgments

I would first like to thank Bill Calkins for recommending me to New Riders as a technical editor; it all started from there. Thanks, Bill: I've had a great time.

Thanks also to Phil Kostenbader and Mary Morris for sharing their great wealth of experience in providing a thorough and comprehensive technical review. Your comments have been absolutely priceless.

Thanks to Ann Quinn at New Riders for constantly providing the encouraging words and for being so patient when the deadlines passed—and passed again! And to Tom Cirtin, who has done a magnificent job of pulling it all together: his insight and experience has made all the difference. And to the rest of the team at New Riders for making it all possible.

Finally, I would like to thank all those people I have worked with over the years, but especially Alan Wakefield (AG), for first recognizing that I had an aptitude for computing and encouraging its development, and Andrew Erving—no one could ask for a better boss. Without the experiences and the memories that I'll carry forever, it wouldn't have been nearly as much fun!

Tell Us What You Think

As the reader of this book, you are the most important critic and commentator. We value your opinion and want to know what we're doing right, what we could do better, what areas you'd like to see us publish in, and any other words of wisdom that you're willing to pass our way.

As an Executive Editor for New Riders Publishing, I welcome your comments. You can fax, email, or write me directly to let me know what you did or didn't like about this book—as well as what we can do to make our books stronger.

Please note that I cannot help you with technical problems related to the topic of this book, and that due to the high volume of mail I receive, I might not be able to reply to every message.

When you write, please be sure to include this book's title and author, as well as your name and phone or fax number. I will carefully review your comments and share them with the author and editors who worked on the book.

Fax: 317-581-4663
Email: stephanie.wall@newriders.com
Mail: Stephanie Wall
            Executive Editor
            New Riders Publishing
            201 West 103rd St.
            Indianapolis, IN 46290 USA

Introduction

Welcome to *Solaris System Management*, the first book to be concerned solely with system management issues in a Solaris environment.

Solaris is the most popular UNIX operating environment available commercially—in this environment, many organizations run mission-critical systems upon which their survival could depend. Management of these systems is of critical importance to ensure that they deliver the required level of service and reliability. *Solaris System Management* provides valuable information for system managers responsible for a Solaris environment.

Solaris System Management focuses on strategic issues, such as security and contingency. These two aspects are crucial in protecting one of the organization's most valuable assets: the data. The system manager is the custodian of the company data and ultimately is responsible for its integrity.

A number of products are available, both commercially and in the public domain, that assist the system manager in delivering better service to the customer and managing the environment. This book identifies and investigates a number of these products, their capabilities, and their uses.

The following sections discuss the intended audience, the objectives of the book, how the book is organized, and the typographical conventions used throughout this text.

Who Should Read This Book?

Solaris System Management was written for the system manager. This book is intended both for the new system manager who has recently taken on the responsibility of a Solaris computing environment and for the experienced system manager who might be managing a Solaris environment for the first time after previously working in other computing environments.

This book is not a system administrator guide, although a senior system administrator considering making the transition into system management likely will find the contents of the text useful. The majority of the concepts and policies described within the book are applicable to other vendor platforms; the solutions, however, are all based on the Solaris platform.

The book also likely will be useful to other managers who need to familiarize themselves with the role and practices of the system manager.

The Objectives

The main objective of this book is to provide information for the system manager on a wide range of activities related to the Solaris computing environment. It is essentially a "hands-off" text, although some examples are used to demonstrate key points.

This book also provides details of products that are available to help the system manager carry out his duties effectively. The intention is to create awareness of the products and their use rather than to provide a technical guide of how to install and administer them.

The majority of books that address system management also contain a lot of detail that is more suited to the system administrator. This book attempts to stay focused on the requirements of the system manager, leaving the system administration aspect to the very many excellent books that are available on this subject.

Organization of This Book

The book is organized into three main parts:

- **Part I, "The System Manager"**—The first four chapters investigate the job of the system manager and cover some general issues that are not specific to the Solaris operating environment, but that are applicable to all system managers.

- **Part II, "Management of the Solaris Environment"**—The next seven chapters look at the policies and strategies that the system manager employs as part of the management responsibility. Included in this part are issues of system purchase, upgrade and maintenance, security and disaster recovery, longer-term management of the systems, day-to-day fire-fighting and routine operation, and interoperability with PC networks. The section concludes with a chapter on shells and public domain software.

- **Part III, "Management of the Solaris Network"**—The final three chapters take a brief look at Internet Protocol version 6 and network monitoring. The last chapter looks at some of the network management tools that can be used to manage a Solaris network.

An appendix at the end of the book provides further reference material, including useful books and references to vast sources of information on the World Wide Web, as well as details on how to get help using the available Solaris documentation.

Conventions Used in This Book

Italics are used to indicate file names or commands. For example:

The packages *SUNWaccr* and *SUNWaccu* must be installed before the accounting software can be used.

The following monospaced font is used to show examples of a computer session containing commands entered and the responses returned:

```
$ getfacl monthly

# file: monthly
# owner: john
# group: managers
user::rwx
user:bill:rw-          #effective:rw-
group::r—              #effective:r—
mask:rwx
other: — -
```

Notes appear like this:

Presentation or Content

The inclusion of command output can affect the presentation quality of the document. Although it is important to present the system documentation professionally, the content and ease of update should be the overriding priority.

Onward and Upward

The role of the system manager is complex and diverse. This book details the skills that are required to be able to do the job effectively, from both the technical perspective and the business perspective. The system manager must possess strong interpersonal skills as well as technical ability, and the correct mix of the two leads to a successful system manager.

I

The System Manager

Job Description

1

THIS BOOK IS CONCERNED WITH THE TASK OF SYSTEM management, particularly with reference to systems running the Solaris operating environment. It should be noted that the majority of the principles discussed in the ensuing chapters are applicable to most computer platforms, not just Solaris. Any examples shown here, however, relate to the Solaris platform only. This chapter provides a gentle introduction to system management and, more specifically, to the job of the system manager.

What Is a System Manager?

The designation *system manager* refers to a role, not necessarily to a specific job title, even though "system manager" is itself a valid title and is used for convenience and consistency within this text. As with many other jobs, the titles can vary enormously, so the title of "system manager" could be taken as synonomous with "IT manager," "IS manager," or "senior system administrator."

Before considering the job of the system manager, however, it's important to get an idea of the system itself. Therefore, this chapter begins with a brief overview of the Solaris operating environment.

The Solaris Operating Environment

Solaris is the name for the UNIX-based operating environment provided by Sun Microsystems. It is often referred to as the Solaris operating system, which is not entirely accurate—the operating system, SunOS, is a component of Solaris, not the whole thing.

This book will be looking primarily at Solaris 7, although it may occasionally make reference to new features becoming available with Solaris 8. The components of Solaris 7 are listed here:

- **SunOS 5.7**—The operating system itself. SunOS comprises a number of packages that manage the system resources and provide network connectivity. The SunOS kernel (as of Solaris 2.0) is based on AT&T's system V release 4 kernel, although it contains a number of additions. Previous versions of SunOS were based on the *Berkeley Software Distribution* (BSD) kernel.

- **OpenWindows 3.6.1**—Sun's own *graphical user interface* (GUI) based on AT&T's OpenLook functional specification.

- **OpenWindows Deskset Tools**—A collection of desktop tools that supplements the OpenWindows software. It provides added functionality to the windowing environment in a standard look and feel, such as a mail tool for receiving and composing email, a desktop calculator, an electronic calendar, and an audio tool (for playing audio files), to name a few.

- **Common Desktop Environment (CDE) 1.3**—CDE comprises a windowing environment and a collection of desktop tools similar to those found with openwindows. CDE however, is based on the Motif specification and can be found on many other UNIX vendors' operating environments. It was adopted as the recognized standard for the look and feel of graphical applications at the time (about 1992) by the major UNIX vendors. Recently the standards have begun to shift with Netscape-based interfaces appearing on the market. Additionally, Linux now ships a graphical interface called the K Desktop Environment, or KDE, containing an integrated HTML display—Motif came closest to becoming a defined standard. Figure 1.1 shows the standard CDE desktop.

- **Solaris Documentation Set**—This includes the Answerbook 2 server software and documentation sets for users, system administrators, and developers.

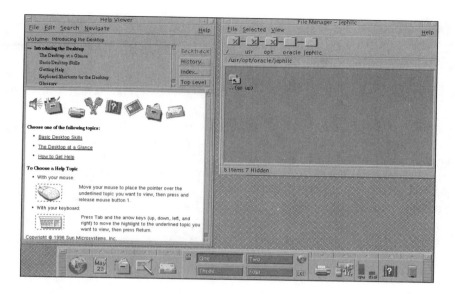

Figure 1.1   The CDE desktop, as it appears the first time it is run.

This list details the core release of Solaris 7, the operating system itself, a choice of two windowing environments with associated deskset tools, and a set of online documentation. This constitutes what is known as the "Desktop Edition" for users just wanting to run the Solaris operating environment on the workstation. The Server Edition of Solaris 7 includes additional software such as Solstice Adminsuite, Disksuite, Backup, and AutoClient. These extra software packages allow server administration and management duties to be performed, something that would not normally be required for a desktop user. If the extra functionality is required, then the server version of the operating environment must be purchased.

Solaris 8, on the other hand, has begun shipping more software with the distribution, such as Oracle 8i, a full enterprise version and a selection of iplanet software. It also includes a CD containing freeware, such as gcc—a freeware C complier—among others.

Warning

The Oracle software, (and some others), is distributed as a noncommercial offering—that is, it cannot be deployed in a production environment. It is provided for evaluation and demonstration purposes. System managers should be aware of this distinction before allowing it to be installed.

The Roles of the System Manager

Most, if not all, businesses today make use of computer systems in one way or another. It might be a very small business with only one personal computer, or a large multinational corporation with huge, complex, networked systems—the principles are the same. They rely, to a varying degree, on computers for their business to function efficiently and effectively.

The increasing reliance placed on computer systems underlines the need for them to be managed properly. In a small business, there probably isn't a system manager as such; rather, a member of the company takes on the role as part of his job. In the larger enterprises, it is a full-time role in itself, with the system manager having responsibility for some or all of the following:

- Computer systems
- System administrators
- Database administrators
- Network administrators
- Technical support department

But that is just the direct, tangible side of system management. There is also another side to this: how the provision of these computing services fits in with the objectives of the business as a whole. The budget for the IT department is often quite considerable. This must be managed properly to ensure that the business gets value for money from the services that it is paying for.

Quite a large proportion of system management is strategic, as in planning for the future of the computer systems. This is particularly relevant with regard to the Internet and the rapid emergence of e-commerce. System security policies are constantly in need of review to ensure that they continue to protect both the computer systems and the data held on them. The formulation of other important policies, such as these, also comes under system management:

- The disaster recovery scenario
- A sensible and realistic backup schedule
- Hardware and software upgrade policies
- Plan for future capacity on the corporate computer network

These are just a few of the issues surrounding system management, but they should give an insight into some of the challenges facing today's system manager. On top of all this, tactical matters also must be handled. These include "fire fighting" specific problems and managing the day-to-day running of the IT department. Remember that system management is not just about computer systems. It is about managing resources, and that includes the staff that the system manager is responsible for.

   The system manager is also a communicator who needs to be able to relate to the customers. At this point, it is worth defining the term *customer* as seen from the system manager's perspective. This is crucial, as you will see in the discussion of service level management in Chapter 3, "Delivering the Goods." The customer is anyone who makes use of the computer systems under the manager's control. This is pretty vague, but it emphasizes the fact that the customer base is potentially very large and diverse.

   The system manager's customers are usually colleagues within the company. Even for a mail-order company taking orders over the Internet, for example, the public is not the customer; the Web sales team is the interface between the system manager and the public, and hence, the customer. Figure 1.2 illustrates the relationships between the system manager and the customer base.

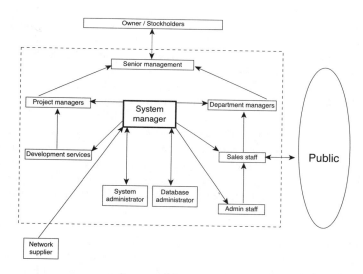

Figure 1.2   The system manager serves his direct customers,
which, in turn, allows them to serve the external customers.

The remainder of this section describes in greater detail the roles that the system manager must assume to be able to carry out his duties. If Shakespeare was right in saying, "All the world's a stage, and all the men and women merely players," then the position of system manager is a one-man play. As you will see, the job of system manager is much more demanding and diverse than you may initially perceive it to be, requiring the playing of many roles with quick scene changes.

As a system manager myself for several years—not just in a Solaris environment, but in others as well, and often in a multivendor environment—I have worn many "hats." I sometimes had to wear several hats at once and resolve the conflicts of interest that can easily arise between them. It is essential that the system manager is acutely aware of which hat he is currently wearing and of the consequences that any actions could have for any of the other "hats" that he will wear in the future. The next section describes the many hats worn by the system manager and the skills employed when wearing them. It also describes the numerous jobs that come under the system management umbrella.

The Manager

First and foremost, the system manager is a manager. The computer systems are his responsibility. It doesn't matter whether it's a single tape or disk, or a multimillion-dollar computer network—they're all part of his domain. Flexibility and versatility are often key attributes that lead to success in this job as well as the ability to remain calm under pressure. This requires someone who can not only react quickly to unforeseen events, but who also can foresee potential problems—and eliminate them—before they happen. It's one of the only jobs in which complex technical issues have to be related to the business as a whole.

The system manager plays a crucial role in ensuring that the IT computer systems provide the necessary services to enable the business to carry out its function. To this end, he must have a good knowledge of the systems, the business, and the corporate objectives and priorities. He must keep abreast of developments within the IT industry and know how they can be used to benefit the business, or be forewarned of an impending threat to the business.

In addition, the system manager is also a manager of staff, which can be quite different from managing the computer systems. Career development and continuing training must be addressed, as well as retention initiatives to try and maintain a stable team. The system manager must be approachable and accessible and have the ability to communicate well with other managers—this is often referred to as "managing across."

Like anyone else in a company, the system manager is an employee and, like all other employees, he works as part of a team aiming to achieve a set of objectives. He will have the same concerns as other employees, including job security, pay raises, and annual assessments.

The system manager has other specific concerns, depending on what role he is playing at a particular time. Some of those roles, and the corresponding concerns, are discussed in the following sections.

Interpreter

In some ways, the system manager can be likened to an interpreter in that technical jargon is translated into plain language. When a problem disrupts service to the customers, senior management will want an explanation at some point of what went wrong and what was done to fix it. The system manager provides the explanation in clear, understandable language, with the objective being to explain things without hearing "And what exactly does all that mean?" from the listener.

It isn't just a case of explaining the problems to management—the system manager also must try to secure the backing and, more important, the money for a new project. The system manager is the person who will fully understand the technical implications and issues surrounding any new venture. He can also relate it to the relevant areas of the business, highlighting the predicted gains to be achieved.

Marketing and Sales Manager

The IT department is one of those areas in which everyone makes use of it to do their own jobs, but it rarely gets an Oscar, much the same as someone working behind the scenes of a major movie production. It falls to the system manager to raise the department's profile and visibility. He has at his disposal a number of opportunities to do this; they must be seized and capitalized on so that senior management is reminded of the important contribution being made to the business. This is crucial if the department is to try to keep up with technological advancements. Some of those opportunities are listed in this section.

Giving a computer suite tour is an ideal opportunity to give the IT department some visibility. It's the chance to tell others how good the department is and how much it has achieved—don't waste it!

The system manager is the perfect choice to present the tour because he has technical knowledge and understands all the jargon, but, more importantly, he can talk about a technical subject to a nontechnical audience and relate it to the business. As an added bonus, he can answer those awkward questions that arise from time to time.

Take an example: The sales director is visiting, has a nontechnical background, and has adopted the Internet sales Web site as his pet project. This is sufficient information for the system manager to know that anything to do with the Internet Web site, or the systems supporting it, will be of interest and will capture the attention of the visitor. Even better, if some improvements have been made by tuning the system to make response times faster, all this will do no harm at all when asking for more money in the budget next year!

But it's not just the computer suite tour that can raise the visibility of the IT department. The system manager will have to provide a regular progress report or summary. This can be a useful vehicle for highlighting instances of considerable success and ensuring that they get the correct exposure to those that matter. It can have a significant impact on the acceptance of future proposals.

In some companies, a regular newsletter is distributed to all employees. This is yet another mechanism for raising awareness. If the system manager contributes a regular column, it lets everyone know what's been going on, especially when relevant to major, innovative projects. A Y2K compliance update was a prime example in the last few years of advertising the success of the IT department.

Financial Wizard

As if managing the systems and staff wasn't enough, the system manager also must be an accountant. The IT budget can be large and complex. Like any other budget holder within the company, the system manager must provide forecast information on a rolling basis throughout each financial year. There is normally pressure to do more with the money that is allocated so that costs can be reduced. It takes a careful eye and considerable knowledge and insight to be able to arrive at the financial year end with the IT budget intact. This topic is discussed in greater detail in Chapter 2, "The IT Budget."

Mediator

The system manager deals with many business functions and with many projects. There will inevitably be times when the priorities and objectives of these different projects collide. To make things worse, the system manager is usually involved with both sides. Here, he must act as the intermediary through whom the problem is resolved. At the same time, he must work to arrive at a solution that is acceptable to both sides. This can normally be achieved through negotiation, but occasionally it may be necessary to offer an incentive to one of the parties so that the work can go ahead.

For example, suppose that one project manager requests that the system be restarted to implement some system changes that have been made, but another project manager maintains that the system should stay up because of important processing that is being carried out. The system manager could resolve this simply by offering to write a quick script that will check every 30 minutes to see if the processing has finished. At this point, the script will alert the system administrator so that the reboot can go ahead at the earliest convenient time. The outcome is that the processing completes and the reboot is also affected; both sides get what they want, and it takes the system manager only five minutes to write the simple script and submit it as a batch job (cron).

This is only a simple example, with an equally simple resolution. Of course, most of the conflicts encountered will not be as easy as this one. This does show, though, that the system manager is in an ideal position to be able to sort out such conflicts.

Financial Responsibilities

In a larger enterprise environment, teams of accountants and financial experts manage the overall company budget, but it is the system manager's responsibility to ensure that the money allocated is spent wisely and in the best interests of the business.

Technical Expert

The system manager is expected to know most things about computers, not just the ones that he is responsible for, but also in general. One of the greatest skills of the system manager is that of troubleshooting. This is based upon a solid foundation of experience and can prove invaluable when trying to resolve a difficult problem that may not have been encountered previously. In this situation, the system manager can identify quickly where the problem lies, based upon experience, thus avoiding wasted time looking elsewhere. Of course, he won't always know the answer, but he should definitely know where to look.

An extension of this role includes passing on some of his expertise to his system administrator(s). This is being done increasingly by companies providing a test environment in which certain faults can be duplicated. In a lab environment, away from the operational pressures, the administrator gets to practice hands-on recovery and diagnosis of problems. This is especially useful for problems that occur very infrequently.

Because the system manager is in charge of all things technical, he often becomes the focal point for all the problems in the office relating to electrical equipment. I have been approached many times by members of staff when the kettle in the kitchen is not working or when the fax machine or photocopier is playing up; the system manager is generally expected to be able to sort them out, one way or another. If someone is using an obsolete piece of software, it is the system manager who will get called to look at a problem with it, even though it may no longer be supported—this just goes with the territory.

Available Training

Sun provides a number of hardware maintenance training courses as part of its training curriculum. Areas covered include desktop (training code SM-210), enterprise (training code SM-240), and storage systems (training code SM-250), as well as a fault analysis workshop (training code ST-350) that guides students through a set of system faults. See the Sun training literature or its Web site (`http://www.sun.com`) for full details of the available training.

The Tasks of the System Manager

As demonstrated, the system manager must be a versatile person who assumes a variety of roles. Now that the basic characteristics of the job have been defined, the next sections cover the tasks that are associated with it, along with the many skills that must be employed in the execution of his duties.

Management of Resources

The system manager carries responsibility for three main resources: the systems themselves, manpower resources, and financial resources. These all must be managed effectively. Financial resources are discussed in Chapter 2 in more detail.

The management of the computer systems, and maybe the network, require the system manager to often make decisions on the proper course of action. The decision could have a significant impact on the business, so he always considers this. This requires knowledge of the business, how it works, and how certain types of change can affect its operation. Not many other positions in the company will have such a comprehensive customer base, ranging from junior office assistant to senior board director.

An example of the type of decision that the system manager might have to make is the provision of application software across the network to the users—say, StarOffice. The system manager can make use of the automounting features of Solaris to make the application available from several different servers; the advantage is that if one of the servers providing the application fails, another will still continue to provide the service to the user. All the user has to do is exit the application and start it again; the connection will be made to another available server. When the failed server is recovered, it simply rejoins the pool of available servers.

As a manager of manpower resources, the system manager has a responsibility for a number of staff members and must make time for them. Staff members are the greatest asset—they can't be put to one side and dealt with when there's some spare time. They need to know that their manager will support them when required. There's nothing worse than a boss who stays locked away in an ivory tower and comes out only when something is needed. He must find time to just have a chat, to see how they're doing, and to let them know that he's around if needed. This makes such a difference.

Learn to Delegate

A good manager learns to delegate tasks to his staff. A busy system manager easily can take on too much and become overloaded. A senior system administrator looking for greater responsibility can lighten the load on a busy system manager and, at the same time, gain valuable management experience.

The Helicopter View

There is a requirement for the system manager, to stand back and take a more global view of things, much the same as a project manager would. A project manager must consider all the implications of a project, not just on the current task or the boundaries of the project, but also on the business as a whole. The same principles apply here as well. The system manager must consider the impact on the business of each change made to the existing infrastructure, especially if implementing a new system.

Taking the "helicopter" view allows him to see much further and, consequently, to see potential problems. These may not be purely technical problems; they could also be political ones.

The system manager must be able to remove himself from the focused day-to-day activity, which can be extremely narrow, and concentrate on the wider implications. A simple example of doing this could be that one department is intending to implement a new system or application to carry out a specific function. The system manager may already be aware that a similar application exists in the company elsewhere. Maybe it could be adapted for this purpose as well, possibly using the existing version across the network, which would amount to significant savings in both effort and money. The importance of the higher-level global view in this example is that neither of the two departments would be aware of the other's intentions. The system manager could pull it all together and would be in a position to make the best use of the resources available. The solution, in this case, could merely be to export the application software from the existing server using Network File System (NFS).

Advocate for the Business and the Customers

The system manager is likely to be required to sit on project boards as the technical authority. He will ensure that a project is in line with the IT strategy and that the necessary standards are being implemented. An excellent example of this aspect of the job is when a larger enterprise is considering consolidation of computer systems onto fewer, larger servers. This is something that Sun Microsystems is encouraging with its recent purchasing initiatives (these are discussed in detail in Chapter 5, "Solaris Installations and Upgrades"). The system manager is the one person who can identify common factors between existing systems and provide the best option for the business.

An important aspect of this job is that there is a link between the IT department and the business as a whole. The link is provided via the system manager. He will have to be able to relate to senior management, other managers, members of staff, and, of course, the technical community. Negotiation and persuasion skills are needed to resolve conflicts; the system manager can very often get caught in the crossfire.

A significant part of the job is concerned with how well the IT department performs, not just from a technical viewpoint, but also from a business perspective. Monitoring the performance is carried out through the use of service level agreements (see Chapter 3 for a detailed discussion of service level management).

The system manager will be central to the creation and implementation of service level management procedures. He needs to be realistic when specifying the level of service that can reasonably be achieved, while at the same time understanding the needs and requirements of the customers to whom he is providing the service. Service level management and service level agreements are discussed more fully in Chapter 3.

The Company's Data Custodian

In a large company, this can be an awesome responsibility. Everybody's data is in the hands of the system manager. This could include confidential corporate documents, financial data, personnel data (which is subject to legal requirements under data protection), data about a new secret product that is under development, and so on.

All the backups that are run on the computer systems are the system manager's responsibility. He must make sure that they are working. The fact that a backup of a system has been performed lures everyone into a false sense of security—it is false because a backup is of use only if it can subsequently be read. The system manager must ensure that regular tests of backups are carried out, which raises confidence in the integrity of the data.

These days, with large corporations relying heavily on computer systems, it is entirely feasible that a company could be ruined if data were to be lost (as a result of data corruption, for example). In addition to the backups themselves, the system manager must consider strategic options, such as contingency planning and disaster recovery. A well-planned contingency and recovery strategy could mean the difference between a company surviving disaster or collapsing completely. Contingency planning, disaster recovery, and backup options are discussed in Chapter 7, "Disaster Recovery and Contingency Management."

Summary

The system manager is a busy and versatile person with diverse responsibility. He has a varied job description and an extremely wide customer base, covering the entire spectrum of users throughout the business.

The system manager must possess a thorough knowledge of the Solaris operating environment and the computer systems at his disposal, as well as the functions of the business as a whole. In addition, he must be able to relate them to each other so that the best possible service is provided.

The job carries a very high level of responsibility in that the system manager is the custodian of the company's data, something that could ruin the business, if lost.

2

The IT Budget

THE SYSTEM MANAGER NORMALLY HAS SOME INVOLVEMENT with the IT budget as part of his job, although the level of involvement depends on the extent of his responsibilities and the size of the enterprise. His budget will form only a part of the overall IT budget, with this budget being the responsibility of a senior manager, such as the CIO or director of IT.

Small businesses do not tend to have a separate IT budget because it is not warranted. Instead, IT expenditure may be itemized as a percentage of the total expenditure, separated out for tax purposes. In this case, the company accountant manages the finances fairly easily.

In larger companies, though, the budget is quite considerable, running from several million to tens of millions of dollars. The finances for IT services must be managed to demonstrate value for money, particularly when service level agreements are present. (See Chapter 3, "Delivering the Goods," for a detailed discussion of service level management.)

This book focuses on larger organizations in which there are probably separate cost centers within the main IT budget and in which the issues are a great deal more complex than with smaller companies. The following list gives a selection of possible areas, in no particular order, that would be covered by the IT budget. The items marked with an asterisk (★) denote those that are normally considered part of the system manager's budget. The remaining items would be managed by other department managers, such as the operations manager or the network manager.

- Development services
- Asset replacement and upgrades ★
- Desktop PC management and support
- Host systems management, support, and administration ★
- Database management, support, and administration
- Application integration and delivery
- Administration ★
- Network management, support, and administration
- Project/stage management
- Infrastructure management/strategy ★
- Computer operations
- IT management ★
- Software licenses ★
- IT manpower resource ★
- Training ★
- Expenses and transport ★
- Leasing of communications links
- Consumables ★
- Research and evaluation of new products

Notice from this list that the IT budget does not merely cover computer hardware and software. A number of "overheads" are often omitted when the cost of providing a service is calculated, with management overhead being a prime example.

This chapter provides an overview of the IT budget, specifically relating to the system manager, covering some of the issues and constraints that he is likely to encounter. It also aims to give some practical guidance when trying to forecast expenditure. The final section in this chapter discusses the *chargeback* method of earning revenue that some companies employ.

Staff

A company's greatest asset is its staff. Without staff members, there would be no company. As the budget holder, the system manager must take into account the financial costs of staffing his department for the financial year. He must be aware of corporate pay increase structures and maybe performance-related pay issues. Both of these can have an effect on the forecast that he is preparing. A further consideration is whether any members of staff are likely to be promoted and, hence, take an additional rise in salary.

As the list in the previous section shows, the system manager's budget does not only involve the technical staff. He might have responsibility for a secretary and administrative staff, such as people involved with planning and coordination, positions that all must be funded from his budget.

The following sections take a brief look at suggestions for sizing the support section for a Solaris network, some options for running a department around the clock, and the question of salaries for system administrators and equivalent roles.

How Many?

The number of staff members required depends on the size and complexity of the systems or network, but the following pointers should help.

The configuration of the desktop workstations can have a significant impact on the number of staff required for system administration and support. The current configurations supported with Solaris 7 are diskless, standalone, and AutoClient. The trade-off with the configurations is between performance, security, and ease of administration. The pros and cons of each are discussed briefly here:

- **Diskless client**—A diskless client performs the worst because it needs a server to provide its resources and because it places a greater load on the network. It is the best for security and also for ease of central administration. All configuration and management is done from the server, and the client is easily replaceable in the event of a failure. There is no requirement for a local backup.

- **Standalone**—Standalone configurations perform the best because they are self-contained—they have a local hard disk containing the operating environment, swap space, and, optionally, data. A standalone workstation is usually connected to the network but does not require it to operate. It is the worst for security and also for centralized administration. The standalone workstation configuration requires its own backup to guarantee the integrity of the filesystems. Replacement of a standalone workstation is more difficult, with a reinstallation of the operating environment or a complete restoration from backup tape being required.

- **AutoClient**—AutoClient configurations perform better than diskless clients because they use cached filesystems stored on a local hard disk. A server is still required, but the load on the network is reduced. Security is better than standalone configurations because no permanent data is held on the local hard disk and no local backup is required. AutoClient systems are also administered centrally. The unit is easily replaceable in the event of a failure.

Of course, diskless and AutoClient systems require the presence of servers, but the administration and support is generally more manageable.

Consider a network with 500 Solaris desktop workstations. If they are configured as standalone workstations, then the administration requirement is much higher, with more visits to the workstation needed to provide the necessary level of support. If the workstations are configured as diskless or AutoClient clients, then administration is carried out centrally from the server. For example, with the installation of a security patch, AutoClient systems can be automatically synchronized with the server, whereas each standalone workstation will need to have the patch installed separately.

To summarize, diskless or AutoClient configurations can be managed with up to 50% less staff than a configuration using standalone workstations.

24×7 Working

Many IT departments are required to support their systems on a 24×7 basis. Some are required to do this without the necessary additional funding that it normally demands. So how can it be achieved? The following sections explore a few possibilities that could be investigated.

Computer Operations

If the department is required to support 24×7 operation, then there likely is already a computer operations staff presence, probably maintaining other systems (mainframes and so on) on a 24×7 shift roster. If this is the case, then it might be possible to make use of them for the Solaris network as well.

That is exactly what I did when working with the diskless client network mentioned previously. Sufficient training was provided to allow some of the staff to carry out basic administration of the systems, with the support section being available (on call) if required. The objective was to make the best use of the resources available. It allowed the operations staff to continue with the normal running of the systems, but with the advantage of having a second-line support on call. This solution was also beneficial because I was sometimes able to talk through resolutions over the telephone rather than tend to the problem myself.

Automation

Through the use of automation tools and procedures, it is possible to reduce the number of staff required to monitor the systems efficiently. As a system administrator, I wrote and implemented two tools for operations staff to use:

- A network monitoring console using the unbundled product, SunNet Manager (now incorporated into Solstice Domain Manager). A graphical representation of all the servers and clients allowed the Sun network to be monitored from a central position. Some additional agents provided extra facilities.

- A GUI-based tool written to allow housekeeping duties to be carried out with superuser privilege (as setuid programs). These included enabling and disabling workstation access, handling shutdown of the servers, monitoring overnight backup logs, and others. This tool was used in conjunction with the SunNet Manager application mentioned previously. It could be invoked from any of the graphical icons on the central monitoring screen.

The provision of these tools allowed the computer operations section to monitor the Sun network beyond normal working hours using only a percentage of one staff member's time. This was absorbed into the normal workload without having to increase the shift complement, so it provided 24×7 coverage while not increasing costs. The only costs involved were for the initial training and some on-the-job familiarization. The whole exercise proved beneficial all around because the operations staff gained valuable UNIX/Sun/Solaris experience that provided them with a new career development option.

On Call

If funding is limited, then perhaps it is possible to have the system administration staff on call beyond normal business hours with dial-in/remote access. This can work extremely well, with staff being paid only for the hours actually worked instead of being present all the time. A standby cost might be incurred, although it is usual for 24×7 coverage to be built into the base salary package.

In any case, having staff on call is significantly cheaper than having extra staff in attendance on a 24×7 basis. Obviously, on some occasions the on-call staff will not be called on at all, representing significant savings. Of course, the practicalities of this option depend on the priority and nature of the systems. One popular method of achieving remote support is to connect the system consoles to a terminal server so that staff members can access them direct from home, further reducing the likelihood of site attendance.

Choosing a Method

The list at the beginning of this chapter is based on personal experience of having to provide 24×7 support to a large Sun network with limited funding. Whether these options are of any use depends on the type of business, the purpose, and the priority afforded to the systems. A large number of businesses are busy during the core hours (say, 0800 to 1800) and then have a quiet time when all the "day staff" has gone home. If this is the case, then the possibilities outlined are viable. If not, and if the level of activity is approximately the same all the time, then you have really only two options: Employ extra staff, or implement some automation tools to reduce the number of staff needed. It may be possible to stretch the reduced resources to form a shift roster.

How Much?

As part of the budget proposal for the coming financial year, the system manager must estimate the cost of manpower resources. It can be a difficult task to recruit the right skills, but it can be even more difficult to know how much the skills are worth. The system manager must find out the salary range that he's expected to pay.

Various publications produce survey results periodically, but by far the most comprehensive survey is that carried out by the SANS organization (http://www.sans.org).

SANS conducts an annual survey to determine the salaries for the following positions:

- System administrator
- Database administrator
- Network administrator
- Security administrator
- Security auditor
- Security consultant

The most recent survey can be downloaded from the SANS Web site and contains information from more than 11,000 respondents based on age, sex, experience, location, and operating system platforms, to name a few. The information contained within the pages of the survey results provides some useful guidance and gives an indication of the salary ranges that could usefully be applied. Individual managers can then adjust the salary up or down, depending on other circumstances. Figure 2.1 shows a typical page of the report, displaying the average salaries, the percentage increase over the previous year, and the percentage of respondents to the survey for the specific role.

SALARIES BY JOB DESCRIPTION

Type	NT			UNIX		
	Avg Sal	Incr %	% Resp +	Avg Sal	Incr %	% Resp +
SEC_CON	73,711	11.7	4.5	75,645	11.1	6.8
SEC_AUD	64,377	9.1	2.9	68,865	10.1	5.0
OTHER	63,178	11.8	11.3	69,760	11.6	8.7
DB_ADM	56,615	12.5	0.7	54,000	6.9	0.4
SEC_ADM	56,797	11.7	3.4	60,808	9.1	8.1
SYS_ADM	51,529	12.0	48.7	61,106	10.3	58.7
NET_ADM	49,486	12.3	28.6	60,639	10.8	12.3

Figure 2.1   A Comparison Between Different Environments, with Useful Information on Trends and Policies.

Figure 2.2 shows a different perspective, displaying the average salary and the percentage increase over the previous year for the UNIX and NT platforms, but this time by geographic regions.

AVERAGE SALARY AND INCREASE BY REGION

Region	NT			UNIX		
	Salary	Increase %	% Resp +	Salary	Increase %	% Resp +
US-Northeast	60,663	12.2	22.8	67.567	10.5	25.9
US-Southwest	58,926	12.1	16.0	69,930	10.1	20.1
Eur: Germ/Aus/Switz	59,187	10.9	0.6	56,500	6.7	0.6
US-South	52,975	11.8	8.2	64,546	10.7	8.4
US-Midwest	52,669	11.8	19.0	61,490	10.0	16.8
US-Southeast	52,571	12.0	11.8	61,562	11.3	9.7
Hawaii	50,840	15.2	0.4	60,214	8.2	0.4
US-Northwest	51,398	11.1	5.7	61,342	10.3	4.5
Eur: UK	49,841	14.0	2.2	67,930	13.2	1.4
Other Asia	47,611	12.4	0.5	66,400	13.4	0.5
Alaska	48,576	9.8	0.4	57,857	6.5	0.2
Eur: Scandinavia/Benelux	45,509	11.6	1.4	51,051	9.4	1.5
Australia	42,844	11.2	1.6	56,720	7.6	1.4
Other South Pacific	45,000	20.5	0.1	—	—	—
Asia/India	—	—	—	42,750	26.8	0.1
Eur: France	44,200	13.9	0.1	—	—	—
Canada - Ontario	42,788	9.8	2.3	43,055	9.2	2.3
Middle East	40,046	18.1	0.5	54,206	20.7	0.3
Eur: Italy	46,000	12.5	0.1	—	—	—
Other West.Europe	41,068	18.5	0.4	43,021	18.6	0.6
Canada - Quebec	39,666	10.8	1.0	42,233	11.4	0.9
Canada - BC	37,527	9.1	1.0	42,358	4.5	1.2
Canada - Other	37,429	8.3	2.0	41,976	6.2	1.4
South America	34,000	20.4	0.4	43,437	9.4	0.5
Other Africa	33,750	16.7	0.1	—	—	—
Central America	33,250	14.1	0.1	—	—	—
South Africa	34,918	19.9	0.3	24,333	10.0	0.2
New Zealand	32,527	12.6	0.4	24,333	3.5	0.2
Mexico	22,000	9.4	0.1	41,600	15.5	0.2
Eur: Spain	20,291	13.8	0.1	33,955	15.7	0.3
East. Eur. & Soviet Repb's	20,416	15.2	0.2	21,111	19.4	0.3

Figure 2.2   The Variation of Salaries Found in Different Geographical Regions.

See the Appendix, "Resources," for details of some other online sites that offer salary information. They are not as specific as the SANS survey, but they still provide useful additional information.

Training

Training courses are expensive, especially when taking into account the cost of paying the delegate while attending the course, the cost of the course itself, hotel bills, and travelling expenses. The system manager must estimate how many training courses are likely to be required and then reserve sufficient funding from the budget to allow for them.

Training is required not only when introducing a new member of staff to the Solaris environment, but also on an ongoing basis so that the department keeps abreast of new software releases and developments. But it's not only the directly relevant technical training needs that must be addressed. For example, a senior system administrator might benefit greatly from some project management training as part of a career development plan. Lack of training has been one of the main reasons for leaving a job. Additionally, the lure of full-training or cross-training can be attributed to staff moving from one company to another.

The Benefits of Training

Although the cost of training courses is high, the added value that the employee brings to the business can often be of greater value in the long term, so training should be seen as an investment in the business. Management sometimes has a problem with funding expensive training courses because it does not see a tangible benefit as a result that can be quantified in financial terms. However, training offers a number of benefits, some of which are listed here:

- Employees become more productive in a shorter time.
- Formal training is more structured than on-the-job training, making the learning curve shorter.
- Employees experience increased confidence in their own abilities.
- Fewer mistakes are made carrying out the duties.
- Greater understanding leads to better performance and motivation.
- Less time is spent seeking advice from the more experienced employees.
- Employees might see new ways of doing the job, resulting in a more efficient operation.
- Employees have the opportunity to learn and practice away from the working environment, where there are often many distractions.

Increasingly, training is being offered as a staff retention incentive or as part of a recruitment package, such as "the opportunity to cross-train to the latest technologies." The problem with most of these options is that they are not sustained. With technology advancing at such a fast pace, the need for continuing development has never been so great.

On-Site Versus Off-Site Training

If there is a fairly large requirement for a training course, it is sometimes beneficial to investigate the option of having the training company deliver the course on the company premises. This can often result in an overall saving because the travelling and accommodation costs are zero. The course can also be tailored to suit the company's individual needs so that the maximum benefit is gained.

Even though the company's own expenses are significantly reduced by arranging on-site training, there will still be some costs involved, such as travel expenses for the instructors to deliver the training, as well as the cost of having the training customized to suit the specific needs of your business. On-site training courses also frequently do not supply sufficient training or practice systems, which reduces the amount of hands-on training and can detract from the overall value of carrying out the training in this way. If the company has a good training system with plenty of machines, then this is definitely an attractive option.

A further benefit with the on-site option is to involve delegates from other departments. For example, if there is a need for a Solaris shell programming course, there might be an opportunity to include database administrators who often use shell programming to create database startup and shutdown scripts or to run periodic checks on specific parts of the database. Some users might benefit from an introduction to shell programming so that they can write procedures to produce, say, daily totals by counting the number of entries in a list of files. The point is that there is a potential opportunity to share the cost between more than one department. As a result, each department gets a better deal than if they were to arrange the training separately.

Capital Costs

Capital costs are usually one-off costs that represent significant expenditure and that are normally implemented as a project. These could include new investments, such as building a new computer room, replacing air conditioning, doing UPS upgrades, and so on.

Sometimes capital costs must be funded over more than one financial year. There might not be sufficient funding in one single financial year, so the project might be designed to span two or even three years.

New Systems

Companies work in different ways, but the purchase of a new computer system can normally be attributed to a distinct project, so the budget of that project would usually pay for the new system and associated software. When the system has been commissioned and tested, it becomes the responsibility of the system manager.

The servers and workstations used by the IT staff in the execution of their duties, however, must be funded by the system manager. For example, the purchase of a new server with a disk array can amount to a significant cost, especially when software products must be purchased as well to evaluate new versions of the operating system and to establish the risk of installing it into the live environment.

Asset replacement is often another area of contention. Some companies have an asset replacement policy in which PCs or workstations are to be replaced, say, every two to three years. Most important, these replacements are funded from a central budget, not the IT manager's budget. Sometimes this is done because the desktop computer that each employee has is deemed "essential office equipment," just like the desk itself. If this equipment isn't funded from another source, then the system manager must ensure that sufficient additional funds are allocated to the budget to allow for asset replacement.

Cost/Benefit of Upgrades

The system manager is responsible for upgrading the computer systems, both hardware and software, so he must decide whether an upgrade is cost-effective and advantageous to the business. Service level agreements often can aid in this decision because they highlight areas of inadequacy that could point to an upgrade that is necessary to provide an acceptable level of service. The SLA can also be used to justify expenditure on upgrades.

Sometimes the hardware and software vendors remove support for either the system itself or the operating system. The justification for upgrading under these circumstances is the risk of running the systems in an unsupported state. Normally the vendors issue desupport notices on older hardware or versions of the operating system. Desupport notices usually are released by the vendor at least a year before they come into force, giving the system manager plenty of time to include it in the budget forecast. It is also worth noting that the vendors are often willing to provide a level of support even when the product is in desupport mode, but the cost is much greater, making it effectively cheaper to carry out the upgrade. Quite often the system manager must present the available options to senior management so that the business can decide whether the upgrade is necessary.

Running Costs

These costs represent the day-to-day running of the operation, the tools that are required to provide services to the consumers on an ongoing basis.

Some of the costs described in this section are frequently either underestimated or overlooked completely. The system manager must take account of the estimated costs that will be incurred. In larger companies, the running costs could amount to hundreds of thousands of dollars.

Two of the major contributing factors to running an IT department are detailed in the next sections.

Support

Vendor support for hardware and software products is essential if any kind of guaranteed service is being provided. If the company is running a 24×7 operation, these become even more critical and, obviously, more expensive. The system manager must decide on the type of support that is necessary for each system, based on the availability requirements and the business priority. It is worth noting that even though there might be a 24×7 operation, it doesn't mean that every system must be covered on the same basis. Other systems might require support only during business hours, with perhaps a four-hour response. It would clearly be a waste of money to support systems around the clock when they are not being used. Chapter 8, "Strategic Management," includes a section on saving money when looking at hardware and software maintenance contracts.

Support of computer systems is only part of the requirement. A controlled environment contains air conditioning equipment, humidity control, and UPS power backup systems. All these require support arrangements as well as regular maintenance. For example, a UPS system must be checked regularly to ensure that the battery backups are in good working order; the backups also must be replaced periodically. A support agreement with the supplier should include all the items listed previously.

Consumables

Budgeting for consumables is often underestimated because it is seen as trivial. Tape cartridges for daily backups of the systems, however, are one of the most important consumables that the business must purchase as they are used to guarantee and preserve the integrity of the data. Saving money by purchasing cheaper, low-quality tapes could be a false savings because the error rates are likely to be much higher. Also, the cost of not being able to restore a file due to I/O errors could be extremely high.

Toner cartridges for printers, CD-ROMS for archiving, and disks are further examples of consumables that must be accounted for. During the course of the financial year, these can amount to significant sums of money.

To illustrate the wide range of consumables that must be purchased, the following list details items considered to be consumable:

- Backup tapes
- CD-R writeable CDs for local backups and archiving
- Toner cartridges for network printers, fax machines, and photocopying equipment
- Special paper requirements for printing, such as photographic paper and transparencies
- Floppy disks or Zip disks for local backups and archiving
- Disk and Zip disk storage units
- Mouse mats
- Screen filters
- Computer cleaning kits

Essential items such as normal printing paper, office stationery and office furniture are excluded from the list because they constitute items that are necessary to do any job, not just one related to IT.

To put things into perspective, consider a Solaris network of 10 servers using DLT tapes as the backup medium, with the cost of one tape being approximately $50. Maintaining a pool of backup tapes to cover a four-week cycle involves 280 tapes at a cost of around $14,000. One copy of the tapes in the four-week cycle is often retained permanently and possibly is stored in an off-site secure area. An additional 120 tapes are required for the year, increasing the cost to $20,000. This example also does not allow for any bad tapes or any other ad-hoc backups. The actual cost of backing up the systems for a year is likely to be in the region of $25,000 for the media alone. Also to be added in is the cost of off-site storage, which might be a standard fixed cost or one that involves a bill each time that a tape is requested for restoration. Similarly, toner cartridges for laser printers located in various offices can accumulate into a significant cost that must be accounted for.

This example shows that if consumables are not properly accounted for, the budget holder could find that funding is in danger of running out before the end of the financial year, putting the service provision to the business at risk.

Forecasting

Forecasting next year's requirements is not an exact science—it can't be because it involves predicting what's going to happen in the next 12 months. The important thing about providing a forecast is to lay down a marker with a value attached to it. It goes without saying that the value attached should be reasonable and based upon some form of evidence, not merely plucked out of the air! The best starting point is the data available from previous years. This is accurate because it reflects what actually happened and is not going to change. For example, consider a system manager trying to estimate the required support budget for his computer systems and administration section. Suppose that last year there were 6 large servers, 300 workstations, 25 printers, and 4 members of staff. After an expansion program, there will be 9 large servers, 400 workstations, and 40 printers.

Some simple arithmetic will show that, theoretically, each member of staff can administer and support 1.5 servers, 75 workstations, and about 6 printers. By creating a spreadsheet, the cost for last year can be used as a basis for this year—say, adding a 10% increase to allow for price rises. Ideally, though, to achieve any reasonable level of accuracy, more than one year's statistics should be available so that a growth factor can be built into the calculations. Many companies have experienced unprecedented growth in recent years because of the Internet and e-commerce, which, if not taken into account, could throw off the figures by a considerable amount.

A possible example is shown in Figure 2.3, using the previous year's data as a starting point for the forecast. Note that the figures used are for illustrative purposes.

Item	1999 cost per element $	Quantity	Total $
Server	10000	6	60000
Hardware Maint	7000	6	42000
Software Maint	1500	25	37500
Printer			
Workstation	1500	300	450000
Hardware Maint	1500	300	450000
Software Maint	47000	4	188000
Staff resource			
Grand Totals	$68,500		$1,227,500

Item	Predicted 2000 cost per element $	Quantity	Total $
Server	11000	9	99000
Hardware Maint	7700	9	69300
Software Maint	1650	40	66000
Printer			
Workstation	1650	400	660000
Hardware Maint	1650	400	660000
Software Maint	51700	6	310200
Staff resource			
Grand Totals	$75,350		$1,864,500

Figure 2.3 Existing Data Provides the Most Accurate Source for Forecasting.

Figure 2.3 shows that $2 million might be a good estimate to include in the budget to support the systems, allowing a little for contingency.

Revenue!

The IT department can also earn revenue by charging individual departments for the services being provided. For example, if a large network is supporting the sales department and the marketing department, then the cost of providing the service can be shared between the two areas. The amount charged to each of the departments would be calculated based on the issues described in the preceding sections, which describe running costs.

Charging for a service is fine until the quality of the service is challenged. Service level agreements challenge the service provider to prove that the consumer is getting value for money. Service level management is discussed in the next chapter, but it is worth mentioning here that, normally, penalties for failing to meet the agreed targets are not financial when dealing internally within a company. This may not be true if an external service provider is charging for the service—in this case, there may well be a financial penalty for providing a substandard level of service.

Recharge Accounts

A recharge account is like a large bucket where charges are deposited. The charges are the costs for the members of staff working in the department that "owns" the budget. The idea is that these costs are debited from the recharge account, but the department also charges for the services that it provides to other departments. The revenue gained from providing the services reduces the deficit in the recharge account. The objective at the end of the financial year is for the recharge account to be at zero. It will never truly be at zero, but for a $5 million budget, a deficit of up to, say, $500,000 would be possible because the manager should not schedule his staff to be more than 80% utilized. This is to take scheduled and unscheduled absences into account—after all, no one works every single day of the year. Staff members take leave, get sick, attend training courses, and so on, but they are still paid, and that money comes out of the system manager's budget.

It often doesn't work like that in practice: Many members of staff find that they are more than 100% utilized and must work longer hours. A significant proportion of the manager's time may also be booked to the recharge account if it is not being attributed to project work. This is the management overhead mentioned at the beginning of this chapter.

Chargeback Systems

Some companies operate *chargeback* systems: Departments within the business charge other departments for the provision of services. Normally, within commercial organizations, a department pays IT a support fee for each system that is to be supported. The system manager must ensure that the total amount charged for the services is sufficient to be able to run the operation—that is, it should cover his own costs. The system manager will need to set aside additional funding to allow for upgrades and hardware failures. An initial figure for this could be derived using the previous years' figures as a baseline.

Another method used, particularly in government, is to assign a chargeback rate to a grade—for example, a system engineer might attract a rate of, say, $400 per day. When the engineer carries out work on a specific project or system, the relevant number of hours are *booked* to that project code or cost center (see the section "Project Budgets," later in this chapter). Under these circumstances, managers are under greater pressure to ensure that the people working in the department are fully utilized so that the maximum amount can be charged to other departments or projects. If the recharge rate is higher than the actual salary being paid to the employee, the manager can appear to make a profit in the recharge account—known as *over-recovery*. A significant over-recovery at the end of the financial year might appear to be very good because it shows the department as highly profitable. This is not necessarily the case, though, because it could mean that the recharge rates are merely unrealistic or that the department is under-resourced and that the staff is being required to work too many hours.

The opposite can occur as well. If an employee is not fully utilized with "bookable" work, then where does he or she book the remaining hours to? The answer is that they get booked to the recharge account. A good example of time being booked to the recharge account is if there is a team meeting. When the cost is not met by charging a department or project, this is known as *under-recovery*—that is, the cost of employing the person for that period of time was not recovered. The system manager usually forecasts the under-recovery figure based on the predicted program of work for the coming year. It must be stressed that this figure can be only an estimate because new requirements could be raised, or a predicted project could be cancelled or postponed.

Recharge Forecasts

Several legitimate reasons might explain why the forecast could become less valid as the year progresses. For these reasons, the budget forecast is compared against actual expenditure on a monthly basis, and the forecast should be adjusted up or down based on current performance. The advantage of doing this is that significant overspending (or underspending) can be identified as early as possible so that remedial action can be taken before the end of the financial year. You may have noticed how many companies suddenly start spending on new computers or furniture just before the end of the financial year. It is because underspending has been identified in the budget—and, as all budget-holders know, if the money isn't spent, even less will be available next year!

Figure 2.4 shows a typical cumulative summary that a system manager might see for a cost center that is under his control. The current date would be sometime in January, and the summary has assumed that actual spending will be the same as the previous month, giving a predicted balance at the end of the year.

Cost Center: D556832 - Computer Manpower

Year: 1999/2000   Opening Balance: $5000000

	Estimated Spend $	Actual Spend $	Balance $
April	40000	37000	463000
May	40000	37500	425500
June	40000	38000	387500
July	40000	39000	348500
August	40000	41000	307500
September	40000	42000	265500
October	40000	42500	223000
November	40000	45000	178000
December	40000	47000	131000
January	40000	47000	84000
February	40000	47000	37000
March	40000	47000	-10000
Totals	480000	510000	-10000

Figure 2.4   The Project Is in Trouble if the Actual Spending Continues to Increase.

Project Budgets

When a chargeback system is in operation, there are associated cost centers and charge codes to which time is booked. This is how the IT department receives payment for the services being provided. Booking time to a code can be thought of as an invoice, billing the customer for the time taken to carry out a function. A budget-holder is normally assigned a cost center code by the finance department. If the manager is responsible for several projects, the budget may be broken down into a number of charge codes, one for each project. Each of the codes is then assigned a proportion of the budget, according to the forecast. The people actually carrying out the work must be careful when completing the timesheets for the week so that the correct number of hours are booked to the correct project cost code. One of the most frequent problems with systems of this kind is that the manager finds hours booked to the code that shouldn't be there. The system manager must manage his budget code(s) accordingly and, on a regular basis, question any dubious entries that he finds.

Another problem that affects this kind of system is that when a job is costed, only the physical action of doing the task is costed; the management overhead, for example, is frequently omitted. As an example, consider the IT section providing an application testing service to the business. Several hundred applications might need to be tested, all of which are to be paid for by the department that uses the application. The IT department bills the relevant project code for each application on a time and materials basis only. The management overhead cost has not been built into the price, nor has the planning effort that has gone into scheduling the applications through the process. This can cause a significant amount of work when deliveries are late, cancelled, or rescheduled. In addition, none of the associated administration has been accounted for, such as the production of a test certificate, troubleshooting, and so on. The system manager is in charge of the section; he manages the resources and yet appears to be working for free.

The objective is to ensure that all relevant costs, not just the obvious ones, are borne in mind when providing a service that is chargeable.

Summary

The IT budget is a complex beast and can easily grow out of control if it is not managed properly. Large companies have specialized accountant staff to manage the corporate finances, but the system manager must keep a close eye on areas of the budget that fall within his responsibility. The budget is not just about budgeting for computer hardware and software acquisitions; it covers a much wider range, including the support and running costs, and the staffing and management of systems and associated administrative functions.

Increasingly, businesses are demanding a continuous service from their IT departments, which has placed increased pressure on the IT budget because system managers are often required to provide this extra coverage with little or no extra financial support. Larger companies may already have a computer operations section working on a 24×7 basis, and it is possible that the system manager may be able to make use of this resource for routine administration beyond normal business hours, backed up by on-call technical staff. The incentive for operations staff is that they receive valuable training and also open up further doors for potential career development.

The IT department can also earn revenue from the service that it provides by charging for its services. Use of the chargeback system allows the cost of providing the service to be apportioned to the various departments making use of the facilities. The other side of the coin, though, is that the level of service being provided to the customer will come under much greater scrutiny via service level agreements, which are discussed in Chapter 3, "Delivering the Goods."

3

Delivering the Goods

THIS CHAPTER PROVIDES A BRIEF INTRODUCTION to service level management and service level agreements. These subjects have become big issues in recent years and have warranted several books. Some references for further reading can be found in the Appendix, "Resources."

Overview

The IT systems and the corporate networks present in today's businesses have become what's known as *mission-critical*—that is, they are crucial to the survival of the business. Unlike a tangible asset, such as a building or production equipment, the corporate network is a collection of assets and services. The networks today are central to supporting the business objectives of the organization.

The system manager is responsible for providing the IT services to the business. He must be in a position to deliver those services in an efficient and effective manner and, more importantly, in a way that is acceptable to the business so that it can survive in today's extremely competitive global market.

The system manager's customers, or clients, are becoming increasingly dependent on the services that he provides. They also are becoming more technically aware, which has given them a much better idea of what they can reasonably expect of the IT department. The client is now demanding more, particularly in terms of the quality of service. Conversely, the IT department is being expected to do more with less. Computer networks are expanding at a frighteningly fast rate, both in size and complexity, but the expenditure and human resources are not increasing at a corresponding rate; they are reducing because of so-called automation tools that have come on to the market. So far, these have shown only limited success, partly because the system management tools and utilities that are necessary for controlling and monitoring the enterprise network are missing or underpowered. As a result, there has been insufficient meaningful data available to be capable of determining the level of success that IT departments are achieving. For a long time, data has been available for various portions of a service, such as individual system performance, network performance information, and so on, but nothing really has been available on the end-to-end delivery of a service. It is this kind of data that will allow the performance to be measured to any degree of accuracy.

The question being asked is this: "How does the business ascertain the level of success, or failure, that the IT department is achieving?"

Previously, the system manager measured success by various factors, which were always related to hardware and software components, such as system availability, performance, and so on. These might have given the impression that all was well, that he was doing a great job, and that all the customers must also think the same.

On the other hand, the client may have had a different opinion. Certainly, the main computer system may have been up and available for 364.99 days out of the last 365, but the network was not, and neither were the printers, so the client lost a lot of time and became increasingly frustrated at the lack of service being provided.

The result is that there is no mutually acceptable agreement between the two perspectives, and that is where service level management comes in.

Service Level Management

Traditionally, IT departments were funded as a corporate overhead—that is, paid for out of a central budget that was not particularly relevant to any specific department. Service level agreements came into existence when IT departments started to charge for the services being provided, normally via the *chargeback* method (described in Chapter 2, "The IT Budget"). So, with each department having to pay for its IT services out of its own budget, it became clear that there would have to be ways of quantifying the service being provided and attaching a reasonable cost to the provision of the service. The consumer also needed to know whether the service being provided was worth paying for—and, if not, how to claim a refund!

The terms *service level management* and *service level agreement* have become popular in recent years because of IT departments being challenged about the level of service that they are actually providing. Questions have been asked, such as, "To what extent are the users and the computer applications being supported?", "Is the reliability of the network and computer systems acceptable?", "Are the IT services being provided in accordance with the business objectives and expectations?", and "Is the IT department providing value for money?"

Of course, these questions could not be properly answered because there was no means of determining the level of success or failure. The system manager could argue based on the performance and availability figures, but the client could counter with a documented list of occurrences when he or she was unable to carry out a required job because the network was down or the system was running far too slowly.

Service level management addresses these issues by ensuring that all parties understand what is expected from each. The system manager probably has to hear some unwelcome news in that he hasn't been doing such a great job as previously thought, and the client may well realize that what is being asked for is totally unrealistic. Either way, the objective is a mutual understanding and, most important, an understanding that is written down and agreed to by all parties concerned.

Service level management is all about *quality of service* and how to measure it. To determine the quality of the service being provided, it is necessary to adopt the view of the customer—that is, the person or persons making use of the service (the consumer). A dissatisfied customer will not want to use your services again. It is the ultimate test of quality, the opinion of the consumer. This is great most of the time, but in our case, there is nothing substantial with which to make a comparison, no baseline that defines what is acceptable. Consider the following example in which quality can be measured:

A car is for sale at the local showroom. The customer can test-drive the vehicle, read the sales literature, compare it to other similar types of car available from different manufacturers, or read reviews about the car in various motoring magazines and journals. In this case, the service level agreement is the warranty that is taken out when the car is purchased. The customer will be entitled to free repairs if a specified fault occurs within a specified period and will have the use of a courtesy car while any repairs are being carried out. The customer, though, must have the car regularly serviced by an approved technician, and no modifications must be made to the car. If a repair cannot be effected, then the customer will be given a replacement car. This agreement is clearly defined and agreed to by all parties. The expectation is that the car will function without any problems for the entire period of warranty. From the customer's perspective, the fact that completing the repair may mean ordering spare parts from abroad is of no concern or relevance. The customer leaves the car with the dealer and expects to have it returned in full working order.

In the same way, the IT department is providing a service to the customer, but the system manager's responsibility might be only a part of that service. To provide the entire service may involve the hardware support technicians, the network team, development services, database administration and central hosts, to name a few. This is of no interest to the customer, and it shouldn't be. The customer wants something, and the IT department (as a whole) provides it. The customer isn't concerned with all the technical bits of computer wizardry that may be involved in providing the service, nor in the fact that there are several sections within the IT department involved—this is irrelevant.

It can be seen that there is a difficulty in defining "quality of service." There is nothing to compare it to—no baseline, no agreed tolerance. The service level agreement (SLA) is created to address this lack of clarity, allowing the service to be monitored and its performance to be measured.

A service level agreement is a contract between a provider and a consumer—in this case, the provider is the IT department, with the system manager being a major part of it. The consumer could be the accounting or sales department. Often, SLAs between internal organizations within the same company would not form legal contracts, but one with a third-party supplier would. The primary reason for their existence is to define, in measurable terms, what is being provided and what is expected, and then to be able to determine how well (or not) the service is being provided.

Perfection is something that is not achievable. The SLA does not try to achieve 100% perfection, but it does define the level of imperfection that is acceptable. It also defines what is desirable and what is possible. Basically, the customer must make realistic expectations. There is no point in asking for something that cannot be delivered because it would undermine the whole process and make any SLA meaningless. A crucial part of setting up any SLA is that a common understanding is agreed and documented by both provider and consumer.

As part of the SLA process, cost must be borne in mind when trying to improve the service. It is quite likely that with financial expenditure, the quality of service could be improved, maybe significantly, but at what cost? It may completely outweigh the perceived benefit. Even though the cost is not directly related to the quality of the service being provided, it must be considered as a potentially limiting factor.

The next few sections provide insight into some of the issues surrounding service level management and the SLA process. This coverage is not intended to be an exhaustive discussion, but it is enough to appreciate the sort of things that are included. An example is included at the end of the chapter.

Provider or Consumer?

As stated before, the SLA is a contract between a provider and a consumer. The two parties can loosely be defined as follows:

- **Provider**—The person or department providing a service for others to use. This may be internal to the company or a third-party supplier.
- **Consumer**—The person or department making use of the service that is being provided.

To complicate matters, the system manager can be, and often is, both a provider and a consumer. This creates a special challenge when trying to draw up a service level agreement with him. On one hand, the system manager is providing the computing services to the business, but on the other hand, he must make use of services provided to him—the network, for example. Here, he is a consumer of a service which may already be the subject of a service level agreement: a telephone company in this case, that supplies the various communications media. This will usually be a third-party supplier and subject to a formal contract with associated penalties for substandard service.

The service level agreement will form a part of the formal contract. The system manager, as both provider and consumer, will have to take this into account when entering into any service level agreement with the business. This is because there is a risk that the provision of the entire service could be jeopardized if this part fails—indeed it may prompt him to seriously review the dependencies that could affect his ability to deliver the service. The third-party supplier managing the network in this case is an extremely important dependency because a network failure would undoubtedly have a significant effect on the system manager's ability to guarantee a level of service.

Database administrators and developers could be further examples of dependencies that the system manager must take into account. If there are no agreements with either of these areas, he will be unable to specify when either a database problem will be resolved or an application bug will be fixed.

From the consumer perspective, this is irrelevant. The consumer makes use of the IT infrastructure and computer systems so that a task can be carried out. As stated earlier, the fact that several sections or departments may be involved in the provision of that service is of no interest to the consumer. However, as part of the negotiation process, the system manager will have to make clear any dependencies that could affect his ability to deliver the required level of service. The consumer, while not interested in the mechanics, will gain useful knowledge of how the service is provided. Value lies in the fact that the consumer's understanding of the issues is enhanced.

This difference in perspective is one of the main reasons why it is necessary to first arrive at a common understanding. The importance of documenting the understanding is to avoid future ambiguities and potential conflicts due to misinterpretation. This will certainly happen if the agreement is not documented.

What Are Dependencies?

Dependencies in this instance can be defined as anyone, or anything, that the system manager relies on in the provision of the required level of service.

Who Needs an SLA?

Any section or department in a company that is making use of a service provided by another department, such as IT services, needs an SLA so that a measurable, quantifiable, reasonable, and attainable level of service can be agreed on between the interested parties. Without the SLA, there is no evidence of performance. The users could complain that the service is slow, and the system manager could respond by saying that it isn't. Who's right? And how do they prove it? Of course, they can't prove it because there is no baseline to compare it to. With an SLA in place, however, the baseline determines what constitutes an acceptable level of service. If the user complains of a slow service, a comparison can be made against what was agreed on, and the necessary proof can be provided. Note that all of this depends on sufficient meaningful data being available.

The users, or consumers, also need an SLA for another reason. It is probably the only place where the user community is represented with authority. They will help to set the standards for the level of service that they require to do their jobs.

Senior management needs SLAs to ascertain the value of a given service and to measure how well the service is performing against an agreed target. This sort of information is invaluable to management, especially when deciding priorities and budgets. It allows them to see easily the value that, in this case, the IT services are providing to the business as a whole. The SLA describes the service in universally clear language that everyone can understand.

Another reason that senior management would favor the use of SLAs is that they often provide the information needed to determine whether outsourcing is a viable option. Part of the SLA process involves gathering and monitoring collected data. A cost element of providing the service should also be available. This cost element can be compared with external suppliers and hence aid the decision for whether outsourcing is an option.

A good way of collecting the required information is to use a time recording system. In this way, time is booked to various tasks by the people carrying them out. Managers then can produce reports to detail how much time (and, hence, cost) is spent providing a specific service. Figure 3.1 shows an example timesheet that has been completed by a system administrator for a working week. A report would contain, say, monthly figures for the total time spent on a specific task and by all those contributing to it.

It can be seen from Figure 3.1 that the system administrator appears to spend his time fairly evenly between the sales and personnel systems. These figures could easily be quantified as a cost if either of them were being considered for outsourcing. Other cost elements to be considered could include these:

- **Maintenance and support costs**—These are the system and software support maintenance contracts. If the service were to be outsourced to a third party, this element would definitely be included.

- **Development services costs**—This is the amount of time required by development services, for example, to fix bugs or provide enhancements. This element would also be included if outsourcing was being considered.

- **Management overhead costs**—This is the necessary overhead that is inherently built into the overall cost of providing the service. This element is often omitted because it is not seen as a *direct* cost. Note that an element of the management overhead would still exist if the service were to be outsourced, although it would be proportionately reduced.

- **Media and consumables**—This element is not normally considered when deciding whether to outsource a service, but it can still be considered as part of the overall cost of providing the service.

- **Administrative support costs**—These costs relate to the production, copying, and distribution of reports, as well as the secretarial duties relevant to the provision of the service. Again, this is another element that is frequently overlooked, but it should be included if an accurate cost of providing the entire service is to be calculated.

- **Clear definition of responsibility**—An SLA defines exactly who is responsible for providing a service or a part of a service. This aspect becomes more apparent when a service is outsourced, especially if more than one supplier is involved. For example, consider an SLA covering several remote sites as well as a central, primary site. If a restore request is received for a file that is resident on a remote system, the SLA provides sufficient information to determine which section carries out the system administration duties, thus preventing the request from "falling through the gap."

CoverMe, Inc. Time Recording System								
Employee: Philcox, John			**Week Commencing:** Sunday April 30 2000					
	Sun.	Mon.	Tues.	Wed.	Thurs.	Fri.	Sat.	Total
Category								
0005 - Administration		0.50	0.50	0.50	0.50	0.50		**2.50**
0006 - Leave								**0.00**
0007 - Sick								**0.00**
0018 - Training (internal)								**0.00**
0019 - Training (external)								**0.00**
A015 - Meetings		1.50		0.75	1.00			**3.25**
B415 - (Sales systems)		3.50	4.00	2.75	4.00	3.00		**17.25**
P441 - (Personnel systems)		3.00	3.75	5.50	3.00	4.00		**19.25**
R141 - Intranet project		1.00				1.50		**2.50**
R148 - Infrastructure project						0.75		**0.75**
Totals	**0.00**	**9.50**	**8.25**	**9.50**	**8.50**	**9.75**	**0.00**	**46.50**

Figure 3.1   A method of tracking time, such as a detailed timesheet, is crucial for managers who need to determine the most cost-effective way of meeting requirements.

The system manager needs SLAs so that the services that he is providing can be well documented and understood. During negotiations, the level of service that can reasonably be achieved becomes apparent. Unrealistic expectations on behalf of the consumer are also highlighted at this stage, and the system manager can work at getting these reduced to a more reasonable level. This focuses on what can actually be done, something that may not have been addressed before. Previously, a lot of the work may have been "firefighting," sorting out problems as they arise. Here, though, is an opportunity to analyze the service in its entirety and to anticipate the potential problems, pitfalls, or network bottlenecks that could cause concern in the future.

A final reason for the system manager to favor the use of SLAs is that it could provide the necessary justification for further expenditure on improvements. The negotiation process and the monitoring of the performance should raise the profile of problematic areas. Using the SLA results, for example, the system manager could not only specify what is needed to improve the service, but also provide the projected improvement in efficiency and throughput that is likely. He will be able to identify this improvement only if there is something already available to compare it with. This will exist in the agreement, as discussed earlier.

Unrealistic Expectations

Unrealistic expectations usually arise because the consumer is not fully aware of what is actually achievable. The following are a couple of examples:

- **100% availability of the application**—This is impossible to guarantee. Even with significant investment, there is still no guarantee. The best possible availability can be calculated only in conjunction with other SLAs (probably with third-party suppliers). The question of availability may not even be negotiable with the consumers because of agreements already active with third-party organizations.

- **Problem calls responded to within 30 minutes**—These calls would be passed on by the help desk system, which is usually also subjected to an SLA. The system manager cannot possibly respond before the call has been passed to his department (by the help desk). The compromise would be to agree on a response time based on the help desk SLA, coupled with a priority mechanism based on the severity of the situation. The priority attached to various types of problems is defined in the scope and terms of the agreement (see later in this chapter in the section "Creating an SLA").

The Benefit

There are three main beneficiaries of a service level agreement:

- **The system manager**—With an SLA, the system manager can gain accurate insight into how well (or not) he is achieving his objectives. The data that he collates as part of his responsibility to the agreement can also be used as justification for further expenditure on the systems, especially if the data reveals that the systems are underperforming in certain areas.

    The system manager also benefits because user departments are much more likely to involve the IT department in the early design decisions of systems. With the users made aware of the costs associated with a system, and its subsequent support, there is likely to be greater focus on longer-term (the complete life cycle) issues. This results in overall savings for the company as a result of better strategic planning.

- **The end user**—The users benefit from SLAs because the IT department is forced to account more accurately for the services being provided. The costs must be based precisely on the performance being achieved, so the user perceives that he is receiving better value for his money.

    A side effect of the SLA is that the applications being used by the user community are prioritized according to their importance to the business. The creation of the SLA forces the focus to be placed on applications demanding the highest level of service, as well as identifying those that can operate with a reduced level of service. With the user department being charged for the services being provided, there is a more concentrated focus on what is being asked for. The user is less likely to ask for more than is absolutely necessary because of the costs that would be incurred.

- **Senior management**—The senior manager reaps huge benefits from the SLA process. He now has a set of clearly defined metrics available from which he can manage the IT department based on performance. It is easier for him to quantify the contribution being made to the business by the IT department and, hence, to identify priorities when allocating funds for additional resources or equipment. The presence of SLAs helps the senior manager when attempting to compare the cost of carrying out a service within the company against that of outsourcing the service to an external supplier.

Of course, the business benefits from the existence of SLAs in that it runs more efficiently and also has the supporting data to provide justification for greater investment. This kind of information can prove valuable, for example, when attempting to convince shareholders or investors of the need for investment in technology.

Creating an SLA

This section discusses the procedures that are followed during the creation of a service level agreement. It is not intended to be a definitive discussion, but it gives an overview of the topics to be addressed.

There are several steps to follow in the creation of an SLA, and these are similar for various agreements—in our case, one between the IT department and another department, within the same organization. The steps are described in detail in the following sections.

Step 1: Gain Agreement That an SLA Is Required

Without this, there is little point in continuing. The fundamental agreement that the SLA is required is the first step to achieving a mutually agreeable solution.

Step 2: Select and Assemble the SLA Team

A team needs to be selected from both the service provider section and the client section. The actual numbers making up the team will vary according to the size and complexity of the agreement being sought, but the guidelines in the following paragraphs might prove useful.

In an ideal world, the chief of each of the departments would be a part of the team, but this is not often possible, so, for the IT department, this may be delegated to the system manager. He can negotiate on behalf of the IT chief and possesses sufficient knowledge, both technical and business-related, to provide positive input to the process. As a general rule, I recommend two initial members from each group, calling on other "experts" as required for specific input related to their field of expertise.

Both parties should send people with sufficient authority to be able to finalize the agreement. Some managers deliberately send delegates that do not possess sufficient authority, but this is negative and counterproductive, and serves no real purpose other than to frustrate the proceedings.

The number of attendees should be balanced from both parties. They do not have to be exactly equal, but deviation should be kept to a minimum. Similarly, there should not be an excess of power on one side—it can be intimidating to be faced with a team that is much more senior than yours. In fact, the less senior party could feel pressured into concessions that make the whole agreement worthless and meaningless. The requirement here is that a mutually understood and agreed contract is drawn up; it is not a competition to see who will win.

Step 3: Prepare for the SLA Negotiation

After the groups have been assembled, there must be some preparation before the start of negotiations. The system manager, for example, needs to identify the processes involved for the provision of his service. If it involves any sections or external providers that are beyond his control, then his ability to provide any guarantee of service is severely diminished. He must first obtain agreements (SLAs, maybe) himself from all of these so that he is then in a position to be able to offer a minimum and maximum level of service.

The system manager must be able to monitor the level of service being provided so that, if required, he can produce evidence to show that targets have been met or exceeded. He cannot promise a level of service if he can't measure it. Conversely, the client group must identify as precisely as possible the service that is required. A certain amount of discipline is required on behalf of the client team: Clients must request the level of service that is necessary to carry out their function, rather than a "wish list" of what they would like to see.

Step 4: Establish the Terms and Scope of the Agreement

Items under this heading include, but are not limited to, the following:

- **Length of the contract**—Typically, this is between one and two years. Given the technology present today, it would be imprudent to try to create any contract lasting longer than two years (indeed, two years is a long time), although, as detailed later in this section, the agreement will be subjected to modification from time to time. A contract start date and end date should be defined here, too.

- **Response times for trouble tickets**—These can vary in priority according to the type of problem raised and must be organized in such a way that the urgent ones are dealt with in a timely manner and in the right order. An example is to have priority 1, 2, and 3 (or high, medium, and low), with a realistic response time attached to each, such as one hour, one day, and one week, respectively. For example, a problem that affects all the users would definitely attract a priority 1 status, whereas a request to add a new user scheduled to join next week would attract a priority 3 response. A priority 2 response could be a problem affecting only one user.

- **Data retention and restoration requirements**—The expectations of how long data is required to be kept (and how and where the data is to be stored) would be included here, in addition to the time taken to restore a specified file (or item of data). For example, if six months of data is held locally, then a restore could be expected within an hour or two. Conversely, restoring a file that is two years old could involve retrieving the backup media from an off-site storage facility and might be specified as taking up to one week.

Resolution and Response

Some SLAs define a resolution time as well as a response time. This can prove to be a dangerous practice for the system manager. Responding to a trouble ticket within a certain time is one thing, but guaranteeing the resolution time is quite different and could potentially cause major problems.

- **Enforcement of quotas**—Any user quotas, usually in terms of disk space storage, should be identified either on a per-user or per-application basis. The system manager needs this information to be able to allow sufficient storage space for the consumers' needs, ensure that the data will be safely backed up, and provide contingency (in the case of high availability requirements) through the use of RAID or mirroring.

- **Identify clear boundaries of responsibility**—When multiple organizations or departments bear responsibility for parts of the system, clear boundaries need to be identified so that each party is aware of the extent of its involvement. This is often a contentious aspect, with disputes arising as to whether a problem is hardware- or software-related and who carries out the initial investigation to determine where the fault lies.

- **Identify the standard path for escalation**—This is the default action to take when nonperformance is identified—that is, failure to achieve the agreed level of service. The escalation path is described in more detail in the section "Penalties for Missed Targets."

The scope of the agreement should be clearly defined so that there can be no misunderstanding between the parties at a later date about what is included in the agreement and what is excluded. Occasionally there will be specific exclusions—for example, if the client group is using an old piece of hardware for a specific function, then the system manager might want to exclude it on the grounds that it is no longer supported and is covered only on a best-endeavors basis.

Step 5: Document the SLA

This is the part of the process in which a mutually acceptable agreement is reached and both parties understand what is being provided and what is being expected. The agreement should possess the following characteristics:

- **Any objectives identified must be within the control of the service provider**—There is no point in trying to set the expectations when the service provider has no direct control. An example of this could be the client group stating that the wide area network (WAN) connections must be available all the time. The system manager might have an agreement with the network section, but it is the network section who will have the SLA with the external communications company, which maintains the WAN connections. However, if the client group requests that there be no more than 60 minutes scheduled downtime on the Solaris servers in a year, this is under direct control of the system manager and is a valid expectation.

- **Any objectives must be meaningful**—This is quite difficult in that an objective initiated by the client group may not be meaningful to the IT department, and vice versa. For example, the number of network collisions or bad receive packets are meaningless to the client group. The client would like to see something such as "a query must be actioned in three seconds or less." The latter will be much more meaningful to both parties; the measurement of it, however, is a different matter entirely.

- **The agreement must be mutually acceptable**—The whole idea of creating a service level agreement is one of it being mutually acceptable. It is unlikely that both parties will always like everything contained in an SLA, but they should find it *acceptable*—there is a distinct difference. If one of the parties finds something that it decides is unacceptable, then this issue should not be agreed to, and renegotiation should take place. This is infinitely preferable to having an agreement made containing items that are unacceptable to one of the parties—it undermines the whole value of having the SLA in the first place. Basically, if the job is worth doing, then it should be done properly.

- **Any objectives must be achievable and cost-effective**—Both parties must realize very early in the SLA process that there is a requirement to be realistic about what is being provided and what is being expected. It is a complete waste of time if the expectations are impossible to achieve with the current system and network configurations. It is also unlikely that any system manager would agree to an expectation that he knows he can't accommodate. If any hardware or software upgrades are required to satisfy the expectation, then they must be justified as cost-effective and beneficial.

- **It must be possible to measure objectively the service being provided**—Some of the client expectations will be extremely difficult to measure accurately without the use of a management tool—even some of these do only part of the job. Data may be available from several sources that, when correlated and analyzed, provides the necessary information to determine whether the expectation has been satisfied. However, both parties must agree on the objectiveness of the data being gathered. The subject of monitoring performance against targets is discussed in greater detail later in this chapter in the section "Monitoring Performance Against Targets."

Step 6: Identify Nonperformance Indicators

As part of the SLA agreement, a set of criteria must be established so that indicators exist when the performance expectations of the client are not being met. To be able to do this, it is necessary first to have established the minimum level of service required.

It could be something as simple as the example in Step 6, that a query should take no longer than three seconds to return the result. This is an end-to-end response time and may prove difficult to measure with any accuracy. The system manager may agree to an indicator as being the availability of the database (on which the query runs). It may be possible to measure the overall availability by using data extracted from more than one management system. It will depend on whether the client accepts the data as being valid, and also how much effort is expended in producing the required information—it may not be cost-effective to do it.

Step 7: Identify and Agree to Corrective Action

Any corrective action should be invoked only as an exception. This section should identify the tolerances that are permissible. For example, if an expectation is that a query should take only three seconds, then what happens if it takes four seconds? And what if this happens only once? It can be seen that it would be unreasonable to invoke a nonperformance procedure for a one-off occurrence. A more representative and meaningful indicator of nonperformance would be if a percentage of queries in a day took longer than six or seven seconds to complete. The tolerances should be reasonable and realistic. As for corrective action, this is discussed more fully later in the section "Penalties for Missed Targets."

Step 8: Determine and Agree to a Review Process

Any SLA that is created will have to undergo a regular review. This is true because, as experience is gained, some of the performance parameters may evolve and be more finely tuned. A regular review should be agreed to and documented. A weekly review may be necessary in the early stages of implementation, but this could probably be reduced to monthly after an initial period.

Step 9: Establish Procedures to Allow Modification and Refinement of the Agreement

As part of the review process, the agreement must be subjected to occasional modification and refinement. This would normally come as a result of experience, or maybe an upgrade to the existing facilities or a new release of the application software. The process for modifying the agreement needs to be addressed here and agreed to.

Types of Availability

There are two kinds of availability, scheduled and unscheduled. *Scheduled availability* takes into account such aspects as routine maintenance and agreed upgrades, and can be easily planned in advance. *Unscheduled availability* includes such things as system crashes and database corruption, and cannot be planned for. It is often important to separate the availability requirements according to these two types.

Monitoring Performance Against Targets

The monitoring of performance is a difficult task and is usually hampered by the lack of accurate data relating to the target. The gathering of data for performance-monitoring purposes will often involve correlating data from more than one management system. For example, to ascertain the performance of the query example described earlier, it may be necessary to obtain network statistics, workstation performance statistics and database/host performance information. Any of these could potentially cause a bottleneck that could result in the SLA targets not being achieved.

Even with the data being correlated from several systems, there is no real guarantee of the accuracy. The IT department may state that queries are being completed in two seconds or less, but the user may disagree, stating that the system is slower than expected and discounting the collected data as invalid. Network monitoring tools have tended to look at only OSI Level 1 and 2 for their performance information, and only report on lost packets, number of retransmits, and so on.

Additional equipment or software may be needed to gather some of the data required for performance analysis. These could include LAN analyzers to examine packet throughput on the network, network-management software (such as Solstice Domain Manager), and the error logs already available.

Some better management tools now coming on the market are capable of monitoring the end-to-end process, something that has traditionally been missing from such tools. Framewatch, from GTE, is an example of the new generation of system-management tools. It uses RMON2-enabled devices that can probe into the application layer of the OSI model and provide comprehensive information relating to the application. (RMON2 is the successor to RMON, Remote Monitoring.) This sort of management information is required to be able to report on the end-to-end performance and provide meaningful data for SLA purposes.

Another source for monitoring the performance of SLA objectives is by using the help desk system. In this instance, the number of calls logged against either a service or an application can be analyzed to gain insight into the level of performance being achieved. This data should be used to supplement other information and should not be relied upon by itself.

The system manager will be required to provide a periodic report detailing the performance levels that have been achieved. The report will be the result of the data gathering and analysis, displayed in a format that the users and senior management can easily interpret. It may be a good idea to produce the report in two forms: in a tabular form because, even though it may be more difficult to read, it will provide accurate figures; and in a graphical form, because it's easier to interpret and shows where any trends lie.

Monitoring trends can be of significant value. The system manager could be fore-warned of deteriorating performance and could address the issue before the impact is felt. Conversely, the senior manager could use the data to aid the forecast for the following year. The data could be used as a basis for the SLA reviews, which is where changes may be made to the SLA as experience increases.

Figure 3.2 shows an example of the type of information that could be included in a typical management report detailing the availability levels.

CoverMe, Inc. Availability Report for: Sales		
Period: April 2000	**Number of Hours:** 220	
Component	**Downtime (Minutes)**	**Availability (%)**
Local Area Network	1.50	99.99
Sales Workstations	7.00	99.95
Sales Local Server	4.00	99.97
Host Systems	5.00	99.96
Sales Query Application	3.00	99.98
Sales Database	8.00	99.94
Product Database	5.00	99.96
Customer Database	20.00	99.85
WWW Server	35.00	99.73
Totals	**88.50**	**99.33**

Figure 3.2   A detailed report provides a more comprehensive picture and also highlights areas requiring improvement. This important data could otherwise be concealed within an overall summary.

The same report is also shown in Figure 3.3 as a graph.

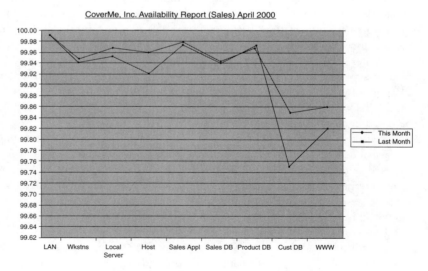

Figure 3.3   The graphical report provides easy-to-understand information and is ideal for displaying a comparison with previous figures.

Penalties for Missed Targets

When the service level agreement is between two departments working in the same company, it is unlikely that there will be a financial penalty for nonperformance. The only time that a financial penalty might be imposed is when the company runs a recharge scheme, or when the service provider is operating as a profit center, charging all its costs to its customers. In these cases, it is reasonable that the client would want to claim compensation for a degraded level of service.

It is worth noting here that if the agreement is between an internal department and a third-party supplier, then financial compensation for failing to meet an agreed target is usually part of the contract drawn up between the parties.

Sometimes the penalty clause is left out of an SLA altogether because the emphasis is directed so heavily on what is expected and required that the parties forget to include a section on what to do if either fails to meet the objectives.

There are alternatives to a penalty clause, and a lot of companies do not like to use the term *penalty*. One option is to include an escalation procedure for nonperformance to identify and resolve the issue. This means that when the objectives of the SLA are not reached and the tolerances are exceeded, an escalation procedure is invoked. This has the detrimental effect of informing management, which can be embarrassing and uncomfortable. The aim of the SLA is not to try to punish, but to provide the incentive to always try to at least meet the targets, if not exceed them.

If the service provider is constantly performing below the agreed level, then the SLA itself might need revisiting because the expectations possibly have been set too high and are therefore unrealistic. This is not always an indication of failure—it could merely be an indication that the negotiation process did not fully achieve a mutual understanding of the service being provided.

It should be remembered that the original aim of setting up SLAs is to be able to define and manage mutually acceptable levels of service. The SLA should identify areas of the service that need improving and aim to focus on these areas instead of looking for ways of punishing substandard performance.

Using an Escalation Procedure

An *escalation procedure* is a defined set of steps designed to do two things: raise the profile of a perceived issue and get something done about it. The means of escalation in this case would probably be in the form of a *service level exception report*, a written report circulated to management highlighting the underachievement. Management, now aware of the problem, is expected to "take ownership" of the issue and exert pressure so that it doesn't happen again.

A more common, everyday example is when, as a consumer, you return to the store to complain about the quality of the goods that you have purchased. When your complaint is not dealt with satisfactorily, you demand to see the manager. You have now *escalated* the situation to a higher authority.

Creating a Service Level Agreement: An Example

The final section in this chapter describes a hypothetical scenario that requires a service level agreement to satisfy the needs of the business. It is intended to demonstrate the kind of issues that must be addressed, as well as provide a good example of the complete process.

Scenario

CoverMe, Inc., is a company that provides life insurance services to the general public. The sales personnel can receive orders and queries via a number of channels:

- Over the telephone
- From the Internet Web site (which are then forwarded using email)
- Via direct email
- In writing by mail (confirmation letters, policy cancellation requests, and so on)

The sales department comprises 25 staff, all of whom have a personal computer connected to the LAN and WAN. Each PC runs an in-house written application to access the sales and inquiry database. The database is held on a host computer system running Solaris 7 and the relational database management software. The host system is physically housed in the computer room, in the basement of the building. The application is GUI-based and makes use of client/server technology.

For some time, the sales staff has been complaining to the manager that it is taking too long to access a customer's record and that they are losing business as a result. This is becoming more evident when dealing with customers on the telephone. The staff members are having to apologize for the delay, which is sometimes greater than two minutes—some customers are even hanging up the phone. The problem is not so critical when dealing with queries or orders from other mediums because the customer is not being kept waiting.

Several calls have been logged with the help desk system regarding the slow response time of the application, but it has not improved, and some of the calls registered are still "open."

At a recent management meeting, the issue was highlighted. The system manager had no knowledge of the problem and agreed to carry out investigations, which resulted in a slight improvement in performance. This was due to the rescheduling of other background work that was running on the host system—it was made to run out of core business hours (which are between 09:00 and 18:30) in an attempt to reduce the load on the system during the working day.

Senior management now has become involved and has suggested that a service level agreement be drawn up between the IT service provider and the sales department. The reasons for this are detailed here:

- A performance problem is costing the company in lost business. This is not quantifiable, but it could potentially affect repeat business from existing customers.

- The IT department cannot produce sufficient supporting data to demonstrate that the systems are providing the required level of service.

- The sales department has not made clear its objectives and priorities.

- There appears to be a breakdown in communication between the help desk and the IT department.

- The business requires a definition of what constitutes an acceptable level of service. It also requests that the necessary monitoring tools be put in place to measure the performance against defined targets. The information is to be used to identify where improvements can be made. A cost/benefit analysis can then be carried out to ensure that any expenditure will provide value for money.

The Service Level Agreement

The scenario described in the previous section clearly shows the need for a service level agreement. This section outlines the step-by-step process of creating a mutually acceptable agreement.

Step 1: Obtain the Agreement

First, before any progress can be made, the senior management from the IT department and the sales department agree that there is a requirement for a service level agreement to be put in place. It is clear that the service being provided by IT is insufficient for the sales team and also that the sales department needs to clearly identify what its expectations are and to prioritize them accordingly.

After a brief meeting involving the two senior managers, the system manager and the sales manager, it is accepted by all parties that the agreement is the only way forward. From the IT department's perspective, the creation of the agreement may have a positive outcome in that deficiencies that are deemed unacceptable can be used as justification for securing additional funding to improve performance. The benefit is recognized as being mainly in the area of telephone sales, where business will not be lost as a result of slow system response times.

Step 2: Assemble the Team

The initial team is selected, comprised of the following:

- **The IT department**—This involves the system manager and a senior system administrator. Input will be required from a database administrator, the PC support section, and the network management team. A member of the development services department will also be required to discuss the workings of the application that is causing the problem.

- **The sales department**—This involves the sales manager and a telesales supervisor. Input will be required from members of the sales team, one from telephone sales and one from Internet-related sales.

- **The help desk manager**—This person will be required to attend at some point in the discussions to describe any existing service level agreements between his section and the business, and to be a part of this one. The relevance in this case is the link between the help desk and the IT department.

Step 3: Prepare for Providing Services

The system manager looks at the service being provided to ensure that any services that he is using are guaranteed, or at least subject to an agreement of their own. If this is not the case, then he is not in a position to be able to guarantee a level of service to anyone else. For this example, the provision of network services and PC support services must be addressed. Host system administration, host system management, and database administration are already his direct responsibility. He also must be sure that any service being provided can be measured. Checking with the networking team reveals that a new system for end-to-end monitoring has recently been installed and can cater to his needs.

Available data can monitor the performance between computer systems, on both the LAN and the WAN. Performance figures are available for both the database itself and the Solaris server, which just leaves the PC on the user's desktop where the application is run from, and for which there is no performance data available. Performance monitoring is enabled on a selection of the PCs to allow information to be gathered. Initial investigations also reveal that the development services section has received problem reports via the help desk, but these have not yet been acted on due to a shortage of resources and other priorities.

The sales team must identify its expectations of the service being provided and also provide clear details of the priorities that exist. Team members decide that the telephone queries must be given the highest priority because there are customers waiting, so the fastest response is required for this type of query or order. Obviously, the team would like an instantaneous response time, but this is not a realistic expectation.

The team carries out some timing tests to identify as accurately as possible the current response times over a period of time, taking the average figure as the current level of service. This figure is calculated as being 1 minute, 35 seconds. The results of the users' tests are shown in Figure 3.4. It is agreed that this is an unacceptable level of service. The level that is deemed to be acceptable is between three and seven seconds.

There is concern that the level of improvement being requested will be too great, so the sales manager talks to the accounting department, which often must run similar types of queries. Discussions reveal that for a simple query to display a single customer's record, the response time is usually less than five seconds. The sales team requirement (between three and seven seconds) is agreed as being acceptable and reasonable.

Figure 3.4   The graphical test report clearly shows that the current system

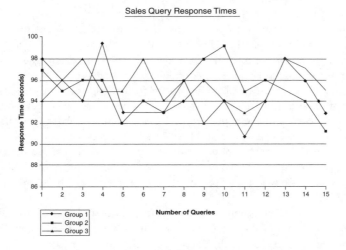

is consistently performing well below the expected level.

Internet- and email-related queries and orders are not as critical as telephone orders, although the slow response times of the system are causing the sales team to build up a backlog of requests and orders. Requests received in writing present the same problems as with Internet orders. Response times are the same as with telephone orders; the only difference is the priority. A drastically improved response time is needed to be able to function effectively.

Step 4: Define the Terms and the Scope of the Agreement

The service level agreement is given a start date, in one month's time, and an end date, in two years and one month's time. The two-year contract is agreed to based on the fact that technology is changing rapidly, so it definitely could not be any longer. There is no guarantee that the SLA will still be valid even after two years, but with the first three months allowing for tuning of the agreement parameters as practical experience is gained, two years is deemed to be a reasonable estimate of the life expectancy. It is generally agreed that an agreement of shorter duration would be of less value to both sides. Additionally, all parties agree that if technology changes significantly enough to affect the value of the agreement, then it will be revisited.

The sales team begins by explaining the process that is carried out when using the system and that the query on the database is looking for only a single customer record. The priority of the telephone queries is also explained, as is the steady buildup of a backlog. Team members mention that the system response time has become steadily worse over the last 12 months. Initially, it was seen as acceptable, probably at about 10 to 15 seconds, because it was a dramatic improvement over the previous system. At that time, approximately 5,000 customer records were held on the database; there are now 50,000, a tenfold increase in 12 months. An acceptable level of service is defined as the response time being between three and seven seconds.

The system manager identifies the service being provided as overlapping between more than one area of responsibility. This, by definition, makes management of the end-to-end process more difficult. He outlines the technical issues concerning the path that is taken by the interchange of data between the client (the user's PC) and the host server (the Solaris server containing the database).

The help desk manager describes the process for dealing with the calls relating to the application. The trouble tickets produced have been passed to development services, the formal owner of the application. At the least, this explains why the system manager had no knowledge of the problem! The help desk manager agrees to revisit his own section's SLA so that a more clearly defined follow-up procedure is invoked, along with a clear escalation procedure. The system manager notes this as an external dependency, which is beyond the control of either party and is the subject of a different service level agreement.

A member of the development services department describes in technical detail how the application works. As a client/server, graphical application, it appears that the design of the application may be the cause of the problem. Usually, with this kind of application, a query submitted from the client (the user's PC) would run on the host server (a much more powerful machine) and only transfer the query results back to the PC—in this case, the customer record. The amount of data being retrieved is trivial and should take only a second or two. The design of the application means that instead of doing this, the entire table is being transferred to the local PC, the query is being run, and the rest of the data is being discarded. It becomes apparent to all parties that the fundamental design of the application is at the root of all the problems being encountered and has caused progressively greater problems as the size of the database has increased.

A member of the PC support services department notes that the PCs on the users' desktops currently have 48MB of memory. For the type of application they are running, they should have an absolute minimum of 64MB, with 128MB being preferred.

Step 5: Document the Agreement

The system manager will not be prepared to agree to the request for the level of service specified by the sales team without additional memory being installed in the users' PCs and the rework of the application so that it performs in an efficient manner.

Only then will it be possible to ascertain an acceptable level of service that is practical and achievable. The current situation does not allow him to guarantee a system response time of less than 1 minute 40 seconds, which is clearly unacceptable to the sales department.

The result in this case is that no agreement can be reached without additional expenditure. The installation of the memory can go ahead because it is a relatively small amount, but the development work required must be scheduled and funded. The SLA negotiations are suspended while the work is carried out. Subsequent testing reveals a substantial service improvement; the response time is within the specified tolerances.

Negotiations recommence, and both parties fully understand what is being provided and the tolerances that exist. The service level agreement can now be formally documented and agreed.

Step 6: Agree on Service Level Indicators

At this stage, indicators of nonperformance are identified and agreed to. The following indicators resulted from discussions:

- Response times for the sales team should not exceed 10 seconds. If nonperformance is encountered, it must occur for at least 10% of all queries during a period of 30 minutes (The 10% threshold allows for blips to occur, which are not indicative of a problem.) The monitoring system provides the necessary management information to measure end-to-end performance.

- PC failures are to be rectified within two hours, by replacing either the entire unit or a specific component. The help desk trouble tickets are to provide the supporting information for this indicator.

- The application must be accessible and usable for 99.5% of the year (during working hours). Availability figures produced on a monthly basis are to be used to measure performance against this indicator.

Step 7: Determine Corrective Action

No financial penalty will be levied with the SLA for nonperformance. Instead, any nonperformance exceptions are to be highlighted in a service level exception report, to be distributed to senior management.

Step 8: Review and Refine the SLA

The SLA will be subjected to weekly reviews for the first three months. Subsequent reviews are to be conducted monthly.

Refinements and modifications to the agreement can be made only by mutual agreement of both groups.

Some Publicly Available SLA Samples

It is often valuable to be able to see real-world examples. They can provide an extra dimension of perspective that might otherwise be missed. The following list shows a number of publicly available examples that can be viewed on the World Wide Web and that may serve as useful references:

- http://cast.stanford.edu/services/
- http://help.oit.unc.edu/ctc/sla/tsld001.htm
- http://etc.nih.gov/pages/etcservicelevelagreement.html
- http://www.ucsf.edu/its/policy/slasum.html

Summary

This chapter is not intended to provide a comprehensive guide to service level management. It is intended to provide sufficient insight into the types of issues that must be addressed.

Service level management is about value for money and quality of service. These two terms are fundamental to the whole process. The provider of the service is expected to deliver a specified, agreed, level of service, and the consumer requires value for the money being spent on the service.

A service level agreement is a contract between two parties that comprises an agreed definition of the service to be provided and a number of tolerances that must not be exceeded. If they are exceeded, however, defined escalation procedures describe how to proceed.

An SLA is only as good as the information available to support it. There must be accurate, reliable, and timely data so that performance can be verified.

The example scenario demonstrates the need for a system manager to be absolutely certain that he can provide the level of service being requested before agreeing to it.

4

Testing

TESTING IS THE ONE PART OF A PROJECT THAT is more likely to be overlooked, particularly if funding for a project is limited. Strangely enough, it is the first thing to be shortened, if not bypassed altogether. Testing has been described as an overhead, although it is actually an integral part of the development and implementation of a system or application. Without it, the company is adding risk to a project—an unacceptable risk that could easily be avoided. There is only one way to ensure that a system or application will work in the operational environment, and that is to test it thoroughly, preferably in an independent test environment in which the "real world" can be simulated as accurately as possible.

Testing is a professional discipline. It requires the services of skilled people, trained to concentrate on the single area of application testing. Historically, testing has been a part of development services partly because the process has a part to play at all stages of development, but also because it didn't fit nicely into any other area. A dedicated test team should be independent and should work in a segregated test environment, completely separate from the development environment. The advantage to be gained from doing this is that testing will be more objective and not subject to political pressure.

Additionally, the application is passed to the test team as a *delivery*. This is an important difference from carrying out testing on the development environment because it requires the test team to install the application on a "clean" system. During development, several tweaks and adjustments might have been made to the system to achieve better performance or to sort out trivial bugs. These may not have been fully documented or included in the final release. Independent, separate testing will highlight any differences that are encountered as a result of a "clean build."

The amount of testing that is carried out varies greatly depending on the size of the business. For example, a small company with maybe three or four IT staff members might carry out only a cursory compatibility test to ensure that the product works and does what it says it does—there may not be any testing at all. In large companies with business-critical applications, a more comprehensive testing policy is more likely, with acceptance testing, coexistence testing, and load testing all being carried out.

The importance of testing is even greater when a third-party supplier is developing an application. The various stages in testing are often used as milestones within the project and payment stages for the supplier—that is, a proportion of the cost of the application is paid upon successful completion of the specified testing phase.

This chapter provides a brief overview of testing, including the lessons that were learned as a result of the Y2K problem. It considers the various testing phases that an application or system might be required to go through. Of course, whether all the phases or just a combination of them are exercised depends on the size of the organization and the effect that an application or system is likely to have on the business. Each stage of testing is described in the text with examples of the benefits to be gained, particularly from the perspective of the system manager.

Quality Assurance

The system manager has a role to play in the testing process, too. It is one mainly related to quality assurance (QA), involving the examination of test results and reports as well as attending various project meetings. The system manager has a vested interest in the success of a new system because it will ultimately be his responsibility to support it. Therefore, he must be sure that the testing has been carried out in a professional manner and in accordance with corporate standards.

Lessons Learned from Y2K

The Y2K issue was itself a huge project and drained resources from the
IT budgets of most companies, forcing a lot of them to put new developments and
projects on hold until all systems and applications were deemed to be Y2K-compliant.
Even then, businesses were reluctant to start new developments because of the uncer-
tainty surrounding the millennium rollover. Y2K was unique in that the deadline was
immovable, and businesses ran the risk of collapsing if their systems were incapable of
functioning correctly.

In January 2000, comments in the media suggested that the Y2K issue was a hoax, a
no-show, and a waste of huge amounts of money in which contractors and IT specialists effectively took industry for a ride. As a Y2K test environment manager for two
and a half years, I believe that without the work done by Y2K programs throughout
the world, there would have been serious disruption to businesses and the environment.

It should be remembered that Y2K wasn't strictly limited to computer systems and
associated software—there were also components that contained embedded processors,
with examples being fire detection systems, intruder detection systems, motor cars,
aircraft, process control devices, weapon control systems, and life-sustaining medical
equipment. Companies had to investigate these devices and either ensure compliance
or have them replaced. People and businesses took the Y2K issue seriously. Dedicated
programs of work were initiated, and professional test teams verified compliance. Y2K
was such a success because all this was done properly—it wasn't luck!

Y2K also produced a number of supplementary issues:

- **The need for better testing**—Y2K testing did not always just reveal noncom-
  pliance; it also revealed other failings within applications. It highlighted the need
  for a more comprehensive testing strategy, with a test team devoted entirely to
  the testing process instead of testing as part of the development function.
  Another important factor was quality assurance (QA)—specifically, that no one
  should QA his own work; it should always be done by someone else. These
  issues were brought to light by the intense testing carried out as part of Y2K.

- **A dedicated test environment**—Many companies realized that a completely
  separate test environment was necessary to carry out compliance testing. It often
  proved impossible to use development environments because of the regular
  changing of system dates and the disruption to normal services that this caused.
  A dedicated test environment has the advantage of being capable of restoring the
  entire system(s) to a known configuration and state. Before testing each application, the system should be reinstated to ensure that it is clean. This is not an
  option in a development environment, but it was a significant factor in verifying
  Y2K compliance. The Y2K-compliance issue made companies aware of the benefits of having a separate, independent test environment.

- **Prioritization of applications**—Because of the immovable deadline of Y2K, businesses had to prioritize the applications to be converted, due to the risk of not being capable of completing them all within the time allowed. The focus on business-critical applications made companies aware (indirectly) of applications that were not as critical as previously thought. Indeed, some applications were dropped from service instead of being made compliant.

- **Patching strategy**—Companies were forced to review the strategy for applying patches to live systems. A large number of operating systems in use required patches to be applied to the system to achieve Y2K compliance. Some decided to install only the patches that were absolutely necessary; others installed them all. My own recommendations were to install all the patches, after checking that there were no obvious conflicts. The advantage of doing this was that if a patch was released late in 1999, then the systems were in a state of readiness to apply it immediately and would not be missing any dependencies. Also, the issue of support from the vendor was relevant. For example, if a support call was logged because of a problem, one of the first things that would have been asked was to confirm the patch status. It was possible that the resolution of the problem could be delayed while the patches were installed.

- **Removal or upgrade of legacy systems**—Old legacy systems and applications that were clearly not Y2K-compliant had to be either upgraded or disposed of. A large number of these systems were still in production because they worked! Y2K focused the attention clearly on these systems, forcing decisions to be made regarding their future.

  The subject of data migration also arose during Y2K. Vast amounts of stored data had been amassed over the years, so companies had to decide whether to migrate the data to compliant platforms or to risk the data becoming unreadable. Data migration was of magnitude significant enough to warrant entire projects being created to deal with it. Some running systems contained only static reference data, often on noncompliant databases. After the data had been migrated to a compliant database, the legacy system could be switched off and decommissioned.

- **An inventory of applications**—The large number of applications that some companies were utilizing meant that a full inventory had to be taken before an accurate assessment could be made of the time needed to achieve full Y2K compliance. It was noted regularly that several different versions of the same application were in production simultaneously, leading to confusion and the potential for unnecessary duplication of effort. An inventory had the advantage of not only cataloging the entire application library, but also assigning a current target version that all users should be adopting. The result was a much tidier application library, tighter version control, and a greatly reduced administration and support overhead.

- **Standards awareness**—Standards laid down by various authorities regarding Y2K compliance heightened the awareness of standards in general. Companies were still developing noncompliant applications as late as 1999, mainly because they were not following established standards. The Y2K issue raised the visibility of standards for application development and the importance of adhering to properly defined procedures and conventions.

- **Investigation into the application delivery and integration process**— The question of how applications were delivered to the user's desktop was another fallout of Y2K. Previous methods had been too unstructured, causing unnecessary support and maintenance, with administrators often having to visit each user's machine to install or modify an application. Central delivery of applications was moved up the agenda of priorities as a potential solution to the vast range of software available on different users' desktop workstations. Additionally, companies looked at standard workstation builds so that each user had exactly the same software configuration. Solaris has made this possible by the use of JumpStart, which brings clusters of workstations up to a standard configuration.

- **Third-party compliance statements**—The Y2K problem demonstrated that statements of compliance from third-party suppliers were occasionally misleading or incomplete. Some applications were strictly only Year 2000–compliant: I personally came across one application that, when the system clock was set to rollover to 2001, displayed 1901, even though it had worked successfully throughout the year 2000. Technically, it was Y2K compliant in that it would work in the year 2000!

Note

The vast majority of third-party supplier statements were indeed accurate and comprehensive. The issue stated previously highlighted the need to ensure that the correct questions were asked and that any possible ambiguities or interpretations were properly addressed.

It is interesting to note from this previous list that a number of the items have nothing to do with Y2K, but they were prompted by the sheer scale of the compliance task. Y2K proved to be an excellent mechanism for companies to carry out housekeeping on a large scale—of course, a further advantage for system managers during this time allowed anything Y2K-related to be charged to a corporate Y2K budget.

A large number of companies are in much better shape following Y2K than they were before Y2K. The streamlining that was necessary to complete everything in time has had a much more permanent effect on companies, many of whom indirectly benefited as a result of the whole exercise.

The Stages of Testing

Testing is involved in several stages during the development of an application:

- **Unit testing**—Modules are tested in isolation during the development process.

- **Integration testing**—Modules are combined and tested together to ensure that they deliver the required functionality.

- **Coexistence testing**—The application is tested alongside other applications to ensure that there is no interference or conflict. An example of this is modifying shared libraries as part of the new development.

- **System testing**—The complete application is tested against the functional specification, which includes installation instructions, guidelines, and administration procedures, as well as the application itself.

- **User acceptance testing (UAT)**—A selection of the user community tests the application in an operational sense. Users run the program in the way that it was intended, and report any problems or issues.

- **Performance testing**—Also known as *load testing* or *stress testing*, this provides the assurance that the application will continue to perform under busy conditions. This is becoming more important as Web-based applications are increasing, with the prospect of many users executing the application concurrently.

- **Implementation**— Larger applications may undergo a pilot implementation in the "live" environment so that comparisons and further checks can be made against results obtained from the current method of operation.

A further stage of testing that is occasionally omitted from the implementation plan is that of end-to-end testing. This topic is discussed in the section "End-to-End Testing."

It is quite rare, however, for a system manager to experience all of these types of testing for a single implementation, except when the delivery is large, expensive, and critical to the business. In this case, the highest level of confidence might be required to significantly reduce any risks during the live cutover. The following list describes the benefit that the system manager might gain from each aspect of testing:

- **Unit testing**—Not much benefit is gained because this type of testing is normally done entirely by the development section or the third party, if the project is being handled externally. For the latter, though, the test results would provide proof that the development is progressing according to the schedule, and it may also be used as a payment point.

- **Integration testing**—Again, the system manager gains no real direct benefit because this testing is carried out within the development section. As with unit testing, however, integration testing could be used as evidence of progress and as a project milestone.

- **Coexistence testing**—This is especially useful when components or modules from several suppliers are used (for example, using GUI applications or forms interacting with Web browsers). Coexistence testing ensures that there will be no compatibility issues and that the new addition will not cause any unforeseen problems with the existing infrastructure.

- **System testing**—The system manager will be responsible for installing the new application or system into the corporate IT infrastructure. He sees that the installation and configuration procedures perform as expected. Also, the fault testing aspect of system testing helps him to ensure that it conforms to the corporate disaster recovery plan and also to test a number of potential disaster scenarios. See Chapter 7, "Disaster Recovery and Contingency Management," for a fuller discussion of these topics.

- **User acceptance testing (UAT)**—The department that requested the functionality ultimately will be paying for it, so user acceptance testing is primarily used in larger developments, particularly those involving external suppliers, in which cost is considerable. UAT is frequently used as a crucial element of a contract with an external supplier—that is, it determines whether the application is "acceptable" or "fit for purpose" to the user community that will be making use of the functionality. The system manager's role in UAT is usually a supporting one in that he will support the UAT environment on which the testing is being carried out. He also will install any patches that result from problems raised during the execution of UAT.

- **Performance testing**—The system manager benefits from this type of testing because it identifies any components, such as servers or applications that might fail as a result of heavy use. Performance testing is also an aid to the system manager's capacity planning strategy, with the results being available for justification for further expansion, if necessary.

- **End-to-end testing**—The system manager will be supporting the system or application when it goes into production, so he benefits from seeing the whole thing, including any interaction with other systems. This type of testing also provides excellent familiarization opportunities for him and his staff to gain a better understanding of how it fits in with the running of the business.

- **Pilot implementation**—This involves the application or system "going live" for a specified set of users, with limited impact if problems are encountered. In addition, this testing provides the benefit of seeing how the application or system performs in the real world. A further business benefit of this is that comparisons can still be made with an existing system that is probably still running in parallel. The system manager can identify performative or administrative issues before they cause an impact in the final transition to operational status.

The numerous stages of testing that are possible for a system or application give some idea of the complexities that can be involved. They also highlight how important it is to carry out thorough testing and to determine the benefits that can be gained from doing so. The fact that many companies either cut testing short or omit it altogether demonstrates the risks that they are leaving themselves exposed to. In these days of competitive Internet trading, a crashing application could prove to be far more costly, in terms of lost revenue, than it would have been if the testing had been fully funded.

Compatibility Testing

Compatibility testing covers several separate aspects of the testing phase, but generally the purpose is to ensure that modules, or components of an application, work both together and with other applications on the system.

Integration and coexistence testing have deliberately been separated here to show the difference between modules of a program working together (described here as integration testing) and the integration of the application into the existing environment, the coexistence element.

A further aspect that fits somewhere between integration and coexistence testing is that of an application in which modules or products are supplied by several vendors. Despite statements of conformability to standards, there can often be problems when a number of different modules are used together, so testing should still be carried out under these conditions.

Unit Testing

Unit testing is the first testing phase that is carried out as part of a development project. A programmer, for example, has written a function. It needs to be tested in isolation, with the objective to ensure that it does exactly what it is meant to do, based on the specification that was provided. Here, the programmer can test his own code to ensure that there are no bugs.

Consider, as an example, the requirement to produce an ad-hoc backup facility for the Solaris servers. One function could be to check that a backup tape is present in the drive and rewind it. The unit testing would involve this function only.

Importance of Testing

The emphasis on testing is normally related to applications that have been written either in-house or by a third-party supplier. It is important to note, however, that even off-the-shelf products require testing to be carried out, particularly coexistence testing and performance testing. These are important to verify that the product will not cause any adverse effect on the rest of the system and that the system is capable of handling the expected demand for concurrent usage.

Integration Testing

Integration testing during the development of an application is carried out in a similar way to unit testing, but it involves a number of modules that interact with each other. Taking the previous example, the integration test would comprise the entire backup program, complete with functions and subroutines. The theory behind integration testing is that it tests the interaction between different units to ensure that they function as expected and as specified in the requirement.

Coexistence Testing

Coexistence testing is a necessary part of the overall testing strategy. It confirms that the new component works in harmony with the existing system, whether hardware or software. In the case of hardware, it could be the addition of a tape drive requiring a patch to be added, a patch that conflicts with another patch already installed on the live system.

In the case of an application, the installation procedure could, for example, modify library modules that subsequently cause other applications to stop working. Coexistence testing identifies these potential problems, which might otherwise go unnoticed, causing severe, unexpected problems when installed in the live environment.

Acceptance Testing

Acceptance testing is the final phase of testing before going live. It is a crucial process and eventually will determine whether a product is acceptable to the business.

When a product is deemed to be acceptable, it progresses through to implementation and becomes operational, but what happens if either the user acceptance or the system acceptance tests fail?

During acceptance testing, problem logs are created when either a bug is found or the application responds in an unexpected manner. The logs are passed to the developer(s) for resolution. An example of a problem log is shown in Figure 4.1. The tester often provides additional information by attaching a screen dump showing clearly the point at which the error occurs. Sometimes the resolution is procedural and may require only a trivial update to the documentation, but on other occasions, a fix may have to be supplied. For the latter, a patch is issued and installed on the system. However, it's not that simple because the fix could invalidate all the testing already done.

Project: C34124/66		Motor Insurance System		
PROBLEM REPORT			No: MIS0034/04	

Test Case:	T/0145 Part II	Severity: 1 - Fatal	(test aborted)	✓
Reporter:	J. Philcox	Severity: 2 - Serious	(test suspended)	
		Severity: 3 - Trivial	(test continued)	
Date:	25 July 2000	Severity: 4 - Cosmetic	(observation)	

Description:
When executing step 3 to enter query criteria, the following error message is displayed as the 'Enter' button is pressed:

Execution Error: Code 45332 - Unable to perform query - object does not exist or you have insufficient privileges - Contact technical support for assistance.

Acknowledging the error returns to the enter query criteria screen and cannot exit the application.

Resolution:

Status: Open

Figure 4.1   The problem log represents a formal document of the testing phase with a unique reference. It is often stored in a database using a program such as PVCS Tracker, allowing further analysis to be undertaken.

Consider the following example: While testing the application, a user receives the wrong results for a query operation. A problem log is raised and passed to the developers to fix. A patch is delivered containing the fixed module. The query module is shared by several forms and is also used to gather the information for the management and financial reports.

Clearly, in this example, the impact of the change is much wider than just the query being tested. The point is that any changes to a system or application under review must include a detailed impact assessment so that its effect is known and understood. In the example, the change is fundamental to the system and may require the testing to be restarted from the beginning. In reality, testing would probably be completed (without installing the patch) so that any other problems can be addressed before rerunning the tests.

Regression Testing

Regression testing is used as a mechanism of ensuring that there have been no unexpected side effects of a change. It allows tests to be rerun, knowing exactly what the result should be, thereby highlighting immediately any deviation. For example, consider an application that calculates the payroll for the employees of the company. Suppose that a new application is being developed to replace the existing one, which cannot handle the increased number of employees since the company expanded.

Using the existing system for calculating the payroll, a test would be devised, using specific test data (say, a dozen employees), and their payroll details calculated. When the new system is installed and tested, the same calculations would be carried out, using the same test data. The results should be exactly the same—if not, then the new system is not functioning correctly.

For an application such as payroll, despite the fact that a new way of doing things has been developed, maybe using a new GUI front end, the functionality—that is, the results of the calculations—should be the same. Regression testing is used for this purpose, to be able to verify that the application still performs as expected. Without the benefit of regression testing, it would be extremely difficult to identify the effects of any changes on other parts of the application, leaving the potential for problems to be found only after the system is live.

System Testing

System testing involves testing all the features of a new application. The IT department carries out the system acceptance and fully tests the functionality against an agreed criteria, usually the functional specification. System testing differs from user acceptance testing in that the management and configuration of the application or system is tested in addition to the functionality.

Some of the types of tests are listed here:

- Installation and configuration procedures, including a QA of the administration and installation documentation.

- Creation and management of user accounts, and management of passwords (if applicable) and permission assignments. For example, a user may be assigned a specific role that will require different permissions, such as query only, query and update, or full administrator.

- Process of exercising each option that is available within the application to ensure that it works as expected. For GUI applications, command-line equivalents should be available for the core functionality of the application so that, for example, GUI sessions are not sent through firewalls when executing the application remotely across the network.

- Configuration of printing from within the application. An example of this is the addition of a new printer or a printer queue.

- Entering of invalid data to check that the error handling functions as expected. The testing looks for errors, so attempts will obviously be made to make the application or system crash.

- Volume testing, to ensure that the system can work under conditions very close to that of the live environment.

- Testing of the security of the system, as part of its security accreditation. The results of the security tests provide evidence of compliance (or otherwise) with the security policy in force.

- Performance of recovery testing, which is necessary particularly in larger systems involving hardware and software deployment. In this instance, the system is deliberately placed in a variety of fault conditions to establish how tolerant it is and how quickly processing can be resumed. For example, in a RAID storage configuration, a good test is to remove one of the disk modules (to simulate a disk failure) and check that a hot spare takes over the role of the failed module.

User Acceptance

The user community must have the opportunity to test the application before implementation. For larger projects, a user assurance coordinator (UAC) should be assigned to the project, normally from within the IT department. As a system manager, I have fulfilled this role. The UAC looks after the users' interests to ensure that the application meets their expectations. UAT should be carried out on a dedicated test environment in which changes to the application cannot be made without being carefully controlled and documented. At this stage of the process, changes are acceptable only when delivered as patches, and these would be as a result of problem logs being created by the UAT team.

This stage of testing is crucial to a project being successful for the following reasons:

- The users run the system or the application as it will be used in the live environment, and exercise it fully so that any deficiencies can be identified as soon as possible. These problems subsequently are rectified before the final delivery. This includes the users entering invalid data, such as bad dates or reference numbers that don't conform to the standard, to check that they will be rejected. The user will determine whether the application will be accepted on behalf of the business. Normally a senior user representative will be a member of the project board.

- The UAC role will be heavily involved in the creation of the acceptance test criteria, the associated acceptance test specifications, and test scripts. These are the documents that will be used during UAT execution. The test scripts that are produced should form a logical sequence that reflects the normal operational usage.

Recovery Testing

Recovery tests can sometimes be extremely difficult to accomplish, particularly with sealed units that can't be accessed directly. Certain tests likely may need the cooperation of the vendor so that the required scenarios can be fully tested.

- UAT enables the user community to see the application running in its final state. It is an ideal opportunity to build user confidence in the product. This is especially vital if the application is new. People are naturally hostile to change, so the UAT provides the chance to gain familiarity and to see the benefits that the new product will offer. Conversely, a badly designed application or a poorly performing system can destroy user confidence. If this happens, then it will be extremely hard to get it accepted.

- UAT will prove whether the user documentation is accurate and usable.

- The users test the user interface as well as the application itself. This is particularly useful for GUI-based applications, in which color schemes and screen layouts are scrutinized.

- Test cases are often executed by more than one person. The same result should be produced each time.

Performance Testing

The other areas of testing discussed so far verify, as much as possible, that the application functions as expected. Performance testing looks at a further aspect that is sometimes less obvious: the testing of the application when under load, or busy, conditions. Performance testing has become even more important since businesses started using the Internet, particularly with reference to Web servers. There might be a point at which the application, or the server, crashes if too many people try to use it at the same time, so the performance capability must be tested so that the anticipated demand can be met. It is extremely difficult to accurately predict the level of demand that a new Web site will generate—companies are often victims of their own success. For example, when an advertising campaign has much greater success than predicted, the increase in demand can be more than the system can handle.

Producing test conditions and data for performance testing can be a time-consuming and expensive business, requiring a great deal of coordination. It often involves creating large amounts of test data, as well as having the relevant technical staff in attendance to accurately monitor the performance as the testing is carried out. From the system manager's point of view, however, the testing can be of great benefit because it might provide firm justification for upgrading a server that was proved to be inadequate, or the purchase of a new, more powerful machine.

End-to-End Testing

The concept of end-to-end testing is that the business function is tested, not merely the application that has been developed. An example of this is a complete sales order transaction. In this case, the end-to-end test would involve the following steps:

1. Creating the sales record

2. Processing the order, from producing the invoice to dispatching the order

3. Adding the customer to a mailing list for future promotions

4. Archiving the transaction after payment has been received

This process could potentially involve several different systems and applications, as well as a significant time delay, as shown in Figure 4.2. It is not uncommon for some end-to-end tests to run for many hours—for example, with the sales record discussed, the archive process might run only once a day overnight. The value of the test is that it runs exactly as it would in the operational environment.

End-to-end testing is a significant area of testing that is sometimes omitted. One reason for this is the practicality of replicating the entire environment: It can prove expensive, although it should be noted that the testing environment can often use smaller, less powerful systems to test functionality.

Sometimes, of course, it is impossible to fully replicate the environment in which an application will run, but the part that is frequently left out involves the interfaces with other systems or applications. In this instance, the new product may receive data from an existing application, then process and forward it to another application, and archive it on yet another system. The testing of the system might involve test data being created to simulate the input being delivered. This is fine for testing the system itself, but not for the interfaces. The new system or application is adding a risk to all the other systems that it interfaces with and could potentially corrupt data on those systems if this aspect is not thoroughly tested.

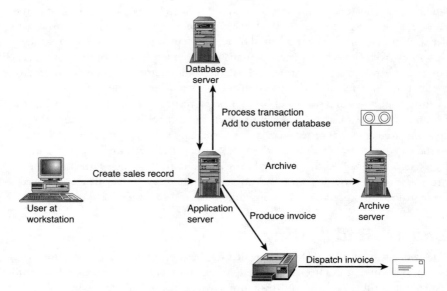

Figure 4.2   The end-to-end test provides the customer with confidence that the new system or application will work alongside existing systems.

Consider an application that runs on a PC—say, a Microsoft Access database. Data is input and processed locally and then is sent to a remote database on a Solaris platform to be used by other sections. The local application generates the necessary SQL code to query or update the records in a table on the remote system. This is known as a pass-through query or a pass-through update. If the code generated is not absolutely correct, the remote database is in danger of being corrupted, despite the local application passing all of its testing.

In this example, the test environment must include a clone of the remote database, as well as the local application and all the associated hardware and software. The significance of the end-to-end test in this instance is that testing encompasses the remote database—which might not even be part of the system under test—to ensure that the data has been inserted or updated correctly.

Final Testing Before Implementation

This testing phase involves the installation of the system or application in its live configuration. To all intents and purposes, the system is live, but with some differences: It is still under the control of the development project, and a parallel element will probably be running. The system or application being replaced might continue to run until the final operating capability is declared. At that point, the new system is truly live.

The final testing phase is often of critical importance because it is the first time that the users get to see the system or application running in the live environment. It is at this stage that unexpected problems are most likely to occur, normally because of something on the operational network that has been overlooked or not considered to be of any consequence. The initial operating capability provides additional time for these problems to be rectified.

Initial Operating Capability

When the system and user acceptance testing has been successfully completed, the system or application can be declared to be in initial operating capability (IOC). This is a state of readiness for full operational status. The system or application is installed, and the users start to conduct their normal business using the new product.

The IOC phase allows the system to run normally, but with the advantage of being monitored by technical staff. Any changes or modifications that are required at this stage must be subject to configuration management and must be delivered as patches, with accompanying documentation. Some initial tuning may be required to enhance performance. This will result in the documentation being amended and redelivered as a new version. At this stage, the system that is being replaced will still be running, and the two might be operating in parallel. Results can be compared as a final check to ensure that the functionality of the new system is correct.

Final Operating Capability

When a new product has completed IOC, its status changes to final operating capability (FOC). This is the point at which the system or application is said to be truly live.

There can be no changes to the system without using the formal change mechanism. The source code for any applications should be under configuration control, as well as all the supporting documentation. At this point the formal responsibility transfers to the system manager or staff members in charge of support and maintenance. Any changes to the software will be delivered in the form of a patch and will be subject to formal authorization procedures, the same as other live systems.

The system or application that was being replaced can now be disabled or switched off.

Summary

Testing is a discipline that requires a high level of skill to ensure that all areas of a system or application are thoroughly examined and exercised. It is also an aspect of system development that is frequently overlooked or shortened because of budgetary constraints.

The Y2K issue highlighted the need for thorough testing and, because of the immovable deadline, forced businesses to identify and prioritize their requirements. The result of carrying out a detailed inventory meant that many companies ended up in much better shape, with a more streamlined and efficient way of working.

The system manager benefits from a number of testing phases throughout the development and implementation of a new system or application, most notably system testing and performance testing, because of the justification that he can provide for requesting additional funding for the systems.

Coexistence testing and performance testing are important because they verify that the system or application will work with other products, that it fits in with the existing infrastructure, and also that it can satisfy the predicted requirement for concurrent usage, allowing for predicted peaks of demand.

Acceptance testing is often used in larger installations, particularly when a third-party supplier is involved and the cost is much higher. The "user community" gets to test the functionality against the original specification, using it as it will be used in the operational environment. The application or system will not be signed off or paid for in full unless the user acceptance-testing phase completes successfully.

The importance of end-to-end testing is fundamental to any new application or system in that it exercises the entire business function, often incorporating several existing systems and processes. It is an excellent means of building customer confidence in the new implementation.

The final testing phase before implementation allows the system or application to be seen in its live environment, but without the risks or impact of full operational running. When carried out in two stages, minor performance issues can be resolved by the system manager before the full implementation takes place.

II

Management of the Solaris Environment

5

Solaris Installations and Upgrades

A MAJOR PART OF THE SYSTEM MANAGER'S WORK involves the provision of new resources and the improvement of existing ones. To this end, the system manager is the person who will investigate the configuration options that are available and will provide the best service for the business.

This chapter covers two main areas: a new installation and an upgrade. A third section at the end looks at the installation of patches, discussing some of the issues that arise when trying to decide on a patching policy, both for the Solaris operating environment patches as well as unbundled product patches and third-party patches.

Businesses face a dilemma these days about implementing new systems. With such a vast array of hardware and software available, all claiming to be the best and all being fully adaptable to the requirements of business, the system manager needs to obtain as much information as possible before committing to any one product. Indeed, some businesses deliberately diversify so as not to be tied to a specific vendor. These environments are known as *multivendor environments*.

A great deal of information can be obtained from the World Wide Web. All the major vendors have Web sites that you can search for information on the various products that they market.

There is a distinct difference, though, between purchasing a new system and upgrading an existing one, which is why these two scenarios form the basis of this chapter.

The following pages discuss new installations and upgrades, providing some useful information on the types of hardware and software services that either are available now or are becoming available. Also investigated are some of the issues that the system manager must deal with when attempting to secure the best possible option for the business. He must be thinking of the future and about the life expectancy of a system, the potential for asset replacement, the required availability, expansion plans, and the purpose for the existence of the system in the first place. A new system must fit into the existing infrastructure and must be in line with the corporate IT strategy—radical changes are frequently perceived as being risky.

A further consideration that is addressed here is the installation into a 24×7 working environment. Internet business is proliferating at an alarming rate, so there is a greater requirement for systems to be running continuously around the clock, every day.

24×7 Operations

24×7 environments are a big subject in today's business arena. This section aims to provide an insight into the types of issues that need to be addressed when establishing a high availability system. The topic warrants an entire book on its own to cover every aspect thoroughly and to consider all the options, but it should prove useful to discuss it here as well.

There is an increasing need for information and application services to be available on a continuous basis, particularly with regard to e-business. Businesses cannot tolerate either planned or unplanned downtime—the only way to provide this level of service is to create a fully operational environment that is available 24 hours a day, 7 days a week.

The continuous environment places a significantly higher demand on the computer systems because they must be constantly available to deliver the level of service that is required. Several issues must be considered when creating a 24×7 working environment, and the major ones are discussed here.

Solaris and Other Platforms

In this chapter, the book begins to focus on Solaris, whereas the preceding chapters largely addressed general system-management topics. It should be noted, however, that most of the principles outlined here are equally applicable to other platforms, although any solutions provided are specifically tailored for the Solaris and Sun environment.

Configuration of the Environment

The configuration of the 24×7 environment is normally determined by two major factors—namely, the level of criticality attached to the requirement, and money, although not always in that order of priority!

First, the critical nature of some services dictates how the 24×7 environment is to be established—that is, the level of replication required, whether to use a single site or to utilize remote sites for added resilience, and so on. The business needs to recognize the importance of the application being carried out and the effect of not being able to carry it out—this is often the deciding factor. A true 24×7 computing environment cannot be achieved using a single system because it creates a single point of failure; there must be at least two systems, and, realistically, they have to be at separate sites. This is because a major disaster, such as fire or flood, could still bring the operation to an abrupt halt if all the systems were housed in the same location.

Sun Cluster software addresses exactly this type of scenario by allowing a number of computer systems to be "clustered" together so that they collectively provide the overall service to the customer. This provides the required availability because, if one computer fails, the others in the cluster pick up the work that was being carried out automatically. This also allows elements of the cluster to be separated by up to 10 kilometers, delivering a high level of contingency against disaster.

A further interesting aspect of this software is that it supports the Sun StorEdge disk configurations, allowing all of the critical data to be housed independently of any one system, adding to the resilience. This is achieved through the use of a storage area network (SAN). A SAN is a dedicated network of storage devices, normally with its own server, that is part of the overall computer network but independent of any of the systems that make use of its resource. This means that if any of the clustered systems mentioned previously were to fail, the data would still be available to the remaining members of the cluster.

The cluster solution is fully scalable, which means that all the systems comprising the cluster do not have to be the same. For example, a four-system cluster could include an Enterprise 10000 server, two Enterprise 5000 machines, and one Enterprise 3000 server. This enables companies to still make use of previous-generation systems, which can be highly cost-effective when attempting to finance the operation. Clustering solutions are discussed again in Chapter 7, "Disaster Recovery and Contingency Management," as part of disaster recovery. Figure 5.1 shows a simple diagram of a possible clustered environment.

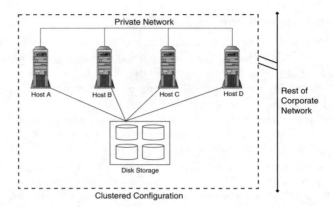

Figure 5.1   The clustered environment provides added resilience and high availability, coupled with automatic failover facilities.

Budgetary Considerations

An extremely important question that the system manager must ask is this: "Who's paying for all this?" Managing and supporting a 24×7 environment is not cheap—indeed, it costs significantly more than just running a "business hours" operation. These costs are not just for computer hardware and software so that high availability can be achieved, but also for additional accommodation (especially when multiple sites are being used), extra staff to support the operation, and, of course, extra management to manage it. Somewhere, someone is going to have to pay for it, and it can't be the system manager. Normally, the requesting department—that is, the person(s) or department that originally asked for the operation—is the best place to start. Companies using the chargeback system, described in Chapter 2, "The IT Budget," should be capable of charging the customer for the services being provided—in this case, a 24-hour computing environment.

Many system administrators and system managers come under pressure to deliver this level of service without being provided with any additional financial assistance. Without lowering standards of service or quality elsewhere, however, this simply isn't possible, which merely shifts the problem rather than solving it.

Staff Considerations

Manning a 24×7 operation involves additional staff: It is not possible to stretch the existing manpower levels to cater to a nonstop operation. Not only must the system administration and support staff be considered, but the management must as well. There is likely to be a requirement for at least one more system manager, who will be responsible for out-of-business working hours. Many organizations employ a formal shift roster, usually with either three or four shifts needed to provide the required level of support. It is important to remember that even shift workers and system managers need to have vacations, just like everyone else, and they are also sometimes ill, so any staffing requirements must account for expected attendance levels. Of course, this is expensive because the number of staff needed for a 24×7 operation will be at least double that of a business hours-only operation—double rather than triple because the out-of-hours shift size can often be reduced. Greater use of automation and management tools can further reduce the number of staff needed, but there is no escaping the fact that each shift must be manned and that attendance factors must be considered, too.

New Installation

A new installation of a system can be a difficult task, especially if it is the first system being purchased from a specific vendor. New contacts must be made, and business relationships must be established. Some new skills also might have to be recruited, or an investment in training might have to be made. All of these things need to be addressed well in advance of the actual delivery.

New System as Part of a Project

Chapter 2 discussed the use of projects. A new system installation is likely to be part of a project, with an associated budget cost code. Any training requirements should be funded as part of the project, potentially saving the system manager a considerable amount of money. Additionally, a project sometimes funds the support and the implementation for the first year or so. Be aware of the potential to charge these costs to the project.

With a new system, the system manager will be heavily involved in the technical assurance of the project. He will have significant input into the specification of the system and the requirements that need to be satisfied. In addition to considering the project itself, he will have to take account of any likely effect on the business as a whole. An example of this is when a new installation threatens to overload the existing power output in the computer room—here, the risk exists that services already being provided from other computer systems residing in the same computer room could be severely disrupted. This example highlights not only the question of who funds any necessary work to provide the additional power capacity, but also the issue of the disruption to operational services while the work is carried out. In mission-critical operations, this will be a serious consideration if all power has to be removed for several hours or, worse, several days. Most, if not all, businesses will simply not allow this kind of interruption to service and will demand a high level of resilience, a requirement that can be satisfied only through the use of multiple sites, automatic failover, and clustering.

The system manager needs to consider the purchase options available for a new system, particularly if it is planned to expand considerably. After a finite period of project support, the new system will become the responsibility of the system manager, so he must take a longer term view of the project, assessing the life expectancy of the system being purchased, the potential for upgrade and expansion, and so on. A purchasing initiative from Sun Microsystems addresses this specific issue. The "capacity on demand suite" enables customers to purchase fully configured systems but pay only for those components actually being used, or to spread the cost over more than one year, thereby allowing better management of the IT budget. (The term *system* does not necessarily apply to one physical computer; it could mean 5 servers and 200 clients, for example, all of which form the system.)

The level of availability required can often dictate how a new configuration will be planned. Larger companies can opt for multiple sites acting in a clustered configuration, providing greater contingency against a disaster, whereas medium-sized businesses might choose hardware redundancy with automatic failover. The small business probably makes use of an uninterruptible power supply (UPS) to protect the system from unscheduled power loss.

The next few sections detail some of the issues surrounding the purpose, configuration, and implementation of a new system installation. A sample scenario sets the scene.

Scenario

The purpose of the scenario outlined here is to identify a number of issues that need to be addressed. It is designed to encourage consideration of how you, the reader, would deal with such a situation. The issues are then discussed in the following sections.

Consider this hypothetical example of a company wanting to expand into a new market:

CoverMe, Inc., the insurance company from Chapter 3, "Delivering the Goods," is expanding into the motor insurance business. The current systems are a few years old and are not capable of supporting the new requirements. It is anticipated that the new motor insurance system will grow by approximately 70% over the next 12 months, but this could be as much as 200% if the new advertising campaign is successful. The requirements for the new system are as follows:

- Provision of servers capable of supporting the additional client workstations
- Workstation positions for 250 staff—150 of these are to be located within a "secure" office area, and the other 100 are to be located in "open offices" that are not secure
- Access to a database for the new motor insurance business
- Integration with existing customer databases
- Access to the new motor insurance application software

The implementation is to be carried out over two sites in a clustered configuration so that the required level of availability and resilience can be achieved. Additionally, a number of Web servers are being installed, but these are being handled by a separate Internet project.

Planning for a New System

A new system requires some careful planning. Several steps are involved in planning for the arrival of a new system, apart from the configuration and purchase of the system itself. Some of them are often overlooked, so they are discussed here:

- **Allocation of accommodation**—The servers need to be housed in a computer room with a controlled environment and guaranteed power. It is always a big mistake to assume that there is space for another system. The system manager must ensure that there is sufficient power capacity for the new computer system(s) to be sited and that the environmental control (air conditioning, humidity control, and so on) can cope with the added load. It may seem quite trivial, but installing a new system into a computer room often requires cutting floor tiles so that the wiring can pass under the floor in ducts. This is frequently overlooked and is done as a rush job at the last minute. When the exact site and footprint of the server(s) have been confirmed, this task should be arranged. Failure to do this can result in the new system being incapable of connecting to the power source or the network, and this can be very embarrassing.

- **Extra resources**—Any new system being implemented could result in the need for extra staff to provide the required level of support and administration. The system manager must address the training needs and ensure that the new staff members are recruited and trained before the delivery of the system(s).

- **Names**—A name for the servers and clients must be chosen. Some companies have a prepared list of names to use for hosts, which must be consulted when a new system is planned. In this instance, names are selected from the list and are registered so that there can be no risk of having duplicate hostnames within the company. The name should be as meaningful as possible to the function that it will carry out and the department(s) that it will serve.

- **Name services**—If NIS or NIS+ is in use, the system manager must evaluate the number of NIS servers to cater to the demand for the new system, especially if a number of clients are included in the new installation. Domain Name Services (DNS) must be taken into account, and the address details must be registered with the DNS server. If this is not done, then DNS will be incapable of resolving the name of your new domain when requests are directed to it.

- **Network connection**—The new system will require a number of network connections. An Internet Protocol (IP) address must be assigned to each computer (or each network interface), and this must be unique within the company and also globally, if communicating on the Internet. The network department normally handles this, but the system manager must place the application to have the address(es) assigned in the first place. A further consideration is whether whether any special requirements, such as positioning on the network, are needed. For example, a server that is providing operating system resources to a number of diskless or autoclient systems should be positioned on the same subnet as the clients to reduce traffic across the network. The exact specifications must be provided to the network department so that it can ascertain whether any capacity issues will arise. Imagine suddenly increasing the network traffic to support 250 diskless clients, which will be running client/server applications to a database server across the network as well as printing and accessing applications servers. For some companies, this could cause major problems, especially if the network is already heavily loaded. It might produce a requirement for multiple network interfaces to be installed on the server(s). Major systems creating a new subnet, or spur, often need to have connections to a router to access the rest of the network. Liaison with the network department is essential so that it can be determined whether there are sufficient "spare" ports on the specified router(s) to cope with the requirement and so that these ports can be reserved. These will also have to be configured when the system is delivered.

Room for Expansion

Many new projects seriously underestimate the amount of growth that will occur in the first year of production. Consequently, they find that the system cannot cope with the demands being placed on it and that an upgrade must be carried out, causing major disruption and loss of availability.

Earlier, this chapter briefly mentioned the capacity assurance suite initiative from Sun Microsystems. This allows the capacity options to be decided early in the project. The options are discussed here:

- **Do nothing**—Continue as before, but try to calculate the perceived rate of growth as accurately as possible. This option will work quite well for businesses with a steady, consistent growth factor, but it will not be capable of catering to a significant increase in business, such as from an extremely successful advertising campaign.

- **Pay as you grow**—This option enables the business to purchase a slightly larger system, fully configured, but then pay only for those components that will be used immediately. The customer then pays more over the next 12-month period as more of the resources are used, in line with demand. There is no need for a hardware upgrade because the extra components are already present in the chassis; they are just "activated."

- **Capacity on demand**—Purchase a high-end Enterprise E10000 server, fully configured, but pay only for those components that are required for immediate use. This option is more attractive to larger companies because it offers a further benefit—namely, the potential to consolidate some other systems to run on the same E10000 server. The E10000 can be partitioned to run as if it were multiple systems; groups of processors (called *domains*) can be configured to work together. The system comes with full fault tolerance and is designed to achieve the highest availability with fully redundant power supplies and online hot swapping of components. The E10000 features automated dynamic reconfiguration (ADR), which allows the reallocation of resources to where they are needed most. This sort of feature addresses precisely those occasions when the system is under heavy load. For larger companies, the capacity on demand option offers significant medium- to long-term savings as well as increased performance and availability.

For further details on purchasing initiatives available via Sun Microsystems, consult the Web site http://www.sun.com, or contact your Sun sales department.

Multiprocessing Capabilities

Sun Microsystems provides unrivalled multiprocessing capabilities, not only in its hardware, but also through the use of its Solaris operating environment, which exploits the facility fully.

Sun provides a range of enterprise servers that can accommodate up to 64 processors and 64GB of main memory (the Enterprise 10000). For some companies, though, this is probably far too large, so other systems are available to cater to enterprises of all sizes. The range of servers and workstations can be viewed online from the Sun Web site.

An interesting aspect of these multiprocessing systems and the operating environment is that a number of processors can be configured to work together as an independent domain. This allows the resources to be directed to where they are needed most, greatly increasing the flexibility that businesses of today require. If a problem occurs, for example, a specific "domain" of processors can even be rebooted without affecting the rest of the system, a facility that enhances the availability of the system. The overall result is that a single enterprise server can be segmented to run different applications independently, while also being capable of sharing resources when required.

Integration into the Existing Infrastructure

Any new installation must conform to certain standards that are already in place within the organization. The system manager is responsible for ensuring that the new system will fit in. This includes allocating physical space in the computer room, ensuring that the power requirements of the system can be accommodated and also that the controlled environment (air conditioning and so on) can cope with the heat output produced by the new system. Network connections are needed to enable the new system to connect to the LAN/WAN, and these must be allocated and configured in advance so that there is no delay when the system is delivered.

Naming conventions also must be adhered to—for example, setup for a new database server running an Oracle database might involve the use of defined *mount points* when creating the database file systems so that consistency across all servers is maintained.

Larger installations and those with external communications facilities, such as the Internet for example, will undoubtedly have a system security policy that all new systems must comply with before being allowed to connect to the corporate network. System security is discussed in more detail in Chapter 6, "Solaris Security."

Purpose of the System

How a system is to be used often determines, to an extent, how it will be configured and managed. The system manager is responsible for ensuring that the required level of service can be provided. The next few sections cover a variety of categories that a large system might be used for. This could be a server providing operating system services to a number of clients, or distributed access to data and print facilities. A database server, for example, will be providing remote access to a database and must be configured to make optimal use of the resources so that acceptable response times for queries and similar items can be achieved. All of these are discussed in the following pages, along with the administration and management overheads that are incurred with each.

Operating System Server

A server that is providing operating system resources to a number of clients must be configured so that it can respond to client requests in a timely manner. Failure to achieve this is normally because either the server has been setup incorrectly, or it is trying to support too many clients. As an approximate rule, a large server would be expected to be capable of supporting only about 50 diskless clients. So, it can be seen from the scenario earlier in the chapter that 4 or 5 operating system servers would probably be required to support the 250 client workstations that are being delivered as part of the business expansion plan.

Mount Points

The use of mount points applies only to databases using UFS filesystems. A popular way of storing the database is to use raw disk partitions and the associated device filenames, but even in this case, there might be symbolic links that adhere to a naming convention.

Two major considerations must be addressed for operating system servers: their physical position on the network and the organization of the disk partitions. Both are these are addressed next:

- **Position on the network**—An operating system server should be physically positioned on the same subnet as the clients to reduce unnecessary network traffic affecting the performance of other systems on the corporate network. Ideally, the subnet should be connected to a router or a bridge so that broadcast messages are filtered out and are not passed through to the rest of the network. Consider the server supporting 50 diskless clients, all of which send broadcast messages to boot up and get all their system resources (/, /usr, and swap) across the network. Figure 5.2 depicts the network configuration for the five servers required to support the 250 clients specified in the scenario earlier in the chapter.

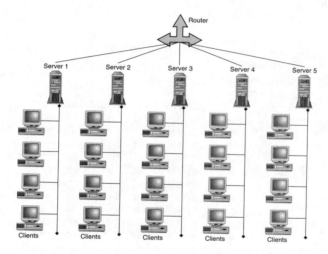

Figure 5.2 Placing the server on the same subnet as its clients dramatically reduces unwanted network traffic that could potentially affect other systems on the network. The router filters out locally addressed packets so that they do not pass through to the rest of the network.

Client Configurations

The clients being supported will be either diskless or autoclient systems. These do not include standalone systems because they require no system resources from a server to function.

- **Organization of disk partitions**—An operating system server supporting, say, 50 diskless clients must provide the swap space for each of those clients on its own hard disks as well as the root (/) file system and the /usr file system, where all of the clients' executables are held. Client swap areas are normally created in a file system named /export/swap/. Because the client swap areas will be heavily used, they should be created equally across the available disks so that the load is evenly balanced across the available disk controllers and disk volumes. Consider the following example:

A server (coverme) supports 50 diskless clients (coverme01 through coverme50). The server has two disks, both 9Gb in size. Each client will have 64Mb of swap space allocated to it. The best way of organizing the disks is to create a file system on each to hold the swap areas for the clients. So, /export/swap contains the swap for the odd-numbered clients, and /export/swap1 contains the swap for the even-numbered clients, as shown in Listing 5.1.

Listing 5.1   Sample Output Showing the Distribution of Swap Space for Even-Numbered Clients

```
coverme# cd /export/swap1
coverme# ls -l total 1704976
-rw——–·  1 root      other      67108864 Jul  2 18:05 coverme02
-rw——–·  1 root      other      67108864 Jul  2 18:07 coverme04
-rw——–·  1 root      other      67108864 Jul  2 18:07 coverme06
-rw——–·  1 root      other      67108864 Jul  2 18:07 coverme08
-rw——–·  1 root      other      67108864 Jul  2 18:08 coverme10
-rw——–·  1 root      other      67108864 Jul  2 18:08 coverme12
-rw——–·  1 root      other      67108864 Jul  2 18:08 coverme14
-rw——–·  1 root      other      67108864 Jul  2 18:09 coverme16
-rw——–·  1 root      other      67108864 Jul  2 18:09 coverme18
-rw——–·  1 root      other      67108864 Jul  2 18:09 coverme20
-rw——–·  1 root      other      67108864 Jul  2 18:10 coverme22
-rw——–·  1 root      other      67108864 Jul  2 18:10 coverme24
-rw——–·  1 root      other      67108864 Jul  2 18:10 coverme26
-rw——–·  1 root      other      67108864 Jul  2 18:10 coverme28
-rw——–·  1 root      other      67108864 Jul  2 18:10 coverme30
-rw——–·  1 root      other      67108864 Jul  2 18:10 coverme32
-rw——–·  1 root      other      67108864 Jul  2 18:10 coverme34
-rw——–·  1 root      other      67108864 Jul  2 18:10 coverme36
-rw——–·  1 root      other      67108864 Jul  2 18:10 coverme38
-rw——–·  1 root      other      67108864 Jul  2 18:10 coverme40
-rw——–·  1 root      other      67108864 Jul  2 18:10 coverme42
-rw——–·  1 root      other      67108864 Jul  2 18:10 coverme44
-rw——–·  1 root      other      67108864 Jul  2 18:10 coverme46
-rw——–·  1 root      other      67108864 Jul  2 18:10 coverme48
-rw——–·  1 root      other      67108864 Jul  2 18:10 coverme50
coverme#
```

Creating the clients can be done easily by using Solstice Adminsuite, a package that provides an easy-to-use graphical user interface (GUI) for system administrators to manage the network. Adminsuite is described in Chapter 14, "Network Management Tools."

File/Print Server

A file server is one that provides access to files or data that are held on the server and distributed to a number of clients. Sharing of the files is achieved using Network File Systems (NFS). A popular use for such a server is for users' home directories and shared areas, such as the online manual pages. When a file server is providing these services to a large number of clients, it must be configured so that it can accommodate the requests being made of it. The server, by default, starts up 16 NFS daemons (nfsd) at bootup. Increased NFS performance can be obtained by modifying the following line in the NFS server startup file /etc/rc3.d/S15nfs.server:

```
/usr/lib/nfs/nfsd -a 16
```

If the value is increased, say, to 32, then 32 NFS daemon processes will be started, which will allow a greater throughput of requests. The actual number of daemons required depends on the number of clients requesting data access from the server.

Another configuration option for file servers is to use the automounter, a facility that mounts remote directories or file systems dynamically only when they are accessed. The directory or file system is automatically unmounted when a specified time of nonactivity has elapsed. One of the features of the automounter is that it provides resilience and flexibility. User home directories, for example, can be easily moved to another file server with minimal disruption, while static data, such as the online manual pages, can be made to use multiple file servers. The advantage of this is that, if one file server becomes unavailable, other users can mount the specified data from the next server in the list. If a user already had a directory mounted when a server failed, then restarting the workstation would enable that user to also mount the data from an alternate server.

A print server is one that provides printing resources to users across the network. The print server holds files for spooling before the actual printing takes place. If a server is being configured to provide printing resources, it should definitely have the /var file system created separately when Solaris is installed.

The /var File System

With Solaris, /var, by default, does not exist as a file system. /var is usually a directory contained within the root (/) file system. It must be manually specified if a separate file system is required.

All spool files are held within the /var directory and can potentially become very large. If a separate file system is not created, then there is a risk that the root (/) file system might be filled to capacity and might endanger the running of the entire system.

Database Server

A database server contains a physical database, or a number of databases, and provides users with access to the information stored within the various tables of the database. Some of the issues surrounding database servers are discussed here, using Oracle as an example of a relational database management system:

- **Memory**—The database server requires a significant amount of memory to function efficiently. The actual amount depends on the number and size of databases held on the server.

- **Kernel configuration**—Some of the Solaris kernel InterProcess Communication (IPC) parameters need to be configured so that the structure of the System Global Area (SGA) can be accommodated. Without these parameters set, it will not be possible to start up any databases because the system will not have sufficient reserved shared memory. (Shared memory here refers to memory that has been specifically reserved for use by the database management software. It is not available for "sharing" with other processes.) The following options contain the minimum recommended values for an Oracle database. They would be added to the file /etc/system followed by a reboot:

```
set shmsys:shminfo_shmmax=4294967295
set shmsys:shminfo_shmmin=1
set shmsys:shminfo_shmmni=100
set shmsys:shminfo_shmseg=10
set semsys:seminfo_semmns=200
set semsys:seminfo_semmni=70
```

Backing Up Before Making Changes

Before editing such an important file as /etc/system, be sure to *always* make a copy so that recovery is possible if any problems occur. To reference the original file, an interactive boot would be necessary.

- **Organization of database storage**—RAID options are frequently used for database servers because they provide resilience and enhanced performance. RAID options are discussed in the next section, but ideally, multiple disk controllers also add to the reliability and speed of access.

  It is advisable to store redo logs on a mirrored pair of disks because of their importance in recovering a failed database. Suppose that the last backup was taken 22 hours ago. and the database becomes corrupt and irreparable. The redo logs can be used to reinstate the processing that has taken place since the last backup; this recovery is known as *rolling forward*, as opposed to rolling back an unsuccessful transaction that failed to complete.

- **Database performance**—One aspect that is frequently overlooked is the creation of database tablespaces and their contents. Some companies create a database with a single large tablespace to contain the data, along with associated indexes. This is highly inefficient usage because there is a high probability of disk contention causing performance problems. The data (tables) should always be held in a separate tablespace than the indexes. Another frequent error is to create users in the SYSTEM tablespace. This is similar to giving all users a home directory of / and then wondering why the root file system has filled up! Most standard database providers recommend the use of a USERS tablespace for this purpose.

- **Host based or client/server**—A host-based server contains the necessary software for accessing the database, such as forms and reports, whereas a client/server implementation allows the database application software to run on the desktop workstation and access the database across the network. The difference is that there is a much greater overhead on the server for host-based implementations because the server's resources are being used for both the database access and the execution of the application software. With a client/server implementation, only the database access is using the server resources; the application software utilizes the resources of a local desktop workstation.

Application Server

An application server provides software resources to a number of clients. In larger installations, there likely will be a number of application servers so that a high level of resilience and availability can be delivered in case a server becomes unavailable unexpectedly. It is quite feasible for large application servers to have hundreds of users running the applications resident on the server, so these need to be fairly powerful, preferably with multiple processors. Because of the large number of potential users that may be using the server, it might be necessary to increase the number of concurrent processes that can be run. This is achieved by modifying a kernel parameter `maxusers` in the file /etc/system, which increases the size of the process table. This parameter is set, by default, to be approximately equal to the number of megabytes of physical memory present in the system. This example shows the line to modify or add to the file /etc/system to change the value of `maxusers` to 256:

```
set maxusers=256
```

The same applies with database servers—a reboot is necessary to make the change effective.

As with file servers, extensive use can be made of the automounter software to enable users to automatically run the application from the nearest available server and can switch to another one if a failure occurs. This will probably require a restart of the workstation if a directory was being mounted from the failing server. For large installations with many applications, I always used to set up a separate automounter map, named auto_packages, which made administration and management much easier.

Using application servers eliminates the need for software packages to be fully installed on each user's workstation—instead, central copies of the software are accessed by many users. The users can also take advantage of the significant processing power available on such a server, relieving the load on user workstations considerably.

Desktop Workstation

Standalone workstations are self-sufficient—they do not require any resources from a server, and they can exist on a network independently of any other Solaris systems. No special configuration options are required for this type of system, but it is neither a server nor a client. A popular use for this type of installation is a network management console. To be capable of monitoring and reporting on other systems in the network, it is of prime importance that this system not rely on any other system for its resources, except for the network itself, of course. A further use for a standalone system might be for an engineer, particularly if using CAD or other technical software, although this use would be primarily for performance.

This type of installation, however, requires a much greater system administration overhead because there is no central control, compared with diskless and autoclient systems. Normally, a standard user workstation making use of shared resources, such as a sales or marketing workstation, would not be expected to be configured as a standalone workstation.

Support of Clients and Architectures

An operating system server, as described earlier in this section, provides the resources necessary for certain types of clients to function—namely, diskless and autoclient systems, both of which are briefly discussed here along with their advantages and disadvantages:

The Standalone Workstation

The standalone workstation configuration is deliberately not considered here, even though it is often termed a "client." This is because it does not require any resources from a server to function. It contains everything that it needs to run independently.

- **Diskless client**—This client is a Sun workstation with no hard disk drive of its own. The only hardware requirement is a network adapter so that it can communicate across the network. A diskless client obtains its root (/) and /usr file systems from a dedicated operating system server along with its swap space. The only thing that it knows about when it is turned on is its own Ethernet address or MAC address. This is sufficient information for the client to communicate with its server and download the kernel so that it can boot up.

  Diskless clients generate significantly more network traffic because all of their file systems reside on the remote operating system server, which is the main reason for locating the server on the same subnet.

  They do have their advantages, though. Diskless clients are ideal for placing in nonsecure areas because they contain no permanent data (because there is no hard disk). Thus, the 100 new workstations mentioned in the scenario at the start of the chapter are more likely to be diskless clients. They are also easy to administer centrally because everything is done from the server.

- **Autoclient clients**—This client is a Sun workstation, as discussed previously, but it does have its own hard disk. Autoclient workstations use the hard disk to store *cached* copies of the root (/) and /usr file systems, and they also maintain their own swap space. Approximately 100MB of local disk storage is required for an autoclient system to function. The root (/) and /usr file systems are downloaded from the operating system server at boot time and are stored in *cached file systems*. Changes to the file systems are replicated in both directions. Therefore, this generates less network traffic than a diskless client and also has the capability to disconnect and still continue to function if the operating system server becomes unavailable. Like the diskless client, autoclient systems are administered centrally, making them easy to manage. In the scenario earlier, the 150 workstations in the secure area would benefit from being configured as autoclient workstations; they are inherently more vulnerable because of the possibility of residual data being left on the hard disk.

Autoclient Versus Dataless Client

The autoclient configuration replaced the dataless client as of Solaris 2.6.

Additionally, an operating system server could be required to support clients of differing architectures. For example, suppose that the 250 clients in the scenario are comprised of the following components:

100 Sparc Ultra 5 (architecture sun4u)

100 Sparc 20 (architecture sun4m)

50 Sparc 10 (architecture sun4m)

The operating system server will have to contain the binaries and support for two architectures, and space must be allocated for this on the following basis:

15MB for each client architecture to be supported

20MB for each diskless client

20MB for each autoclient client

RAID Options

This section runs briefly through the more popular options for configuring storage arrays, usually referred to as Redundant Array of Inexpensive Disks (RAID) arrays. RAID arrays provide advantages through increased performance and higher availability.

Most larger companies use a RAID type of configuration for management of their disk storage. The more popular options use a storage management subsystem in which the intelligence is provided via additional hardware. It is possible, however, to implement a pseudo-RAID configuration through software using a product such as Solstice Disksuite, which is covered briefly later in this section.

The concept of RAID is that a number of physical disk modules are bound together to form a logical unit, sometimes referred to as a *stripe*. It is worth noting that to make a RAID configuration truly reliable, multiple SCSI controllers and storage processors (SPs) should be used to ensure that disk access is maintained in case of a controller failure, creating a dual access to the disk modules. Storage processors are part of the RAID device; they control the physical access to the RAID elements (disks). Multiple SPs improve the resilience further. The Clarion storage subsystem supplied by EMC is a good example of such a device. The following subsections describe the more popular RAID configurations, along with some of the recommended uses for each of the configurations.

RAID 0

This option is sometimes called a nonredundant array. It is not a true RAID configuration because it does not have any fault tolerance. Figure 5.3 shows how a RAID 0 stripe is organized. RAID 0 offers significantly improved performance through simultaneous I/O to different disks; the data blocks are written to and read simultaneously and independently. Data is written sequentially in blocks across the stripe, spanning all the physical disk modules. RAID 0 does not offer any enhanced reliability, so the failure of any one of the disks means that the whole stripe is lost. Recommended uses for this type of configuration might be video editing and related applications requiring high bandwidth. It is not recommended to use this option for mission-critical data.

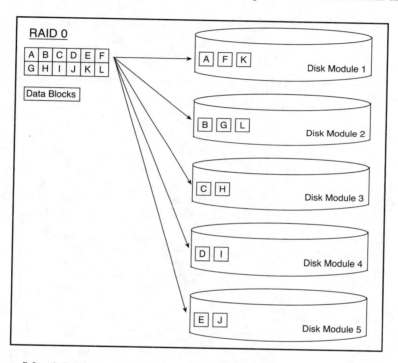

Figure 5.3   A RAID 0 configuration provides significant performance improvements, but the failure of one module will render the whole stripe unusable.

RAID 1

In this configuration, also known as a mirrored pair, two physical disks are bound together. The hardware writes the same data to both disks, thereby creating a mirror. Reading from the mirror is done from either disk. This option is highly fault-tolerant and is ideal for storing mission-critical data and for applications requiring very high availability. If one of the disk drives fails, the other continues, while copying to a replacement module (see the upcoming section "Hot Spares"). A further use for this option is the system disk, that is, the disk containing the root (/) and /usr filesystems. Figure 5.4 shows the RAID 1 configuration.

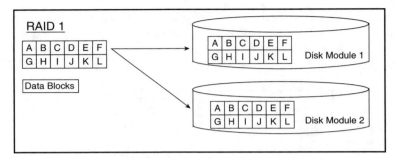

Figure 5.4   The RAID 1 configuration writes to both modules
and is ideal for protecting critical system information.

RAID 1/0

This RAID configuration provides the reliability that RAID 0 fails to offer. It is
essentially a combination of a RAID 0 stripe that is duplicated in a RAID 1 configuration—that is, a mirrored RAID 0. The RAID 1/0 stripe is shown in Figure 5.5.

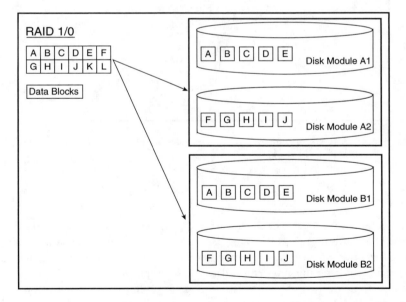

Figure 5.5   A RAID 1/0 configuration is a good compromise for RAID 0,
providing performance enhancement and also reliability, in case of failure.

RAID 3

RAID 3 maintains one of the physical disks for parity information. It provides the necessary fault tolerance if one of the disk modules fails because the replaced module can be re-created from the parity information, and the user does not lose access to the data (including data that was stored on the failed module). However, performance is degraded during the module rebuild, which could take several hours. Any application that requires a high throughput would be suitable for this option, although single-task applications are best suited. Figure 5.6 demonstrates how the data blocks are organized in a RAID 3 configuration:

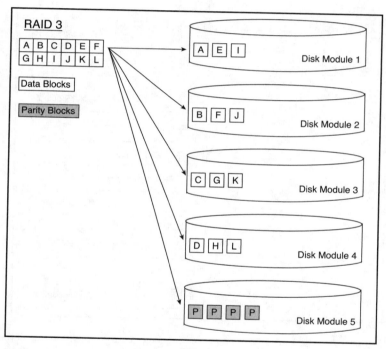

Figure 5.6   RAID 3 is good for single-task applications, such as CAD, in which a high throughput is required. Multitask applications will suffer because of all the parity information being stored on a single module.

RAID 5

This is the most popular option for larger systems, especially those using relational database applications. The data is striped across multiple physical disk modules, but unlike the RAID 3 configuration, parity data is stored on each of the modules, providing high availability and reliability. Again, if one of the disk modules fails, the disk can be re-created from the information contained on the remaining disks, allowing users to still access the data, including data that was stored on the failed module. As with RAID 3, performance is degraded while a failed disk module is rebuilt, and the process could take several hours to complete. File servers, application servers, and systems using databases benefit from using RAID 5, but in the case of database systems, it is generally recommended to store online transaction logs (redo logs) on a mirrored pair of disks for added resilience (RAID 1). Figure 5.7 describes how the RAID 5 configuration is implemented.

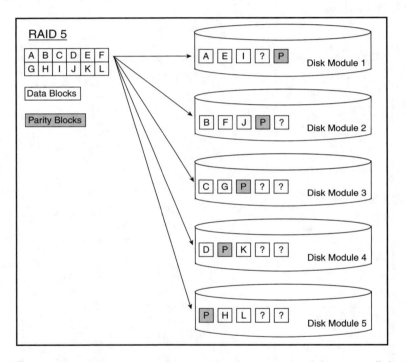

Figure 5.7 The RAID 5 configuration distributes parity and data across all the modules, providing enhanced performance and reliability.

Hot Spares

Hot spares are essential for any storage subsystem to make full use of the fault tolerance that is made available by these configurations. A hot spare is a disk module that is managed by the storage hardware and allocated as a "spare." Frequently, there will be a pool of hot spare disks in a larger array configuration, allowing the system to continue operating even if several disk modules fail.

If a failure occurs, the storage subsystem dynamically allocates one of the hot spare disks to replace the failed module and initiates the rebuild onto the spare disk module. The advantage of doing this is that the failed disk module can be replaced at a more convenient time, and the system continues to operate throughout.

Figure 5.8 shows a typical disk array configured with three hot spare modules. Notice that the configuration displayed consists of more than one RAID stripe and more than one RAID configuration. A hot spare disk module automatically replaces any of the modules in the array that suffer a failure.

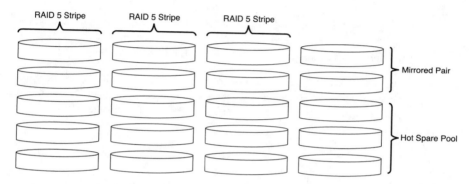

Figure 5.8   Hot spare modules allow dynamic replacement of a failed unit without having to interrupt the operation of the system. The failed unit can be replaced at a more convenient time.

Solstice Disksuite

Solstice Disksuite is a software solution for emulating disk mirroring and striping, but without the added hardware normally associated with a RAID configuration. It is normally used in smaller systems where SCSI disks can be grouped together into structures that resemble RAID arrays. It also allows the creation of logical volumes that can span multiple physical disks; this, in turn, allows a file system to be larger than one physical disk, something that the standard Solaris implementation does not facilitate. Figure 5.9 shows the concatenation of several disks to create a large file system that is also mirrored.

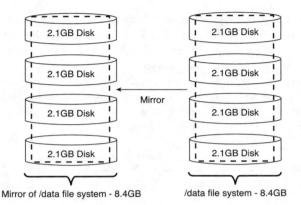

Figure 5.9 Even though the concatenation of multiple disks through software does not provide the same performance enhancements found in true RAID configurations, the pseudo-array can be cost-effective for smaller companies.

Upgrade

An upgrade is significantly different from a new installation. From the outset, a restriction inherently exists that a system already is running, unlike the new installation discussed in the previous section, where the system is being created from scratch.

The upgrade carries a greater risk than the new installation because a working system is being changed, file systems will be overwritten, and the potential exists for unforeseen problems to arise.

Thorough testing of the upgraded system in a test environment significantly reduces the risk of serious problems occurring, but it does not totally eliminate it. Another major difference between the upgrade and the new installation is the requirement for a fallback procedure, a way to recover if things go terribly wrong. If the upgrade fails and cannot continue, there has to be a way of restoring the entire system to the state that it was in before the upgrade commenced.

The following sections address some of the issues that need to be considered when undertaking an upgrade of an existing system.

Preparation

Thorough preparation and testing are key elements in reducing the risk of failure when carrying out an upgrade. The following list provides some useful tasks that should be carried out:

- **Test environment**—Any upgrade, whether it is for the entire operating system or an application, should first be carried out on a test environment so that problems can be resolved before the live upgrade. The mere action of performing the upgrade is not the only important part; testing the upgrade also is important, so development of comprehensive test packs is essential to reduce the risk of unforeseen problems as much as possible.

- **Compatibility**—The system manager must ensure that the system meets the minimum hardware requirements for the upgrade to proceed. Sometimes it is assumed that because the current version runs normally, the new version will, too. A simple example proves the point: An old Sun IPC workstation (architecture Sun4c) with 24Mb of RAM runs Solaris 7 quite happily. It's fairly slow, but it runs. If you now try to load Solaris 8 on the same machine, it will fail, not only on the architecture not being supported any longer, but also on the insufficient amount of RAM.

- **Upgrade path**—The normal progression of upgrades for the Solaris operating environment is fairly straightforward. However, if you have any doubts about jumping from, say, Solaris 2.4 to Solaris 7 in one go, then a call to the Sun Helpdesk will verify whether you should be aware of any special issues.

   In the case of application software, especially software supplied by a third party, this aspect can become increasingly important. Some vendors insist that a scheduled upgrade path be followed. In this case, the system manager cannot jump several versions of the software without invalidating the support warranty. This should always be checked with the supplier because it is possible that a number of interim upgrades may have to be performed to arrive at the target version. A further aspect of third-party software is that when you are upgrading the operating system, you should seek confirmation that the application is fully supported under the new version of the operating system.

- **Patches**—Upgrading to a new version of the operating environment might mean that, in addition to the installation of the operating environment, some patches are needed. For example, when doing an upgrade from Solaris 2.6 to Solaris 7, you should determine that Solaris 7 was available during 1999. The Sun Year 2000 Product Compliance Status Table shows that three patches are required to achieve full compliance. In addition, a patch cluster containing recommended and security patches should be applied to the operating environment. The system manager should be aware of the details of the patches and also of any patching policy that exists within the organization (patching is discussed in more detail in the next section).

- **Fallback procedures**—One of the most important preparatory tasks that needs to be carried out is including a plan for restoring the system if a failure requires the upgrade to be aborted or postponed. In this instance, there must be a capability to restore the entire system to the state that it was in before the upgrade started. The section "Backups," later in this chapter, provides details on how to provide this capability.

Policy on Stability of Product

Some companies adopt a policy of extreme caution when looking to upgrade the operating system, especially if the upgrade is a major revision. For mission-critical businesses, there is a risk that the new version will not properly interact with the existing systems on the network—even though a significant amount of testing can be carried out on a test environment, it is often difficult to replicate everything!

Other companies, however, move to a new operating system version virtually as soon as it becomes available. This is fine when a new system is being installed, but it presents other problems when upgrading an existing system. Some of these problems are outlined in the following paragraphs:

- **Clustered failover systems**—Certain kinds of configurations display problems of their own, particularly in a master/slave setup. Normally, one of the slave systems would be upgraded first and left to run for a period of time to see if any problems were encountered. If so, then that system could be reinstated without too much disruption to the operation of the business. The difficulty arises when a failover must occur onto the newly upgraded system in the live environment, which is necessary to upgrade the master system. If problems are encountered at this point, then the whole system is in danger of crashing and becoming unavailable. Careful consideration is needed in this instance, along with extremely thorough testing.

- **Third-party application software**—Sometimes a third-party supplier needs to provide a new version of the application software to run on the upgraded operating system. If this new version is not available, then it can become impossible to carry out the upgrade without incurring serious risk with no guarantee or warranty from the supplier.

- **Mission-critical nature**—The mission-critical nature of some installations dictates that a new version of an operating system must be declared stable before any kind of implementation is even considered. The difficulty here is defining what is "stable." Some companies wait for the second release—that is, an interim release that fixes the majority of the bugs already identified; others, such as government departments, may wait until a central body declares it to be stable after it has carried out extensive research and testing.

Backups

Before an operating system upgrade can take place, a guaranteed backup of the system must be performed.

Ideally, the backup should be performed with the system at a single-user state—that is, with no activity and no users logged in. Any databases should be shut down, and the backup should be verified. It is critical that the backup is capable of being read because it could be the only means available to restore the system if the impending upgrade failed.

The final contingency is to actually restore the system from the backup media onto a test environment. By doing this, the integrity of the backup is proved, and the capability exists to restore the system in the event of a failure.

It should be normal practice to regularly test backups, but in the real world, this is rarely done. Management and users alike are satisfied and confident as long as a backup of the system is taken. They assume that because the backup was done, there will be no problem in restoring the necessary files, if needed. Without testing, there is no guarantee that a backup can be read, particularly when the backup is written to magnetic tape.

A further option for obtaining a system backup if mirroring is being used is to break the mirror—that is, disable one half of the mirrored pair, creating a static copy of the system disk in its current state. The static copy could then be used to reinstate the operating system to its former state if the upgrade failed, and it would also be much quicker than having to restore from backup media.

Type of Installation

Four methods exist for installing the Solaris software on a system: interactive, network, Jumpstart, or Webstart. Each of these options is discussed further here:

- **WebStart**—This installation option is only for initial installations and cannot be used for upgrading the operating environment. It is included here for completeness only. WebStart is Sun's Java-based installation program. It provides a point-and-click interface to install the operating environment as well as other software that is bundled with Solaris.

- **Interactive**—This is the preferred option for system administrators building a single system, and it is discussed in the next section.

- **Network**—In this option, the operating environment is installed over the network. Ideal for a computer without a local CD-ROM drive; a CD-ROM drive is required for a Solaris installation because this is how the software is delivered. A remote install can be carried out using a remote system's CD-ROM drive, or an image of the Solaris CD-ROM copied to the remote system's hard disk. This option is very useful when there is no local CD-ROM drive, and this is also the recommended method for the E10000 system.

- **Jumpstart**—This is a method of automating the Solaris software installation process on a number of systems. This option is discussed in the upcoming section "Multiple Systems."

Single System

The installation of a single server is more easily carried out using the *interactive installation method*. This still appears to be the most popular method among seasoned system administrators, partly because it is the method that they have always used, but also because it provides the system administrator full control and flexibility.

Using the interactive method, the system administrator can *preserve* file systems so that they are not re-created during the installation—a process that would lose all of the current data—and manually change only those file systems that will be directly affected by the installation process. The option of preserving existing file systems speeds up the whole process, reducing downtime.

Multiple Systems

A large number of companies now tend to use "standard builds" for their networked desktop PCs. The advantage of this is that each desktop PC is configured in exactly the same way, so this saves a lot of time because the build can be done with very little or no intervention. In much the same way, the Solaris software can be installed on multiple machines using a predefined set of configuration files. This method of installation is known as *Jumpstart*.

Imagine a company with 50 servers, all requiring an upgrade to the latest version of Solaris. Suppose that 10 are application servers with 1024MB (1GB) of memory, 25 are operating system servers with 512MB of memory, 8 are file and print servers with 768MB of memory, and 7 are database servers with 2GB of memory. Rules can be configured so that, in this case, the amount of memory decides how the server is to be installed—that is, the Solaris installation options. Instead of the system administrator having to carry out 50 complete installations, this can be done automatically. One significant advantage with this option is that it eliminates the possibility of human error, an important factor when considering 50 separate installations because this can maintain consistency across many servers. This also saves on the resource and time needed, as well as greatly reducing the operational impact on the business.

A further point to note with Jumpstart installations is that scripts can be automatically called to run both before and after the installation takes place. For example, a script might be run to back up the system before the upgrade, followed by another script to restore the data file systems after the upgrade has taken place. See the Appendix for further reading on the Jumpstart option.

Recovery from a Failed Upgrade

If an upgrade fails, then there has to be a means of restoring the system to its former state—that is, the state that it was in before the upgrade commenced. This can be done in one of two ways:

Small Versus Large Installations

The interactive installation method is useful for a scenario in which a system administrator supports only a few systems. For larger installations in which many tens or hundreds of systems are being configured, this option quickly becomes impractical and also increases the risk of human error.

- **Restore from backup**—If file systems were preserved during the upgrade, then only the Solaris operating environment file systems need to be restored from the backup media—that is, root (/), /usr, and maybe /opt and /var, if they are separate file systems. Of course, the system boot block would have to be re-created on the system disk, but apart from that, this is a fairly simple process and doesn't take too long.

- **Use a mirrored pair**—The "Backups" section earlier described a method by which a mirrored pair of disks containing the essential operating environment file systems could be effectively broken so that a static copy remained. If the upgrade then failed, it is easy to reinstate the broken half of the mirror as the master and use it as the live system disk to recover the system. If a RAID configuration such as this is in use, then this option provides a much quicker recovery, dramatically reducing the downtime and the impact on the operation.

Patches

A patch is a fix, provided by a supplier as a temporary solution to a problem. It is temporary in that it fixes a problem, which will be integrated with a future release of the software, in the same way as a homeowner might plug a leaking pipe until the plumber arrives. A patch can be for both software and hardware—it might provide support for a new type of hard disk device, but it is implemented through the software. This is an important part of the installation and, although the system administrator will install the patch, the system manager will decide on the correct policy to adopt on patch installation.

Sun provides access to its patches via two media: the Sunsolve Web site on the Internet, and on regularly updated CD-ROMs. The Internet option provides security and recommended patches for all customers. For customers who have a support agreement, there is access to many other patches and a database of patch information, bug reports, a searchable symptoms and resolution database, and a comprehensive range of white papers and early warning notices. The CD-ROM distribution (currently at four CDs per month) is available to customers with a support agreement and contains the same information as mentioned, along with a periodic updated CD containing archived patches, mainly for older revisions of SunOS.

In recent years, three main patching policies have been identified within businesses. These are listed along with the advantages and disadvantages of each:

- **Install all patches**—This strategy follows the advice of the supplier and installs each recommended patch. This policy is a sensible one because it ensures that the system is always up-to-date with the latest fixes. It can also fix problems that may not yet have been encountered and is a preventative, proactive policy. Some caution is encouraged, though, so that patches are not just blindly installed when they are clearly irrelevant. The installation information supplied with each patch must be clearly noted to see if there are any dependencies—other patches that must already be installed before installing this one—or any conflicts; these are clearly labeled in the documentation. A significant advantage of this policy is that a fault call raised with the supplier can be dealt with more quickly, avoiding unnecessary delays. The only disadvantage is the extra time needed to ensure that the system remains up-to-date.

- **Install only those patches necessary**—This policy installs only the patches needed to resolve the current problem. This is a reactive strategy and deals with faults and failures after they have already occurred. The only advantage to adopting this policy is that less time is spent analyzing and installing the required patches. The advantage is easily outweighed by the disadvantages: A problem must occur before it is resolved, which could mean downtime and potential loss of data. A serious problem requiring a call to the supplier can be delayed while patches are installed to bring the system up to the required level. Indeed, the installation of these patches could—and often does—resolve the problem.

- **Resist as much as possible**—Some companies refuse to apply any recommended patches on the grounds that their applications work correctly without them. I noticed this especially with a few third-party suppliers providing applications running on the Sun/Solaris platform during the run-up to Y2K. One company refused to apply the /usr/bin/date, patch stating that it wasn't used! Needless to say, the application itself was certified as Y2K-compliant, after thorough testing, but with a caveat stating that the platform it was running on was definitely not Y2K-compliant. This policy is extremely short-sighted and could cause significant downtime, as well as make fault resolution much more difficult than it should be.

The next two sections outline the application of patches for both the Solaris operating environment and for unbundled/third-party-supplied patches.

Operating System Patches

Sun Microsystems delivers operating system patches in a consistent format, similar to that of a software package in that they can be easily installed or uninstalled (the latter being known as "backed out"). Patches are provided both separately and as clusters. The recommended patches are often delivered in a cluster to aid installation. This means that all the necessary patches can be installed in one go rather than having to do them one at a time.

After deciding on a patching policy as outlined in the previous section, the system manager should ensure that the systems that he is responsible for are patched accordingly. Installation of the actual patches themselves will be carried out by the system administrator, but the system manager may have to decide on particular issues when there are possibilities of conflict. An up-to-date list of the patches already applied to the system should be readily available as part of the system documentation (see

Chapter 8, "Strategic Management," for a discussion of this aspect) so that any potential discrepancies or conflicts can be easily identified. A sample of the output from the
command `patchadd -p` for an Intel box running Solaris 7 with the recommended
patch cluster installed is shown in Listing 5.2.

Listing 5.2 Sample Output Listing the Patches Already Applied to a System

```
# patchadd -p

Patch: 107545-03 Obsoletes:  Requires: Incompatibles: Packages:  SUNWcsr SUNWcsu
Patch: 106542-08 Obsoletes: 106833-03 106914-04 106977-01 107440-01 107032-01
107118-05 107447-01 Requires: 107545-02 Incompatibles: Packages:  SUNWarc
SUNWatfsr SUNWcar SUNWcsl SUNWcsr SUNWcsu SUNWdpl SUNWesu SUNWhea SUNWipc SUNWkvm
SUNWpcmci SUNWpcmcu SUNWscpu SUNWtnfc SUNWtoo SUNWvolr
Patch: 106794-03 Obsoletes:  Requires: Incompatibles: Packages:  SUNWcsu SUNWhea
Patch: 106961-01 Obsoletes:  Requires: Incompatibles: Packages:  SUNWman
Patch: 107039-01 Obsoletes:  Requires: Incompatibles: Packages:  SUNWdoc
Patch: 108375-01 Obsoletes: 107882-10 Requires: Incompatibles: Packages:
SUNWdtbas SUNWdtdte SUNWdtinc SUNWdtmad
Patch: 107023-05 Obsoletes:  Requires: 108375-01 Incompatibles:  Packages:
SUNWdtdmn SUNWdtdst SUNWdtma
Patch: 107457-01 Obsoletes:  Requires: Incompatibles: Packages:  SUNWcsr
Patch: 107588-01 Obsoletes:  Requires: Incompatibles: Packages:  SUNWaccu
Patch: 107637-03 Obsoletes:  Requires: Incompatibles: Packages:  SUNWxi18n SUNWxim
Patch: 107888-08 Obsoletes: 107002-01 Requires: Incompatibles: Packages:
SUNWdtdst SUNWdtdte SUNWdtma
Patch: 108344-02 Obsoletes:  Requires: 108375-01 Incompatibles:  Packages:
SUNWdtezt
Patch: 107201-11 Obsoletes:  Requires: 108375-01 107888-08 Incompatibles:
Packages:  SUNWdtdst SUNWdtma
Patch: 106945-02 Obsoletes:  Requires: Incompatibles: Packages:  SUNWcsr
Patch: 106953-01 Obsoletes:  Requires: Incompatibles: Packages:  SUNWbnuu
Patch: 106979-09 Obsoletes:  Requires: 107457-01 Incompatibles:  Packages:
SUNWadmap SUNWadmc
Patch: 107116-03 Obsoletes:  Requires: Incompatibles: Packages:  SUNWpcu SUNWpsu
Patch: 107260-01 Obsoletes:  Requires: Incompatibles: Packages:  SUNWvolu
Patch: 107452-02 Obsoletes:  Requires: 107118-03 Incompatibles:  Packages:
SUNWcsu
Patch: 107455-03 Obsoletes:  Requires: Incompatibles: Packages:  SUNWcsu
Patch: 107685-01 Obsoletes:  Requires: Incompatibles: Packages:  SUNWsndmu
Patch: 107793-01 Obsoletes:  Requires: Incompatibles: Packages:  SUNWcsu
Patch: 107973-01 Obsoletes:  Requires: Incompatibles: Packages:  SUNWsutl
Patch: 108302-01 Obsoletes:  Requires: Incompatibles: Packages:  SUNWcsu
Patch: 106737-03 Obsoletes:  Requires: Incompatibles: Packages:  SUNWoldst
Patch: 107339-01 Obsoletes:  Requires: Incompatibles: Packages:  SUNWkcspg
SUNWkcsrt
Patch: 107894-04 Obsoletes: 108123-01 108238-01 Requires: Incompatibles: Packages:
SUNWtltk
Patch: 106935-03 Obsoletes:  Requires: Incompatibles: Packages:  SUNWdtbas
Patch: 107181-12 Obsoletes:  Requires: Incompatibles: Packages:  SUNWdtdte
```

continues

Listing 5.2 Continued

```
Patch: 108220-01 Obsoletes:   Requires: Incompatibles: Packages:   SUNWdtbas
Patch: 108222-01 Obsoletes:   Requires: Incompatibles: Packages:   SUNWdtdmn
Patch: 107886-06 Obsoletes: 107220-02 Requires: 106935-03 Incompatibles:
Packages:   SUNWdtdst SUNWdthev SUNWdticn SUNWdtma
Patch: 108483-01 Obsoletes:   Requires: Incompatibles: Packages:   SUNWcsu
Patch: 108663-01 Obsoletes:   Requires: Incompatibles: Packages:   SUNWadmfw

#
```

This sample output clearly shows whether a patch conflicts with any other patch (in the "Incompatibles" section, which in this case are none) and also whether a patch obsoletes another patch. This information is valuable to the system manager if a specific problem requires a patch to resolve it. If a conflict is identified, a call to Sun will obtain the necessary advice on how to proceed. If the patch were to just be installed, then the system could suffer adverse affects and further complicate the problem.

Each patch supplied by Sun contains important installation information, including any dependencies—that is, any other patches that must be installed before this one—as well as the information relating to potential conflicts. Always ensure that this information is read and checked against the list of patches currently installed on the system. It could save a lot of time.

A final noteworthy point about operating system patches is that, when using the Jumpstart utility to install Solaris on a number of systems, it is possible to prepatch the Solaris image on the install server. This means that each system installed will already contain the necessary patches and so does not have to be done individually. In the same way, servers providing operating system resources to diskless or AutoClient systems can also be patched at the server level once and then replicated to each of the clients. For example, a server supporting 25 diskless clients and 25 AutoClients can apply the patches once to a spool directory and then synchronize all the clients so that they are also using the patches. These clients do not physically store the operating system software on local disks; it is kept in a file system on the server and is accessed over the network. (See the Appendix for further information on the Jumpstart utility.)

Testing Patches

Any operating system patch should be installed first in a test environment that mirrors the live environment as closely as possible. The patch should be thoroughly tested before being deployed operationally to ensure that there are no unforeseen problems.

Unbundled and Third-Party Application Patches

Patches supplied by Sun Microsystems for unbundled and application products are normally supplied in the same format as the operating system patches. They should be subjected to the same treatment as outlined in the previous section.

Patches from third-party suppliers, however, can be slightly different. They may or may not be supplied in the package-type format. Decisions on whether to install these patches need to be given particular attention because there might not be enough information provided on potential conflicts with either other patches or other applications.

A patch from a third-party software supplier should be subjected to the following procedures:

- It should be installed only if the supplier or Sun Microsystems states that it is necessary.

- Any patch should be treated with caution and thoroughly checked for viruses.

- Look for any supporting documentation provided by the supplier for an indication that it has been thoroughly tested.

- Confirm that the patch is for the correct version of the Solaris operating environment.

- Always install the patch in a test environment and carry out rigorous testing; also reproduce some of the tests that may be documented (if any). The test environment should mirror the production environment, as closely as possible, including any other third-party and unbundled software applications.

- Read all of the installation instructions that accompany the patch carefully, particularly where they may involve altering kernel parameters or installing other patches.

- If in doubt, always contact Sun for confirmation.

Failure to carry out these procedures could seriously jeopardize the integrity of the system and possibly the network. Of course, it is the system manager's responsibility to ensure that these duties are carried out and that the company is not exposed to any unnecessary risk.

Third-party Suppliers

The term *third party* refers to any software supplier that is not part of Sun Microsystems. It should be noted that this includes software from a licensed software house as well as that available in the public domain.

Summary

The implementation of a new system can often be a complex task, frequently aggravated by financial constraints and pressures. The system manager should be able to offset a number of costs to the project or department requesting the implementation. The complications are much greater when a continuous operation is required, on a 24×7 basis. Staff, management, and financial considerations all play a part here and need to be resolved satisfactorily to provide the required level of service.

A new system creates a number of issues relating to its environment, such as its accommodation in the computer room, the power requirements, environmental control, and so on. All of these can have an effect on the existing systems already present in the room, so the system manager must be mindful of the current operation and must take special care to avoid disruption wherever possible.

Upgrading existing systems carries a different risk from the new installation in that an operational system is being modified. Clustered solutions, such as the Sun cluster software, greatly assist the system manager in reducing the impact on the business and eliminating downtime of the operation. This is achieved by having a number of systems share the workload so that when one is removed from the cluster to be upgraded, the others merely take on the work that was being carried out by that system. On completion of the upgrade, the system simply rejoins the cluster, and the operation continues uninterrupted.

The system manager must always consider contingency in case of a failure. Part of his preparation for an upgrade has to be the consideration of fallback plans so that he can quickly restore the system to its former state, if required. The use of a test environment helps in the evaluation of potential problems, and a full backup provides the contingency that is needed; however, the backup must be tested before declaring its integrity.

Most companies have a policy on applying patches. They either install all the patches available, install just the patches that directly affect their operation, or don't install any. I always recommend the first option of installing at least the recommended patches and the security patches—it could make a lot of difference when trying to resolve a problem via the Sun help desk.

6

Solaris Security

BUSINESSES AROUND THE WORLD ARE MAKING as much use as possible of Internet technologies to break into new global markets. As companies become ever more dependent on the Internet for their business relationships, the importance of computer security increases as well. More and more people and businesses are connecting every day, and with that comes more potential for security threats.

Single-site, centralized data centers, with equally centralized security requirements, are fast disappearing and are being replaced by new, modern, distributed corporations with sites not just in different towns and cities, but in different countries as well, all communicating together and sharing confidential company information. It is a system cracker's paradise if there is no security policy in place—they can just march in and wreak havoc.

Hacker or Cracker

The term *hacker* is usually referred to in the news as an external malicious attacker of computer systems. Within the IT industry however, the term *cracker* is used to define the malicious attacker or virus perpetrator. A *hacker* is someone who is not malicious but who, through unsupervised access, can often cause unintentional damage to a computer system, normally because of inexperience rather than a deliberate action. That distinction between the two concepts is used in this text.

But it's not the external cracker who actually causes the most damage; those instances are merely the most widely reported. Perhaps surprisingly, various studies have shown that by far the largest cause of security incidents comes from within—that is, someone already authorized to use the computing resources of a company, such as a disgruntled employee who was passed over for promotion or was refused a raise. This employee could do something as simple as delete important files, for example, but a more sophisticated employee could write and introduce a destructive virus into the system. The possibilities are many.

The Computer Crime and Security Survey, carried out each year in the United States by the Computer Security Institute/Federal Bureau of Investigation (CSI/FBI), analyzes and highlights the effect of computer crime/abuse. The findings clearly show a marked increase each year. To put this into perspective, Figure 6.1 shows the average financial loss suffered for the last four years as a result of computer crime. The average loss is taken from the number of companies that were able to put a dollar value on the loss encountered.

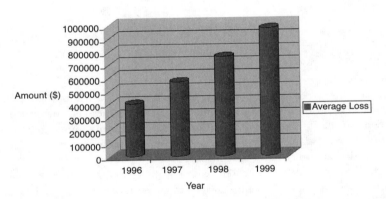

Figure 6.1   The disturbing upward trend toward computer crime highlights the need for increased computer security and incident reporting.

The system manager is responsible for maintaining the integrity of the systems that he manages and for ensuring that there is no unauthorized access to confidential data. In larger corporations, the system manager might be assisted by a dedicated computer security section, whose role is to implement a company security policy. Sadly, a large number of businesses do not have a corporate policy, and various departments implement their own ad hoc computer security, often lacking consistency and the capability to ensure that it is enforced.

This chapter aims to address some of the issues surrounding the need for better security in a Solaris environment, and it takes a brief look at some of the security products that are available—both with the Solaris operating environment and also from the public domain.

Strategic Planning and Techniques

Computer security is a strategic issue, although some tactical measures can be taken on a per-system basis; these are discussed at the end of the chapter. Computer security requirements should be addressed as part of the IT strategy and should be budgeted for accordingly. Too little value is placed on security, probably because there is no "tangible" benefit, or return from investing in it, unlike the launch of a new product. The threat from both inside and outside the company is very real and is growing. A company should address the issue from the perspective of not being able to carry out business. For example, suppose that an external cracker penetrates the system and trashes the customer and orders databases, or perhaps a malicious e-mail is sent to each of the customers in the database stating that the company is no longer trading, and recommending a competitor instead. The losses incurred could undoubtedly cause bankruptcy in some cases.

A good computer security strategy needs to be initiated by professionals who have experience in dealing with such an important issue. When the strategy has been devised and implemented, it needs to be regularly assessed to see if any modifications or enhancements are required. Each version of the Solaris operating environment is becoming more secure, providing a good reason for carrying out upgrades as soon as it is practical to do so, in line with the corporate IT policy regarding the stability of products (refer back to Chapter 5, "Solaris Installation and Upgrades").

This section discusses how the strategic security policy can be implemented in the Solaris environment, and examines a number of security products that are available to assist the system manager in securing the systems under his control. The products include those shipped with the Solaris operating environment as well as unbundled security packages from Sun Microsystems and others that are available in the public domain.

System Security Policy

When dealing with security issues in a network environment, it is the security policy that pulls everything together and identifies how the security of a network and the systems contained within it is managed.

Most companies implement a security policy, some on a per-system basis and others on a corporate basis. Larger organizations use a dedicated computer security section to manage the entire security issue, taking a perspective from a much higher level. The policy is then implemented for each system that is installed and connected to the network—indeed, a condition of connecting to the corporate network is that compliance to the security policy is demonstrated and verified. The system manager must ensure that security issues are taken into account when implementing a new system. He also serves as a regular liaison with the computer security section.

The development of a good security policy, however, is not solely about protecting the systems at all costs. It needs to be a careful balance between the security itself and the restrictions that it imposes on running the business. The user community must be considered as part of the bigger picture, particularly the effect and inconvenience that the security measures have on them. Of course, the best security policy is to deny everything to everyone, but this is not a practical solution. The system manager (and the computer security section, if applicable) must take into account the needs of the business and the users to see if the proposed policy is more of a dictatorship than a preventive measure. After all, the users are carrying out the core business functions, and they will often provide a valuable insight into what is practical and realistic and what is unworkable. It is no use having a brilliant security policy if the company cannot function as a result.

There are a number of important steps to take in the formulation of a security policy; these are discussed briefly here:

- **Identify what needs to be protected**—This includes but is not limited to hardware, software, data, and documentation.

- **Carry out a risk assessment**—Each item identified in the previous section should be examined to see the associated risks and then should be ranked by the level of severity attached.

- **Apply weightings**—After assembling a list of resources that require protection, each item needs to have a weighting associated with it so that it can be prioritized as to its importance. This, in turn, defines how much is spent on protecting the resource.

- **Keep the policy acceptable and realistic**—Despite the risks and severity, the security policy needs to be workable and acceptable. There is no point in having a stringent security policy that stops the company from carrying out its business in the most effective manner. The cost-effectiveness of a security policy can often be determined by the effect that it has on the operation of the business.

- **Establish a violation procedure**—While trying to protect the resources, a security policy also has to consider what to do if the network or system is breached. The type of incident reporting, the level of auditing, and the escalation procedure for when to inform the authorities are all examples of things to be addressed here.

- **Educate users**—One of the best ways to protect the resources is through educating the users in matters relating to security. A formal training program coupled with regular bulletins keeps the user aware of security considerations. It also demonstrates to the users that the company takes security seriously.

Unauthorized User Warning

Whenever a user logs in to a computer system, a statement should be displayed that says something like, "Only authorized users can use this system." Otherwise, you are providing an intruder with an escape route when prosecutions start—on the grounds that it never said he couldn't or shouldn't have access!

A more local issue for the system manager to address as part of the security policy is that of managing the access for internal users, or employees of the company. It has to be recognized that in any computer network environment, there must be an element of trust; otherwise, nobody would be allowed to do anything, and the business would not function. Consider, for example, how you would protect against a corrupt system administrator with full superuser privileges. The answer is that, realistically, this is virtually impossible, which is where the element of trust comes in. For the rest of the users of the system, though, the system manager must analyze the potential risks to the security of the system (and the data) and determine how to provide them with sufficient access to carry out their jobs without compromising the system. The system manager needs to ask himself a few fundamental questions about each user (or group of users):

- Does the user need to have command-line access (a shell)?
- Does the user have potential access to sensitive data?
- Does the user require any special privileges?

These questions are deliberately broad in their scope, and companies should be able to ask more direct questions depending on the type of business being carried out. Still, these cover the major risks that a user could potentially gain access to more than they are legitimately entitled. The system manager could consider three general solutions: a restricted shell, captive accounts, or nonprivileged user accounts with enhanced auditing facilities. Each of these is discussed briefly here:

- **The restricted shell**—This option is realistically useful only when a user carries out an extremely limited function, such as logging in to collect or deliver data. Using the restricted shell, there can be no traversing of the system directory structure. The command set that is available is very limited, too.

- **Captive accounts**—For users who run specific applications, this is a more popular option. For example, the sales staff might use the system to access the sales and customer databases. In this case, when logging in to the system, the user is taken straight into the application, with no opportunity to enter commands at the prompt. When the session is finished and the user quits the application, he is immediately logged off.

- **Nonprivileged accounts with auditing**—When access to the command line is required, the best solution is to provide a nonprivileged account, reducing the amount of damage that the user can cause. For functions requiring greater access to the system or enhanced privilege status, the use of software such as Sudo provides the necessary privilege while also limiting the access and auditing everything that is done. (Sudo is discussed in detail later in this chapter in the section "Products Available in the Public Domain.")

Shared User Accounts

Never allow users to share user accounts. Every user of a system must always be assigned a unique account that is to be used only by that person. As soon as users are allowed to share logins, accountability is diminished and the security is compromised.

For further references on security issues, two excellent sites on the Internet provide regular bulletins and newsletters, as well as a wealth of security-related information:

- The SANS Institute, at `http://www.sans.org`
- CERT Coordination Center (originally called the Computer Emergency Response Team), at `http://www.cert.org`

See also the Appendix, "Resources," for recommended further reading and other Internet sites relating to Solaris security.

Out-of-Hours Policy

When computer systems are running continuously, 24 hours a day, 7 days a week, there needs to be a policy in force for the hours when offices are unattended. Consider the scenario in which Sun workstations configured as diskless clients are left in open office space. If an intruder can gain physical access to the client, then it can be turned on. It will automatically boot across the network and end up displaying the login prompt. Meanwhile, the intruder, watching the boot sequence, can gain all sorts of information concerning the network setup, such as the hostname, the IP address, the Ethernet address, the daemon processes that are running, and so on. If left long enough, he may be able to log in!

One way of stopping this with clients that boot across the network is to disable them from the server. This is accomplished simply by renaming a single file in the directory /tftpboot on the operating system server that provides the client's resources. The client's boot filename is made up of the hexadecimal equivalent of its IP address and the kernel architecture. For example, a Sparc Ultra client with an IP address of 210.127.8.10 would have a file named D27F080A.sun4u. By appending, say, .old to the filename, it will fail to boot. When the file is renamed back to its original name, the boot will succeed.

Setting such a policy is simple to implement and can be done automatically through the use of a shell script, even using cron to schedule its execution at the required times.

Firewalls

Most businesses allowing external connections make use of firewalls. Many suppliers produce firewall hardware and software, so it is perhaps suitable that a short discussion of the concept of firewalls appears here.

There is a point where the company's private network and an external network, such as the Internet, meet. This is the point at which a firewall is inserted. A firewall system consists of a hardware and software configuration (collectively known as a firewall). It resides at this point and controls access both into and out of the company's network, much like a security guard at the entrance to a company's premises.

A firewall need not be used only for external connections; it can also be implemented to restrict access to specific systems within the company, such as the accounting system. In this instance, the company might want to separate this system from others on the network and allow only a specified list of users to access the system.

Sun's Firewall-1

Sun Microsystems produced a product called Firewall-1 which has now been retired and incorporated into the Solstice Sunscreen security product. Solstice Sunscreen is discussed later in the "Unbundled Products" section.

There are two main types of firewalls—a packet-filtering firewall and an application firewall (also known as a proxy server). Both are described in the following sections.

Packet-Filtering Firewall

This kind of firewall "filters" packets that it receives according to a predefined set of rules, allowing only packets that match the rule criteria to proceed through to the company network. Two slightly different policies might be applied to this kind of firewall, either to allow all packets unless specifically denied by the rule set, or to deny all packets unless specifically allowed by the rule set. The choice will depend on the overall security policy for the company, but obviously, the latter option is more secure.

A packet-filtering firewall offers less protection than an application-level firewall, but it is cheaper and might be appropriate for a low-risk environment. It usually doesn't support authentication, nor does it have any reasonable logging facility. Packet filtering can be implemented on the Internet router(s) or, if a Sun system is connected to the Internet, by using the freely available package ipf. For further reference on this package, see the Appendix, "Resources."

Application-Level Firewall

This is a much more sophisticated kind of firewall, demanding a separate system to run server programs (called proxies). These programs receive external requests and analyze them for authenticity, forwarding only legitimate requests to the internal network.

A major distinction between the two kinds of firewall described here is that the application-level firewall supports full authentication and logging. It is a more secure option than a packet-filtering firewall and is suitable for medium-high-risk environments. It also has the capability to "hide" the name and address of any computer communicating through the firewall. This means, for example, that the IP address of a computer is concealed from any potential intruder "listening" on the other side; all communications "appear" to have originated from the firewall.

Creating a DMZ

You can combine packet-filtering and application-level firewalls in series, one after the other. This has the advantage of increased protection from a greater variety of attacks. If you then take this one step further, using two packet-filtering routers and an application-level firewall in the middle, the most secure firewall can be created through the use of a *demilitarized zone* (DMZ). This creates a separate, isolated network between the private company network and the external network (the Internet).

An advantage of this type of setup is that direct transmission across the DMZ is prohibited, denying any attacker direct access to the company network. It is in the DMZ that a company might place public data or a download area because external users can still legitimately access the publicly available company information, but the private company network is protected, while still retaining the capability to communicate on the Internet.

Security Products

This section provides an insight into some of the security products that are available for Solaris. It is not intended to be an in-depth discussion; it will serve more to raise awareness that will prompt system managers to investigate products of interest more thoroughly. Some additional resources are shown in the Appendix. This section covers three main aspects: those that come as part of the Solaris operating environment, those that are provided by Sun Microsystems as unbundled products, and, finally, some products that are available from third-party vendors or in the public domain.

Bundled with Solaris

The first list comprises those that come bundled with the Solaris operating environment and that are available immediately following the installation of the operating environment. An advantage that these products possess is that no additional configuration of the system is required to make use of them right away.

Password Management Features

Solaris, by default, provides a number of password management features. These are discussed briefly here:

- **Validation of passwords**—The password entered by a user at login is compared with the password stored in the file /etc/shadow; see the following bullet "Shadow password file" for an explanation of this file. If the two match, then the user is allowed to proceed with the login.
- **Aging of passwords**—The system administrator can force the user to change his password after a specified period of time, warn the user that a change is imminent, and prohibit him from immediately changing it back to the old password. When selecting a new password, the user also is prevented from using a previously selected password. The mechanism ensures that a newly selected password meets the specified criteria—that is, the correct number or characters or symbols.

- **Shadow password file**—Earlier implementations of SunOS contained the encrypted password as part of the file /etc/passwd, so it was visible to non-privileged users. The file /etc/shadow now contains the encrypted passwords for users and is also a hidden file, which is readable only by the root user.

- **Expiration of user accounts**—The system administrator can set the expiration date of a user account. This feature automatically disables the user account when the expiration date is reached. One of the most frequently overlooked password administration duties is disabling user accounts when a member of staff leaves the company or no longer requires access to the system. This feature goes some way to closing this potential loophole.

Automatic Security Enhancement Tool (ASET)

ASET is a set of utilities that can be used by system administrators to check the basic security of the Solaris system. It provides warnings where potential security loopholes are detected and, depending on the level of security selected—low, medium, or high—makes corrections.

When you run ASET, a number of reports are generated, which you can inspect to see the results. Details of any actions taken can also be found here.

As an example, I ran ASET on a Solaris 7 machine with deliberate security holes. The results are shown in Listing 6.1 as a concatenation of all of the *.rpt files in the directory /usr/aset/reports/latest.

Listing 6.1 **The Output Produced from Running the ASET Command**

```
#cat *.rpt
*** Begin Checklist Task ***

No checklist master - comparison not performed.
... Checklist master is being created now. Wait ...
... Checklist master created.

*** End Checklist Task ***

*** Begin EEPROM Check ***

EEPROM security option currently set to "none".
<< There is no security on the boot prom. This
                                                    Should at
least be set to 'command'.
*** End EEPROM Check ***

*** Begin Environment Check ***

Warning! umask set to umask 022 in /.profile - not recommended.
    << should be set to 077 so that the default is no
                                                    permission for
```

continues

Listing 6.1 **Continued**
_____

anyone other than the owner
Warning! umask set to umask 022 in /etc/profile - not recommended.

Warning! "." is in path variable!
<< path variable is open to malicious attack
Check /.profile file.

*** End Environment Check ***

*** Begin Firewall Task ***

Task skipped for security levels other than high.

*** Begin System Scripts Check ***

Warning! /etc/hosts.equiv contains a line with a single +
<< the system trusts all remote hosts
This makes every known host a trusted host, and is therefore
not recommended for system security.

Warning! The use of /.rhosts file is not recommended for system security.
     << If this has to be used, keep it at individual

                                                    user level,

certainly not in the root directory.
Warning! Shared resources file (/etc/dfs/dfstab) , line 12, file system exported
with no restrictions: **<<**
       share -F nfs /usr/opt/oracle
blindly sharing file systems as read/write

*** End System Scripts Check ***

*** Begin Tune Task ***

... setting attributes on the system objects defined in
    /usr/aset/masters/tune.low

*** End Tune Task ***

*** Begin User And Group Checking ***

Checking /etc/passwd ...

Checking /etc/shadow ...

Warning! Shadow file, line 15, no password:
<< Users with no passwords assigned
       john::11146::::::

```
Warning!  Shadow file, line 16, no password:
      bill::::::::

Warning!  Shadow file, line 17, no password:
      frank::::::::

... end user check.

Checking /etc/group ...

... end group check.

*** End User And Group Checking ***
```

The example output shows that significant security holes have been found, and these have been annotated accordingly on the text, but the system has not attempted to modify any of them. This is because, by default, the security level is set to low. Experienced system administrators can modify the configuration for each of the security levels to suit their own installations. The relevant files can be found in the directory /usr/aset/masters.

Access Control Lists

The standard UNIX file and directory permissions allow three categories of access to be specified: the owner of the file or directory, the group, and everyone else (known as "other"). Sometimes this is insufficient, particularly when individual, specific access is required. Consider the following example:

The system manager (user: john) is compiling a management report file named monthly, but he requires input from another manager, the network manager (user: bill). The file is owned by user john and is group-readable by the group managers. The requirement is for the other manager to be able to write to the file, but some managers in the group should not be able to write to it, so the option of allowing group write permissions is not acceptable. Of course, one alternative is to give the user bill his own copy of the file. This is inefficient, though, because it creates multiple copies of the same file, both of which will end up being different.

The access control list (ACL) provides the answer to the problem. ACLs provide a finer level of file and directory access permission and easily solve the problem outlined. User john can now give explicit write access to user bill in the form of an ACL, as shown here.

The original listing shows the permissions as originally stated:

```
$ ls -la monthly
-rwxr----- 1 john      managers 2872175 Jul  8 15:24 monthly
$
```

User john executes the command to give user bill the required access, to be able to write to the file:

```
$setfacl -s user:bill:rw-,user::rwx,group::r--,other::---,mask:rw- monthly
$
```

The listing now shows a "+" at the end of the permissions listing, indicating that an ACL is in force:

```
$ ls -la monthly
-rwxr-----+  1 john      managers 2872175 Jul  8 15:24 monthly
$
```

By executing the command getfacl, the precise permissions can be displayed, as shown in Listing 6.2.

Listing 6.2 **Sample Output Showing the Full ACL for a Given File**

```
$ getfacl monthly

# file: monthly
# owner: john
# group: managers
user::rwx
user:bill:rw-          #effective:rw-
group::r--             #effective:r--
mask:rwx
other:---
```

ACLs can be extremely useful when explicit, limited access is provided to a restricted subset of users, while retaining the desired level of security. The ACL facility is automatically included when Solaris is installed, so it can be used immediately without any further configuration necessary.

Pluggable Authentication Module (PAM)

The PAM software comprises several authentication modules that are dynamically loaded—that is, loaded into the kernel as they are required. One of the benefits of PAM is that the system manager can implement a separate authentication process for each of a number of services (login, su, and telnet being good examples). In this way, a more extensive security authentication procedure can be put in place, depending on the perceived security risk that the service displays. Also, the authentication of a user can be covered by more than one method and in a flexible order. For example, consider the following sample lines from the PAM configuration file /etc/pam.conf:

```
su      auth  requisite  /usr/lib/security/pam_inhouse.so.1
su      auth  required   /usr/lib/security/pam_unix.so.1
login   auth  required   /usr/lib/security/pam_unix.so.1
login   auth  optional   /usr/lib/security/pam_inhouse.so.1
```

Notice, for example, that the su command is authenticated twice, once using an in-house authentication method and then also using the standard UNIX authentication. The third column defines the severity of the authentication, so again for su, if the requisite authentication fails, then the other authentication will not even be carried out, and the su request will fail.

A final advantage of the PAM feature is that further modules can be plugged in and configured without needing to modify the applications.

SunShield Basic Security Module (BSM)

The Basic security module is enabled by a simple script. It makes a modification to the kernel, which disables the STOP-A key combination (used to halt a running system), disables the volume management facility, and installs a full auditing facility that is highly configurable, depending on the level of audit required. The system manager can choose to audit functions, such as deletion of files, and also users. BSM includes utilities that enable the audit trail data to be analyzed, even generating reports of events that have been logged.

Figure 6.2 shows the default audit_class file, which displays the standard auditing categories that can be used immediately.

```
# cat /etc/security/audit_class
#
# Copyright (c) 1988 by Sun Microsystems, Inc.
#
#ident  @(#)audit_class.txt 1.4     97/01/08 SMI
#
# User Level Class Masks
#
# Developers: If you change this file you must also edit audit.h.
#
# File Format:
#
#       mask:name:description
#
0x00000000:no:invalid class
0x00000001:fr:file read
0x00000002:fw:file write
0x00000004:fa:file attribute access
0x00000008:fm:file attribute modify
0x00000010:fc:file create
0x00000020:fd:file delete
0x00000040:cl:file close
0x00000080:pc:process
0x00000100:nt:network
0x00000200:ip:ipc
0x00000400:na:non-attribute
0x00000800:ad:administrative
0x00001000:lo:login or logout
0x00004000:ap:application
0x20000000:io:ioctl
0x40000000:ex:exec
0x80000000:ot:other
0xffffffff:all:all classes
#
```

Figure 6.2   The categories available for auditing allow the majority of events to be captured, producing full accountability. Auditing is highly configurable for specific requirements.

As an example, suppose that the Oracle database has crashed. Upon initial investigation, it is found that the main tablespace data file is missing—this is called system.dbf and is an essential part of the database. By interrogating the audit logs, which contain the attribute **fd**, it is possible to ascertain exactly what happened. The record in question is reproduced here, with the fields of interest highlighted in bold:

```
header,129,2,unlink(2),,Sat Jul 15 00:45:59 2000, + 509999500
→msec,path,/usr/opt/oracle/oracle/system.dbf,attribute,100600,oracle,dba,838
→8621,25540,0,subject,jephilc,root,other,root,other,701,350,0 0
→aries,return,success,0
```

The scenario goes like this:

- The file in question was /usr/opt/oracle/oracle/system.dbf.

- It was owned by user oracle and group dba.

- The operation carried out was unlink, which is the rm command, executed on Saturday, July 15, 2000, at 00:45:59, on the host named aries.

- The user in question turned out to be jephilc, who had managed to become the superuser root.

- The result of the operation was success—it worked, and the file was successfully deleted.

This example demonstrates how useful the auditing facility can be, particularly when considering that the majority of security incidents are actually carried out by members of staff within the company, as mentioned in the introductory paragraphs of this chapter.

> **Audit Only as Needed**
>
> Be very careful configuring the file audit_user, where the categories for auditing the users are selected. If all is selected, then vast amounts of disk space will be consumed—approximately 20–30Mb when a user logs in and starts up the window system. If the system does not have a separate /var file system, then there is a risk that the root (/) file system will fill to capacity.

Secure Network File System (NFS)

Sharing file systems across the network is potentially dangerous, particularly when shared globally with no restrictions. Solaris provides a mechanism for using enhanced authentication of users when trying to mount file systems across the network using NFS. An option to the share command is included, sec=mode. Currently, Solaris provides support for three modes (the mode none is not supported for NFS mounts): sys, dh, and krb4. Each is briefly discussed here:

- **sys**—This is the default authentication method used by Solaris. It uses the AUTH_SYS authentication, in which the user ID and group ID are checked by the NFS server before allowing the mount to proceed.

- **dh**—This is the Diffie-Hellman public key encryption system. This is a standard public key system that creates a secret key between two hosts.

- **krb4**—This method uses the Kerberos version 4 system for encryption and is freely available from the Massachusetts Institute of Technology (MIT). It is also available as a product from several different vendors. Kerberos is described later in this chapter in the section "Products Available in the Public Domain."

Unbundled Products

The security products listed in the next sections are available from Sun Microsystems but are not part of the Solaris operating environment distribution. They must be purchased as separate products and installed as packages. The list is not exhaustive, but it is intended to give you good insight into the products and facilities that can be implemented if a company requires additional security functionality to that provided by the standard Solaris release.

Trusted Solaris

This is a security-enhanced implementation of the Solaris operating environment that provides a fully configurable security policy that is incorporated within the software. Trusted Solaris extends the security that is normally provided with UNIX, such as sensitivity labels. These determine a level of security that a user possesses when logging in to the system and, in turn, can restrict the access available to the user.

Trusted Solaris also limits the use of the root user in traditional UNIX systems. Instead, there are other user accounts, such as secadmin, the security administrator, and admin, the system administrator, who sets up, for example, nonsecurity-related portions of user accounts.

Further information on Trusted Solaris can be found on Sun's Web site or gained from your Sun sales department.

Sunscreen Secure Net

Solstice Sunscreen is a package that provides the combined functionality of a firewall along with network-level authentication, also known as Simple Key management for IP (SKIP).

Sunscreen consists of two main components, a screen and an administration station. The screen component carries out the firewall functionality, screening packets and performing the necessary encryption and decryption, while the administration component is carried out by the administration station, based on configured security policies.

Sunscreen employs a stealth architecture that allows companies to effectively set up a virtual secure private network across a public network, such as the Internet. The stealth aspect of this product relates to the fact that the screen can be configured so that it cannot be accessed using an IP address. Therefore, it can pass packets across the network without recording any indication that it ever existed because there is no IP address. Because of this, a potential intruder cannot access the machine running Sunscreen, which makes it very difficult for it to be attacked. For internal network connections, the stealth mode need not be used, so a second mode, routing, is also available, which is much faster and would normally be used to segment the network internally within the company. The stealth mode screen would be used for the external perimeter—that is, the point where communications meet the outside world, the Internet.

Figure 6.3 displays a company network employing the use of Sunscreen Secure Net.

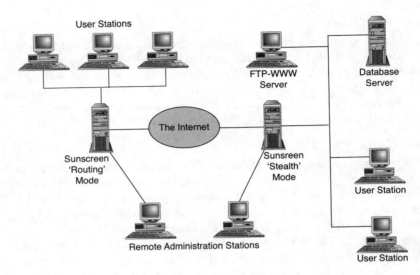

Figure 6.3   The flexibility of Sunscreen is demonstrated by the added functionality of remote administration.

Sun Security Manager (SSM)

SSM provides the type of security that corporations require when running mission-critical applications in a distributed environment. It delivers advanced access control for clients, servers and applications, as well as a centralized management facility.

One interesting aspect of SSM is that it supports *Secure Single Sign On (SSSO)*. This facility is important in today's multi-system distributed networks. Users are being forced to remember more passwords as they have access to more systems and applications. A consequence of this is that there is a higher probability that they will be written down or made easy to remember, which makes them less secure. The capability to use a single password for all access means that the user can remember the password, and the fact that it may have to change regularly is not a major issue.

Sun Security Manager also provides support for high availability in a 24×7 environment. A master server holds the security database, while a number of slave (redundant) servers hold read-only copies of the security database. Any of the security servers can respond to requests, and updates are automatically distributed to the slaves when made to the master database. If the master security server fails, then any of the slave serves can easily be converted into a master.

Products Available in the Public Domain

The following products are available in the public domain from a variety of sources. Refer to the Appendix for a list of the more popular sites where these products can be obtained.

Sudo

Sudo is a freely available software package that provides the facility for specific users (or defined groups of users) to run either some or all commands as the superuser (root). Additionally, it can be configured so that commands are run as another user. All commands and their arguments are written via the syslog process, which can be regularly audited. This can be modified so that all Sudo messages are written to a specific file that can be closely monitored. Configuration of syslog for such purposes is discussed in more detail in Chapter 9, "Tactical Management," in the section "System Logging."

Sudo presents a number of advantages for the system manager:

- It is an ideal way to give enhanced access to specified users for a particular purpose.

- Limited superuser (root) access can be granted without having to reveal the superuser password, which would allow blanket access to the whole system.

- The audit logs can be used to track privileged command usage and hence see what was done, by whom, and when it was done, providing increased accountability.

- It is an excellent tool for junior system administrators who are learning the job because it eliminates the risk of them making an error while logged on as user root.

- A double-check is made when users run Sudo commands. First, a user is required to provide his own password when using Sudo commands. After the user is authenticated, no password is required unless a Sudo command is not entered for 5 minutes (although this interval is also configurable). As a second check, the program verifies that the user is allowed to run the required program.

- Sudo is simple and effective, and its use can be easily modified through the use of a single configuration file, the sudoers file.

Control of privileged commands is carried out through the use of the sudoers file, which is installed by default into the directory /usr/local/etc, although it is a good idea to configure the installation to place this file in the /etc/ directory. A sample sudoers file is shown in Listing 6.3:

Listing 6.3 **A Sample Configuration of the sudoers File, Containing a Fundamental Flaw**

```
# sudoers file.

#

# This file MUST be edited with the 'visudo' command as root.
#
```

continues

Listing 6.3 **Continued**

```
# See the man page for the details on how to write a sudoers file.
#

# Host alias specification

# User alias specification
User Alias   OPS=jephilc,operator,frank,bill
User Alias   DBA=jephilc,oracle
User Alias   SADM=jephilc

# Cmnd alias specification
Cmnd Alias   ADMIN DB=/app/oracle/product/8.1.6/bin/svrmgr1
Cmnd Alias   EDITHOSTS=/usr/bin/vi /etc/inet/hosts
Cmnd Alias   LISTALL=/usr/bin/ls
Cmnd Alias   KILL=/usr/bin/kill
Cmnd Alias   BACKUPS=/usr/sbin/ufsdump,/usr/sbin/ufsrestore
Cmnd Alias   MOUNT=sbin/mount,/sbin/umount
Cmnd Alias   SHUTDOWN=/sbin/shutdown

# User privilege specification
root  ALL=(ALL) ALL
SADM  ALL=(ALL) ALL
Jephilc      ALL=EDITHOSTS
DBA    ALL=ADMIN DB
OPS    ALL=SHUTDOWN,KILL,MOUNT,BACKUPS
```

This file shows that several user aliases have been set up along with a number of command aliases. The section of the file headed "User privilege specification" dictates exactly who can run what.

The listing declares that there is a fundamental flaw in the file, namely the line `Cmnd_Alias       EDITHOSTS=/usr/bin/vi /etc/inet/hosts`. By providing access to the vi editor, the whole system has been left wide open because vi has a shell escape option. In this case, user `jephilc` could gain access to the command line as user root and have full superuser access. For this reason, the administrator of the sudoers file must be extremely careful when considering the entries to be added and also determining who will be allowed to use them.

Kerberos

Kerberos is a network authentication system that allows entities communicating over networks to prove their identity. It also prevents eavesdropping by potential intruders because the communications are encrypted.

Kerberos works by providing users or services (known as principals) with tickets that are used to identify themselves to other principals. It also provides secret cryptographic keys for secure communication with other principals.

When a user wants to use a service, these steps are followed (they would normally be carried out as a script or as part of the service requests, not manually):

1. The user runs kinit and requests a ticket-granting ticket (TGT) and a session key from the Key Distribution Service (KDS), which is the Kerberos server.

2. KDS receives the request and returns an encrypted TGT and the session key, which are encrypted using the user's password. The user enters the password to decrypt the TGT and the session key.

3. User now runs klogin, which requests a service ticket from the Ticket Granting Service (TGS). The user sends the TGT received from KDS, the session key, and a service request.

4. The TGS authenticates the request by examining the session key. The TGS then sends back a service ticket and a service session key to the user, who decrypts them both.

5. The user sends the service request to the provider of the service, along with the service ticket obtained from the TGS and the authenticator, similar to a reference, proving that he is who he says he is.

6. The service provider decrypts the TGS ticket and authenticates the request. The service now starts.

Figure 6.4 shows the kerberos authentication process in action. The numbers on the diagram refer to the steps in the process just listed.

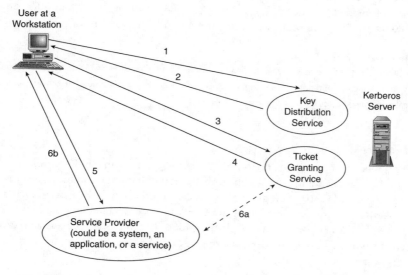

Figure 6.4 The authentication process of kerberos is similar to obtaining a reference from a trusted person known to both parties.

Crack

A number of system administrators and system managers are reluctant to use tools such as Crack because they are utilized by crackers to try to gain unauthorized entry to computer systems. Crack attempts to obtain passwords by comparing them to dictionary words. It has been stated that more than 30% of the average password file entries can be broken the first time this program is run.

If the system manager arranges for the program to be run against password files, then weaknesses can be identified and rectified, possibly before the cracker tries. The old saying, "Forewarned is forearmed" comes to mind, and in this case, it is particularly true.

Crack is successful only on systems in which the encrypted password is held in the file /etc/passwd along with all of the other user details. Solaris 2 versions utilize the shadow password entry, which is secure and beyond the reach of programs such as Crack. However, older Solaris systems running Solaris 1.x are at risk from this program, as are systems that are part of an NIS domain.

SATAN

SATAN is an acronym for Security Analysis Tool for Auditing Networks. Used to detect security risks, SATAN is run remotely from a computer against either another system or an entire network. As with Crack, some companies are reluctant to use this kind of tool because it is not necessary to have access to the system or network being tested. However, the same reasons for using Crack apply here.

An extremely useful feature of SATAN is that when a security risk is identified, a tutorial is provided that not only explains the detail of the risk, but also offers advice on how to fix it. The tutorial also details the potential impact of not fixing it.

Sinning with SATAN

Be aware that there are severe legal implications for using a tool such as SATAN to assess a network or system to which you do not have legitimate access. As a security prevention tool, it can be useful in identifying weaknesses in your own system or network.

Tcp Wrapper

Tcp Wrapper is a freely available tool that provides monitoring and control of network services. It is installed and configured so that when certain communications ports are connected to, the Wrapper program runs instead of the intended daemon, such as Telnet. Authentication can be carried out in addition to detailed logging before passing successful connections to the original daemon. Tcp Wrapper delivers an extra level of security, which is essential when allowing external connections via the Internet to the corporate systems.

Tripwire

Tripwire is a company producing security software designed to maintain the integrity of a system or a number of systems. The majority of companies rely heavily on the integrity of their data and need to know immediately if it has been compromised in any way. Tripwire can be used in a variety of applications; the main uses are described here:

- **Intrusion detection**—Tripwire software notifies the user when an intrusion is detected. It does this by noticing that files have changed or been tampered with. When Tripwire is run for the first time, it takes a snapshot of the files or file systems that it has been configured to monitor. This counts as a baseline for future, regular comparisons to be made, effectively creating a digital fingerprint of the system. As soon as the software notices that a file has been changed, it notifies the user and identifies exactly what has changed and what needs to be done to undo the damage.

- **Unauthorized software check**—In the same way that the software checks for an intruder modifying or altering files on the system, Tripwire also acts as a verification tool that a system has not had any unauthorized software installed on it. This is something that a cracker might want to do to install a virus.

- **Assessment and assistance with recovery**—If an attack is taking place, the Tripwire software produces violation reports so that the files requiring repair or replacement can be quickly identified.

- **Evidence reporting**—The reports produced by the Tripwire software can be utilized in forming a chain of events for data intrusions, specifying what happened and at what time. They are useful for providing formal evidence of the intrusion.

- **Configuration verification**—The Tripwire software can also be used to verify configurations across several different systems. Suppose that there are 10 servers with similar configurations. Tripwire makes a database using as a template a configured server. It then checks against the other servers to see that they are using the same applications, for example, or are using up-to-date versions of software. In this way, the software can monitor systems, watch for the abuse of software licenses, and monitor which applications are installed. It also has the advantage of noticing when untested modifications are made to the system because the difference between the modified system and the template will be flagged to the user.

The Tripwire software is extremely useful for maintaining the integrity of software and data. In addition to the uses provided here, Tripwire can also be used across the network to centrally manage systems throughout the enterprise. Tripwire HQ Connector contains the integrity software along with a communications agent, allowing it to communicate with a management console—this is known as HQ Manager. Using HQ Manager, a single position can act as a central point for integrity management for hundreds of different systems.

Tactical Options

A number of tactical options are available to the system manager of a Solaris network to help tighten up the security and make it much more difficult for unauthorized access to be gained. Some of these are discussed in the next sections. This is not an exhaustive discussion, but it provides a good indication of the type of action that can be taken to protect a business from malicious and, in some cases, accidental incidents.

Routing Options

By default, Solaris runs the routing daemon (in.routed). It allows routes to be dynamically added to the routing table instead of statically routing through a known gateway. Greater security and control of network routes can be achieved by creating the file /etc/defaultrouter and adding an entry containing either the name or the IP address of the primary router that the system uses. When the system is next rebooted, only the default route defined in this file will be used. Further routes can be manually added using the `route` command.

setuid and setgid Programs

Quite a number of programs make use of the setuid and setgid features of Solaris. Some, such as the `passwd` command, are needed, but others are not. setuid programs are not normally recommended because they pose added security risk. Also, when there are a large number of them on the system, it is difficult to spot a potential cracker adding one more!

The system manager should have a policy whereby setuid programs are closely managed. One good way of doing this is to collect a list of setuid and setgid programs and then compare them regularly to see if any unauthorized ones have been added.

To obtain a list of programs that have the setuid bit set, use the following command:

```
find / -perm 4000 -print
```

Or, another way:

```
find / -perm -u+s -print
```

The lists should be saved in a secure location and be used as a baseline template for comparisons to be made.

If any programs have the setuid or setgid bit set, then they should be reviewed to see if this is really necessary. Those that are not deemed necessary should have the bit(s) removed. As an example, consider the program ufsdump in the directory /usr/lib/fs/ufs. The only time that this program is used is by the superuser (root), and the program is already owned by user root. The setuid bit can easily be removed from this program without causing adverse affects on anything else.

Logging of Repeated Failed Login Attempts

Detailed logging of failed login attempts can be obtained by creating a file called loginlog. These three commands set this up correctly:

```
touch /var/adm/loginlog
chmod 600 /var/adm/loginlog
chgrp sys /var/adm/loginlog
```

The addition of this extra logging causes an entry to be written to the log file if five failed login attempts occur. The majority of the time, it is simply a user that has forgotten the password, but it could also alert the system manager (or administrators) to an intruder trying to guess passwords.

Disabling or Removing Unnecessary Services

If a particular service is not required, it should be disabled and then removed. By leaving it, the company could be exposing itself to an avoidable risk of intrusion. For example, if NFS is not being used, then comment out or remove the relevant entries in the /etc/services file, and rename or remove the scripts in /etc/rc2.d and /etc/rc3.d that automatically start NFS at system startup.

Many network facilities are started via the inetd process, its configuration file being /etc/inetd.conf. Each of the facilities listed in this file should be inspected to see whether it is appropriate for the specific environment—if not, then disable it by commenting out the entry or removing it. For example, if a company requires a more secure system, then it is a good idea to replace the standard /etc/inetd.conf file with one that just allows Telnet and FTP services (if these are required). A very good example of a network service to disable is finger because it has been known to have security problems.

Making Use of Groups

When administering user accounts, many companies create the accounts with a group of staff or general. This is less secure and potentially allows user accounts to have access to files and data that should be restricted. It is a better policy to create groups for relevant sections or functions, and then modify them as necessary when further access is required. For finer management of permissions, a combination of groups and ACLs (mentioned earlier in the "Bundled with Solaris" section) can be used.

For example, when defining groups for sections, possible candidates could be sales, marketing, or personnel. Here, the accessibility of unauthorized data is immediately reduced, preventing staff from sections outside of personnel from reading sensitive files. The other popular alternative for grouping user accounts is by function, such as sysadmin, which provides greater privilege for system administrators yet does not require them to always use the superuser account (root). Management would be a further function grouping allowing managers from various sections to share information requiring limited access, such as sensitive reports or financial data.

Summary

Network and system security have become increasingly important as more companies make use of public networks such as the Internet. The increased business and profits must offset the increased risk from unauthorized intruders; the latter could prove to be extremely costly.

Several products are available from Sun Microsystems, either included with the Solaris operating environment or as unbundled products. There are also an increasing number of products available to run on Solaris from third-party suppliers and in the public domain. Some tools available publicly are also those used by crackers to try to gain unauthorized access to systems and networks. System managers are well advised to be aware of these products so that any potential security holes can be filled at the earliest opportunity.

A central part of dealing with the computer security issue is formulating a security policy. This is the document that draws everything together, the resources that need protection, the risks associated with them, and the way in which they should be protected. It also contains the procedure to follow if an attack on a system or network is detected.

Disaster Recovery and Contingency Management

A DISASTER CAN OCCUR AT ANY GIVEN TIME—there may not be any warning, and the effect could be catastrophic. But what constitutes a disaster? It doesn't have to be something straight out of a Hollywood movie, with raging torrents or blazing infernos. It could be quite different, such as a digger cutting through the main cables supplying power to the whole site, or a key member of the staff leaving the company—the disaster scenario is depicted by the effect that it has on the company and that company's capability to continue operating.

In the context of computing and business, disaster is difficult to define accurately, so for our purposes let's define it as *an event or an incident that causes major disruption to the operation of the business for an extended period of time.*

In recent years, *disaster recovery* has become a frequently used buzzword in IT circles, as has *business continuity*. The whole recovery/continuity concept has developed into an industry of its own. This reflects the change in attitude that businesses have undergone; they are now realizing the importance of being able to resume (or continue) working in the event of a disaster. Previously, a data center consisted of a large centralized room with mainframe computer systems and batch processing. Today, with the development of distributed networks and environments, the main computer systems are often scattered across several sites.

Companies have become so reliant on their computer systems that these can frequently be the deciding factor in determining whether a business survives or collapses. With this in mind, it is quite astonishing to find that a large number of companies still have no formal disaster recovery plan in operation, despite knowing the risk. Senior management of a business has a responsibility to both the stockholders and the employees to protect the assets of the company as much as possible. Legal responsibilities also must be considered, such as personnel data, financial data for tax and auditing purposes, security logs, and so on. If a company loses all of this data as a result of a disaster, it could face prosecution or lose the business.

With an ever-increasing number of companies appearing on the Internet, there is an increase in demand for computer systems to be running and doing business continuously. The existence of a tried and tested disaster recovery plan, therefore, is essential for this to be a feasible objective. At the very least, it requires two separate sites, where all of the facilities are duplicated. However, as the rest of this chapter will show, the computer systems themselves form only a part of the overall disaster recovery and contingency plan; other aspects, such as clear procedures, thorough documentation, and good planning, are equally important.

A disaster recovery plan does not guarantee that the company will be unaffected by a disaster; that is never truly achievable. What it does, though, is put the company in the position of being prepared so that it won't be the end of the world if a disaster happens. A company with a tested (and current) disaster recovery plan has a much higher likelihood of surviving and continuing to do business than a company without such a plan.

This chapter addresses some of the issues related to disaster recovery and contingency, and how it relates directly to the Solaris computing environment. The chapter is divided into two broad sections. The first covers disaster recovery, the types of disaster that can be encountered, what a disaster recovery plan is, and the benefits of having one. The second part focuses on contingency management and the various ways in which the impact of a disaster can be reduced with some alternative options. The end of the chapter presents a section describing the steps to take in creating a disaster recovery plan and reinforces some of the ideas discussed in the text. The Appendix, "Resources," also lists some further readings and useful Web sites for disaster recovery and contingency information.

The Expansive Data Center

A data center can no longer be described as being a collection of computers in one physical location. It is a concept or a logical entity that can be spread across multiple sites, maybe multiple countries and that, taken as a unit, provides the mainstay of the computer support for a given company.

Disaster Recovery

The objective behind disaster recovery is to provide a means of restoring normal operations as quickly as possible if a disaster strikes. It attempts to minimize the impact by being prepared. A frighteningly high proportion of businesses that suffer a full-on disaster, such as total network loss or massive data corruption, go out of business permanently, and a percentage of these fail to recover from the disaster at all.

As an example, imagine a business selling computers and components on the Internet, a competitive business with several rivals. If the Web site becomes unavailable, then a potential customer is highly likely, with one swift click of the mouse, to move to a competitor's site. The sale is lost, and the chances of further business from the same customer are significantly reduced.

The most damaging factors for companies that suffer a disaster are negative cash flow, because even if they are insured for loss of business, they may not be able to afford to continue functioning until the insurance pays out. In the meantime, consumer confidence and stock prices could plummet, and customers could go elsewhere. A good disaster recovery plan could have the business up and running very quickly, even if it is in a degraded state, and capable of continuing its trading.

Types of Disasters

Disasters come in varied shapes and forms, not always how many would envisage them. Some of these are identified here, listed in no particular order of importance:

- **Natural**—Also called "acts of God," these are the more obvious disasters, such as earthquake, flood, fire, hurricane, or tornado.

- **Political**—This category covers terrorist attacks and espionage where a political motive might be designed to destabilize or harm the economy.

- **Man-made**—This could include a toxic chemical spill caused by a road accident that forces the entire building to be evacuated, or a digger cutting through cables supplying power and communications resources to an entire block.

- **Malicious**—In this case, a hacker deliberately tries to sabotage the business, infestation from a virus occurs, or a disgruntled employee seeks revenge.

- **Human**—Here, a key member of staff resigns, taking years of experience with him that exist only in his head because they were not documented, or critical data is accidentally deleted.

- **Criminal**—This involves the theft of critical computer systems or components, or the theft of critical data for financial gain (industrial espionage).

- **Equipment failure**—Disaster here includes the loss of a major server, a hard disk crash, or the loss of communications between the systems and the Internet.

The Disaster Recovery Plan

In an ideal world, a disaster recovery plan would automatically be built in to any new computer system or network that was being implemented. This section deals with reality though, and the fact that, for the majority, this is not considered at the time of implementation. A new system is more likely to be included in an existing plan (if there is one) at the next review, which could be too late if something happens in the intervening period.

The system manager is someone who is heavily involved in strategy and is responsible for the provision of IT services to the business. It is highly likely that he might be the instigator of a disaster recovery plan for the IT systems, if one does not exist, because he has a good understanding of how a serious failure could affect the company as a whole, not just a particular section or department.

What Is It?

A disaster recovery plan is a survival strategy. It is a plan designed to return a company to normal operating capacity as quickly as possible following an interruption to services—the disaster. The disaster recovery plan identifies key elements of the company and critical tasks that must be completed. It also identifies areas of high risk that need to be addressed to reduce risk.

The disaster recovery plan contains extensive contact information, something that could be very difficult to find in an emergency, and is kept in a central, accessible location. In fact, the plan is normally held at several key locations. Members of staff or external resources are assigned to various tasks. Their responsibility will be to instigate and implement the recovery of the company; because this has been planned and thought about in advance, it is less likely that bad decisions will be taken by someone in a state of panic.

A disaster recovery plan is a plan for recovery; it is a document, or a series or documents, that collectively comprise the survival strategy. However, it is not enough to merely have the plan safely in a cupboard. The task of building the plan is as important as the plan itself. It is the "doing" activity that provides familiarization, which in turn raises confidence levels. The process of creating the plan could also highlight areas of particular vulnerability in existing procedures that themselves could lead to an interruption to service. In this way, potential disasters of the future can be prevented.

Global Recovery Standards

The disaster recovery plan for the IT systems would probably be integrated into a corporate-wide disaster recovery strategy, although it might be addressed separately. It is worth checking to see if any standards exist before proceeding.

Benefits of a Disaster Recovery Plan

The existence of a disaster recovery plan brings several benefits, some of which could save a business from collapse. These benefits are described in the following list:

- **Minimizes downtime**—The downtime and unavailability suffered as a result of a disaster can be fatal to some companies. Sun cluster software provides an excellent means of maintaining high availability, allowing clustered nodes to be located at separate sites (Sun cluster was discussed in Chapter 5, "Solaris Installations and Upgrades"). By maintaining continuous high availability, the company can do business when others would have ceased completely.

- **Keeps the staff**—If a disaster occurs, it is possible that the business won't be capable of continuing to pay its employees; if this is the case, they will leave and find work elsewhere. A good disaster recovery plan should have most of the employees gainfully employed within one or two days—most employees would welcome the chance of an extra day or two off.

- **Retains an acceptable level of cash flow**—One of the major causes of businesses collapsing is that they run out of money—ironically, this happens before the insurance claim can be settled. The sooner the company can resume an operating capability, the better the cash flow situation and the better the chance of survival. The existence of a disaster recovery plan indicates that advance planning has been carried out and that an alternate way of continuing business has been investigated or implemented.

- **Maintains customer confidence**—In the highly competitive world of Internet commerce, customer confidence can be shattered very quickly. If the Web site of a company becomes unavailable or the company cannot trade, the customer will merely look elsewhere, so business is lost. When the company is a public company trading on the stock exchange, customer confidence becomes even more important. By simply publicizing the fact that a disaster recovery plan has been tested and implemented, confidence will rise (maybe the share price, too) as the stockholders see that the business is serious about protecting its assets—and their investments.

- **Satisfies legal requirements**—For some of the data held by a company, legal requirements govern retention and security of the data. The disaster recovery plan demonstrates that everything is being done to protect the information (by storing backups in a secure off-site storage facility, perhaps). Conversely, the absence of a disaster recovery strategy might result in legal penalties on the grounds that the executives did not make adequate preparations to protect the company's assets and legally required data.

- **Reduces insurance premiums**—Demonstrating to an insurance company that a disaster recovery strategy is in force within the company could reduce the premium payments. This is because of the prevention options that have been taken, as with home contents insurance policies—hoomeowners often pay reduced premiums when certain approved security measures to their property are implemented, such as intruder alarms and fire-detection equipment.

- **Raises employee education and awareness**—The creation of a disaster recovery plan raises staff awareness of potential dangers and risks. It has the side benefit of educating all those who are involved in the process on disaster management. It can be quite disturbing to members of staff when they realize exactly what could happen if a disaster struck the business, focusing attention on areas of weakness and vulnerability and, more importantly, what can be done to improve the situation.

As with the year 2000 problem described in Chapter 4, "Testing," an exercise of this magnitude produces other side effects as the project progresses. One of these is that the company assesses exactly what is critical to the survival of the business and what is less critical, so priorities can be set accordingly. The information might be used by managers to justify other future projects. Many companies find the exercise useful as an information-gathering process; the employees learn more about the function of the business, how it all fits together, and the impact of a certain function being unavailable. All this has an indirect effect on the general running of the business.

Finally, the action of creating a disaster recovery plan highlights, in some cases, precisely how vulnerable to disaster the business is, prompting positive decisions to be taken to improve the situation. The vulnerabilities might not all be directly related to disasters—for example, an analysis might reveal a security weakness in the Solaris operating environment currently installed. Upgrading to the next release might fix the problem, and other extra security measures that had not even been considered could be implemented. This might have been completely overlooked if the impact analysis had not been carried out.

Contingency Management

For a long time, risk assessment and risk management have been topics associated with projects that must be addressed in the project plan. A disaster recovery plan is no different in that it is effectively a project. It involves a number of stages and carries a number of risks. A risk is something that might happen, such as the database server crashing or the computer room being destroyed by fire. Each risk that is identified must be managed—that is, it must be addressed, and the best solution, usually based on money, must be found to somehow resolve it. As with project management, four main options can be applied:

- **Do nothing**—the risk is accepted, and the company hopes for the best. This is not an ideal option, but it's an option nonetheless.
- **Avoid the risk**—Here, the risk is eliminated completely and no longer presents a problem. For example, because of its location, a business could be deemed to be at risk from major. Housing the computer systems in the basement of the building flooding is considered to be high risk, high impact, and high probability. To avoid this risk, the computers could be moved to the top floor of the building. This might pose other risks, but the risk of flooding no longer exists.

A much simpler example related to everyday life could be the risk that you will get wet if you go out today and it rains. To eliminate the risk, don't go out!

- **Reduce the risk**—The concept of risk reduction is to make the likelihood that the risk will materialize much smaller—that is, preventive measures are taken. The risk is not totally eliminated, as with risk avoidance, but the chances of it happening are reduced. For example, a business might have a critical database server that is deemed a high-risk, single point of failure. Deciding to purchase an identical server, locate it at another site, and install the Sun cluster software is an instance of risk reduction. Even though the server might not now constitute a single point of failure, it is still possible that both servers could become unavailable at the same time, but it's much less likely. Similarly, one of the servers becoming unavailable has a significantly reduced impact on the operation of the business—in fact, there would be no impact because the remaining server would provide the company with a continuing operation while the failed server was being fixed.

  In the real-life example, the risk of getting wet could be reduced by watching the weather forecast or taking an umbrella.

- **Transfer the risk**—The remaining option is to pass the risk on to a third party, normally by outsourcing to a supplier or by taking out additional insurance. By using the outsourcing option, the computer systems could be managed by a third-party company in a data center owned and maintained by the company. In this instance, the supplier remains responsible for all aspects of the mission-critical systems, including planning for disaster recovery. The insurance option means that the business will be fully covered against loss of income as the result of a disaster, with resources (and money) being available immediately following the disaster to ensure that the business survives until normal operating status is resumed.

  The real-life example here would mean that you would get someone else to go out for you and hence take the risk of getting wet on your behalf.

Contingency is an essential part of any disaster recovery plan in that it identifies the measures that are to be taken to protect the company. Unlike the discussion earlier in the chapter on disasters, where the focus is clearly on identifying key areas of vulnerability, this aspect focuses on what to do about them to reduce the impact of a disaster. It is intended to ensure, where possible, that the business stands the best possible chance of not only surviving, but also being able to resume normal running at the earliest opportunity—or, better still, to continue running throughout.

The remainder of this section looks at potential contingency options for a business and shows how they can be used to maximize the chances of early recovery. They are not discussed in any particular order of importance.

Backups

Chapter 1, "Job Description," mentioned that the system manager is the custodian of the data for the company, and this is an awesome responsibility. Given the responsibility that this carries, it is amazing that the backups of a system are often viewed as a chore instead of an essential process.

Backups are crucial to the survival of the business, especially when considering the mission-critical, 24×7 systems in use today. Imagine a disaster striking the company only to find out that the backups haven't actually worked for the last two months—and even if they had, the tapes were being kept in the computer room, which has just been destroyed.

It is not just the data relating directly to the business activities that needs to be backed up; there might also be legal requirements for the retention of audit trails, or financial information for tax purposes. Remember that these requirements cover several years, and the data may need to be restored, if required, during a future investigation or audit.

To guarantee the integrity of the system's data in any way, the system manager must have a reliable and tested backup policy. The media used for the backups must be stored securely, and—probably the most important aspect of all—the backups must be tested at regular intervals. If they are not tested and are subsequently unreadable, then it really doesn't matter whether they are stored in a secure location because they're useless.

Sun Microsystems has a fully scalable product called Solstice Backup that is designed to deliver the best possible protection for a company's data. For example, it will accommodate a small business with a single system (the Server edition), a medium-sized business with a number of clients distributed across the network (the Network edition), or a large enterprise environment with many systems at remote locations (the Power edition). Choosing the correct edition of the software depends on how much data is needed to be backed up and how efficiently it is to be done. Solstice Backup supports concurrent devices so that multiple tape drives, or jukeboxes, for example, can be written to or read from at the same time, greatly enhancing performance and reducing the time needed for a system backup.

Solstice Backup doesn't just provide a good backup utility, it also includes a Storage Node Module. This module allows the central control server to make use of further tape devices located on remote machines. There are two main advantages to this: The capability is significantly enhanced (as is the performance), and, more important for disaster recovery strategies, it provides an automatic failover facility if the backup devices become unavailable. And for systems using relational database management systems, there are add-on database modules for Oracle, Sybase, Informix, and Microsoft SQL.

If all this wasn't enough, other add-on modules enable Solstice Backup to work in a true heterogeneous environment, delivering support for clients from various architectures, including desktop PCs (Microsoft Windows 95/98/NT), NetWare systems, a number of other UNIX architectures, and Macintosh.

Figure 7.1 shows a possible backup configuration that would deliver a high level of resilience.

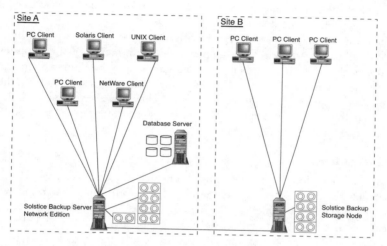

Figure 7.1 The Power edition of Solstice Backup provides not only resilience, but also flexibility in supporting a wide range of architectures, including online protection for databases.

Carrying out the actual backup is only part of the solution. A number of further issues need to be taken into account to guarantee, to any degree, the integrity and recoverability of the data stored electronically. These issues are discussed next.

Devising a Sensible Backup Policy

How often is a backup done? What data or file systems are backed up when one is done? Ideally, a full backup of everything would be done every day, but this is not always a practical option; it could prove a waste of resources and could undermine the reasons for the backup in the first place:

- The result could be that the system spends the majority of its time executing backups instead of running core business applications.
- Static data—that is, data and file systems that haven't changed since the last backup—are being backed up, wasting time and media.
- The real business-critical data might fail to be backed up in favor of noncritical, static data, which could prove to be extremely damaging.

A good, practical strategy is to first back up critical file systems containing operating system data at specified periods, preferably with the system at single-user mode to ensure that there is no activity other than the backup process itself. These backups would normally be carried out using the standard Solaris backup and restore commands (`ufsdump` and `ufsrestore`). It is also good practice to have the operating environment on different disk partitions rather than the actual data. This makes the restoration of the system software much easier and manageable because its content rarely changes (unlike the live data).

When it is not practical to carry out a full backup on a daily basis, the best strategy is to do a full backup once a week, supplemented with incremental backups every other day of the week. Remember that if high availability is required, then clustering and RAID configurations should already be implemented, greatly reducing the need for the backup tapes to be required. In an emergency, however, when a whole building is destroyed, the capability to restore the entire system from the backup tapes exists, and the actual loss will be very small.

Media Rotation

After devising a backup regime that is both practical and sensible, it would be a shame to neutralize the effect by continually writing to the same tapes. The result will be unreadable backups—worthless. Each backup tape has a finite life expectancy. Determine what this is, and replace the rotating tapes before the specified number of uses is reached. This simple task can significantly reduce the risk of I/O errors on tapes.

A further consideration when discussing the rotation of backups is the percentage of backups that are kept permanently. Some companies have a rotation policy of, say, four weeks—every four weeks, the backup tape is overwritten as part of the backup cycle. The result, for example, is that a file that was accidentally deleted six months ago cannot be restored. Other companies have a policy in which, for example, every fourth *full* backup is retained permanently (and the entire backup set for that day is replaced with new tapes). The result here is that a file from six months ago can be restored, if required.

The reason this is mentioned is that frequently, when a member of staff either deletes a file accidentally or that file becomes corrupt, there might be a considerable time lapse before it is noticed. A bimonthly report, for example, would require information from the previous two months to actually compile the report, and the data required might have already been recycled.

Restoring Solaris Backup Software

The operating system backup would include the Solstice Backup software, which is installed as a package, probably in the /opt file system. In the event of a serious failure requiring a full restore, Solstice Backup itself would have to be restored (or reinstalled) before it could recover the rest of the system's data.

If this kind of data is likely to be required, then perhaps a further add-on module to Solstice Backup is the answer: Hierarchical Storage Management (HSM). Data is automatically migrated to the backup device based on specified policies and is also available for recall when needed.

Storage of Backup Media

The beginning of this section mentioned that there is little point in achieving a good backup strategy if the backup media is subsequently destroyed in a fire. This scenario is likely if the tapes are stored at the same location as the computer systems from which the data is taken. A good disaster recovery plan should state that off-site, secure storage is vital for any business-critical data. Any backup tapes that are stored on-site should be done so in a certified fire-proof vault.

One further point about off-site storage is worth mentioning here. If a serious disaster strikes the business, the data stored in an off-site facility must be accessible. Suppose that there is a serious disaster on Friday evening—it is possible, if this has not been investigated, that you would not be able to retrieve the valuable backup tapes until Monday morning.

Scheduled Testing of Backups

Unfortunately, the most common error with regard to backups is that the company is lured into a false sense of security, purely because a backup has been taken of the systems. The real proof of a good backup is the capability to subsequently read the tape and restore the contents of the backup. This aspect is frequently overlooked until it is too late, when it is really needed. A periodic test to ensure that the tapes are readable should be a part of every backup strategy. It is not necessary to restore the entire contents of a tape; selecting a small sample of files will demonstrate its readability.

Media Storage Warning

When considering fire-proof safes or vaults, always examine the temperature rating of the safe to ensure that the media is fully protected in case of a fire. It is extremely important to know how cool the safe will keep the media and to ensure that this is within the tolerances of the media itself.

Alternate Site

If a serious disaster, such as a fire, occurs it may not be possible to use the site, in which case an alternate site is needed. For larger companies, relocating the entire operation at a moment's notice is no easy feat; in some cases, this could prove to be impossible. Disaster recovery terminology defines three types of alternate sites, depending on the state of readiness—hot, warm, and cold sites:

- **Hot site**—This is essentially an alternate site that is ready for business. It includes sufficient hardware, networking, and so on so that it is capable of providing immediate backup support to the business. In a distributed clustered environment, where the operation is mirrored at each node location, the transition to another site is much less painful.

- **Warm site**—The warm site is not as prepared as the hot site, but it is partially equipped with hardware and networking. Greater effort is required to achieve operational status, but generally the company could be up and running within 48 hours of a major disaster.

- **Cold site**—This could be empty commercial space belonging to the company, or even a mobile trailer, for example, providing electricity, a controlled environment, and communications access. The space is used to install, configure, and operate replacement systems.

As an alternative to providing its own alternate site, a company can make use of a third-party company that specializes in disaster recovery. A prime example for Sun computer networks is Sungard Recovery Services, Inc. (http://www.e-recovery.com), the world leader in enterprise recovery solutions. With a network of so-called megacenters across the United States, Sungard provides continuous support on a 24×7 basis for companies during a disaster situation. Sungard was notably active during the World Trade Center bombing, Hurricane Floyd, and the San Francisco earthquake, to name a few. Its facility in Philadelphia is the largest of its kind in the world, comprising more than 350,000 square feet of usable operations space. Figure 7.2 shows a picture from the Sungard Web site of the second-floor space.

Figure 7.2 The huge expanse of usable space can accommodate the largest requirements for business continuity.

Not only does Sungard provide the space for a company's recovery, but it can also provide the systems, including the complete range of Sun servers, right up to the E10000, Sun's flagship server. Office space for the continuity of business is included in addition to the space for the systems themselves. Sungard also offers a fleet of mobile Metrocenters in most metropolitan areas that can be delivered to the company's site within 48 hours and that accommodate an office environment of approximately 50 people. Figure 7.3 shows what a Metrocenter looks like.

Figure 7.3   The Metrocenter can be deployed virtually anywhere, providing the most flexible solution for a company requiring urgent recovery facilities.

Sungard is ideal for large companies running business-critical applications, requiring continuous 24×7 access. The company has high-availability facilities to ensure, as far as possible, that the business survives the aftermath of a major disaster.

Emergency Replacement and Spares

Of course, an alternate site is necessary only in the event of a major disaster that destroys the current site or makes it unserviceable. An option that provides contingency when components of a server or network fail is to establish an agreement with the provider of the support contract, if it isn't with Sun themselves, so that a fast-track replacement of critical components can be delivered. For the simpler field-replaceable units, such as disk modules, controller cards, memory, and so on, it might be desirable to hold a stock of emergency spares.

Replacing Server Components

Only qualified, trained staff should attempt to replace components of a server. Sun Microsystems offers a number of hardware maintenance training courses, although it may still be necessary for a field engineer to attend for component replacement. Consult your hardware support vendor for advice.

Creating a Disaster Recovery Plan

This section identifies the broad steps that are needed to create a disaster recovery plan based on thorough preparation and teamwork. The intention of this section is not to produce a specific recovery plan, but to provide information on the type of activity that should be carried out and the sort of data that an IT disaster recovery plan should contain.

A disaster recovery plan is not created during one short meeting held late on a Friday afternoon. It can take up to two years to create and implement a solid plan. This is a complex document that addresses a number of broad objectives, such as the following:

- Protecting the lives of company employees (and maybe members of the general public)
- Reducing the risk to the business
- Protecting the company against potential legal backlash from stockholders
- Maintaining consumer confidence
- Recovering critical business functions

The following steps provide a broad outline of how to tackle the task of creating the disaster recovery plan.

Step 1: Obtaining Agreement and Support

This is probably the most fundamental of all the steps to take: management support. It can also be one of the most difficult to achieve. A disaster recovery strategy will be effective only if it has the backing of senior management. One problem is that a disaster recovery strategy yields no tangible return on investment, and it could prove quite costly in terms of money and manpower resource. Management can be reluctant to approve this kind of expenditure for this reason; it is often viewed as unnecessary and overkill.

A justification in terms of potential impact (in hard cash terms) could go far obtaining the necessary support. For example, quantifying the actual loss of revenue for, say, a 24-hour period of unavailability, taking into account the fact that the staff still has to be paid, raises a number of eyebrows in the higher echelons, especially when the business is turning over millions of dollars per day. Management buy-in to the concept is essential for one other good reason: This should be funded as an overhead, not out of the system manager's budget—that is, funding should come from a corporate budget or a company's contingency budget.

Step 2: Assembling a Committee

The creation of the disaster recovery strategy and associated plan should be run as a project. Therefore, a project manager should be coordinating the operation and guiding the project through its various stages. The project manager needs to identify key areas of operation and assign members of staff who are familiar with these areas to an emergency response committee. Examples within an IT disaster recovery scenario could include the system manager, the network manager, a member from the computer security department, and so on.

After assembling the committee, a recovery team should be identified, comprising key personnel and resources involved with the IT department. It is worth noting that this does not solely mean the computer staff. It needs to include, for example, an electrical engineer, the network supplier (telephones and data), and any suppliers that might be needed in the event of a disaster. The person elected to be the head of the recovery team must have sufficient authority within the company to make urgent decisions if it becomes necessary.

Step 3: Seeking Professional Advice

The design and implementation of a disaster recovery strategy is a complex issue and needs to be addressed properly to have the best chance of being effective. While the employees of the company know the business, and a qualified expert knows about disaster planning, the combination of the two forces ensures that the best possible option will be identified. For example, take a look at the organization Survive (http://www.survive.com), the leading forum for business continuity and recovery expertise.

Step 4: Carrying Out an Impact Analysis

An analysis of the business-critical systems and functions must be carried out to identify areas that are key to the survival of the organization. The analysis should answer questions such as these:

- What is the impact if this business function is unavailable for an extended period of time?
- What is the effect on this business if the database server were unavailable?
- What is the financial impact of this business function?
- Does this business function depend on any other business function?
- What are the infrastructure dependencies of this business function? Does it require the Internet, a DNS server, or something else?
- Does another business function depend on this one? If so, what is the financial impact of the dependent?

These are just some example of questions, but in reality, a full analysis would have to include all the business functions, all the computer systems, the computer network, and communications equipment such as telephones, faxes, and so on.

Step 5: Carrying Out a Risk Assessment

An assessment of the different kinds of disasters should be carried out to ascertain whether the location or type of business might be prone to any particular types of disaster. Examples of these could be if the company was geographically located in an area prone to earthquakes; another could be if the company carried out work for the defense industry and could be a target for terrorist attack. The result of the assessment would identify those elements posing the greatest risk and, conversely, those posing no risk—as an example, a company located on top of a hill would not be at risk from flooding.

Step 6: Collecting Required Information

Before the plan can be put down on paper, some necessary information must be obtained and collated. The sort of information that is needed includes the following:

- A callout list for management and disaster response team members
- A floor plan showing the location of computer equipment and associated computer network infrastructure
- A list of vendor contacts to be called in the event of a disaster
- An inventory of the hardware listed by type, model number, configuration information, original cost, date purchased, and associated software for each system, including the version number
- An inventory of the software, listed by cost, date purchased, license key codes, details of the system acting as the license server, and number of licenses purchased
- Copies of hardware and software maintenance contracts
- An inventory of mobile telephones held by members of staff, along with copies of the agreements
- Any special information that might be required, depending on the type of business

The majority of the information listed here would be better placed as a series of appendices to the disaster recovery plan itself, with references to them within the document. The advantage of organizing the plan in this way is that changes are much easier to make without affecting the entire plan; the relevant appendix can merely be updated.

Step 7: Creating the Plan

Keep it simple and as nontechnical as possible. The instructions contained within a plan might have to be implemented by a nontechnical person if key members of staff are not available or are incapacitated. The plan needs to identify what to do for the following time periods, clearly referencing the information already collated in Step 6.

Initial Response: The First 24 Hours

This is the most crucial time when the emergency authorities will be contacted, along with the disaster recovery team. Communication is vital so that key members of the organization are kept informed of the current situation. During this time, the alternate site, if required, should be activated, and hardware and software vendors need to be contacted to arrange for replacement systems and network infrastructure to be delivered. A detailed log should be started to record the events and actions. This material will provide vital details for the learning process after the disaster is over.

Of course, the employees of the company also need to be informed of the situation so that they can be diverted to the alternate site or directed as appropriate to the particular instance. In larger companies, this can often be achieved via a tree network—managers are informed and contact the supervisors, who contact the members of staff for which they are directly responsible.

The Next 48 Hours

This is the interim period during which the replacement hardware should be delivered and installation can commence. Procedures for recovering critical systems need to be clearly identified, including the complete restoration from the most recent set of backup media.

There should be a clear priority established, designed to restore the operating capability of the business as soon as possible. The instructions should be easy to follow because, as mentioned previously, the recovery might need to be undertaken by someone who is not part of the system administration team.

Resumption of Normal Business

Depending on the extent of the disaster, this period could last for days or weeks. The plan should identify the procedures, such as the members of staff requiredto work in the alternate site, to ensure that business continuity is achieved. This also should resolve issues such as what to do with excess staff that cannot be accommodated at the alternate site, maybe setting up a sort of shift system, in which employees work fewer hours but at different times of the day. Employees might have had to travel farther to reach the alternate site, so there may be additional accommodation issues and traveling expenses.

Return to Normalcy

This is when the original site is declared open again. The procedures must identify the sequence of events for relocating the business back to the original site. This includes doing final backups, restoring to the new replacement systems at the original site, and clearing out the alternate site, including making sure that it is left secure.

Step 8: Reviewing the Plan

When the disaster recovery plan has been created, the first thing to do is to have it reviewed, preferably by an independent party, for objective analysis. Comments and suggestions that result from the review should be addressed; if necessary, the plan should be amended to reflect the decisions made. The disaster recovery plan should be reviewed at least every year, but more frequently if changes are taking place within the organization.

Step 9: Rehearsing the Plan

The members of the disaster recovery team, the management, and key members of staff should all be made familiar with the contents of the plan. They should all be aware of where copies of the plan are kept, specifically copies that are kept off-site because these will be required if the building burns down. A rehearsal will make the recovery team more confident of the procedures to follow. As a result, gaps in the plan may be identified, and the plan can be amended accordingly. The rehearsal will not be anything like the real thing, but the more prepared the members are, the better they will react if it does happen for real.

The best rehearsal, though, is to have a drill. For example, the system manager arrives at work in the morning only to be denied access to the computer systems and informed that they have all been destroyed. His senior system administrator has also been incapacitated as a result of the disaster (the administrator would actually be maintaining the systems while the drill is in progress). In this situation, the system manager would have to invoke the disaster recovery plan as if it were the real thing. The members of a disaster recovery team often learn the most from drills like this because problems that occur can be noted and rectified, adding to the value of the overall plan. The simulation also allows errors to be made—all part of the learning process—without the consequences that would have resulted had it been for real.

Summary

A *disaster* need not be a "disaster" if sufficient preparation and planning are carried out. It is a frightening reality that many companies have no contingency plans in place. The existence of a disaster recovery plan could keep the staff employed, satisfy legal requirements, reduce the insurance premiums, ensure that the company has a sufficient cash flow for survival, and highlight how vulnerable the company actually is.

A key aspect of planning for disaster is a good backup strategy—without the company data, there is not much to recover. But a backup is only as good as the capability to restore from it, if it becomes necessary. Secure storage and regular testing of backups guarantee the integrity and readability of the data.

A number of steps are involved in creating a good, solid disaster recovery plan:

- Obtain management buy-in.
- Assemble a disaster recovery team.
- Seek professional advice.
- Analyze the impact of a disaster on the business.
- Assess the risks to the business.
- Gather the required information.
- Create a logical plan that deals with the initial reaction to a disaster, the ensuing 48 hours, the resumption of business activity, and the return to normal operation.
- Practice the implementation of the plan, and improve it.

Many professional business continuity and recovery companies can provide expert advice as well as resources. A company can choose whether to use corporate-owned premises for an alternate site or a third-party site, fully prepared and ready for the contingency operation. With the resources available to businesses today, a successful recovery from a disaster should always be achievable. The only reason for failure, is the lack of preparation and planning.

8

Strategic Management

As part of his duties, the system manager must ensure that the systems under his control are being managed in a cost-effective yet efficient manner and that they can deliver the level of service required by customers.

Computer systems tend to evolve into collections of systems, and from there into complete environments. This could be the result of the addition of new projects, a corporate reorganization of departments, or a number of other reasons, but the result is the same: The responsibility lies with the system manager. The system manager could quite feasibly inherit, for instance, 10 systems with 10 support agreements from 10 different third-party vendors, each requiring renewal at different times of the year. Failure to manage this important environment could seriously jeopardize the system manager's ability to obtain the correct support if a failure occurred.

A large number of systems that I have personally encountered have little or no documentation—or, if there is any, it is frequently out-of-date. An interesting analogy can be drawn to a homeowner renting a house to a third party during an absence abroad. Certainly the homeowner would take a detailed inventory so that any items missing or damaged could be easily identified and so that appropriate steps could be taken to obtain compensation or replacement. Likewise, computer systems can be worth millions of dollars, especially when housing vital corporate data, and yet there is no inventory detailing the makeup of the system or how it is configured.

The system manager also needs to address the issue of configuration management. The majority of development projects use a means of version control, such as SCCS, that is tightly managed between releases of the application. However, scripts and programs written by the system administration staff or the database administrator frequently exist in an unmanaged state, often in a user's home directory. These scripts and programs usually are run by privileged users and are infinitely more powerful than most application software because they can cause severe disruption if inappropriate changes are made without testing. (System backup scripts are a prime example.) Without configuration management and a central repository for such elements, it is virtually impossible to apply any kind of control.

For the system manager to be able to manage his environment in a cost efficient and effective manner, he needs to provide management information that shows how the systems are being used—or not used. That information can be used to make appropriate, justified decisions on future expenditure and capacity planning, as well as options for continuing support.

This chapter discusses these issues and identifies the options available to address them, including a real-life example of reducing unnecessary support costs through simple analysis and consolidation.

Saving Money

All managers seem to be under constant pressure to cut costs where possible, do more with less, and generally to conjure up huge savings out of thin air. Consider a new system manager eager to make a good impression. It might be easy to impose too-severe cost cutting and put the department in jeopardy—and it might not become apparent until it is too late.

In a large company, saving, say, $20,000 might be considered fairly trivial when taken as part of the overall expenditure, which could amount to tens or hundreds of millions of dollars. However, the system manager can put the savings to good use so that he actually manages to do more without requesting additional funds. For example, more research on new products could be carried out, which might benefit the business by doing the job more efficiently. Or, perhaps additional disk upgrades could be purchased or additional training could be provided for members of staff. As any manager is no doubt aware, when the budget is under-utilized, it is generally acknowledged that less will be available for the following year—and that could be in addition to any budget cuts that have already been planned!

Maintenance Contracts

When a new system manager takes up this position, it is a good idea to examine the maintenance contracts that are in place, particularly for a large computing environment. There are significant advantages to doing this:

- **Familiarization**—The maintenance agreement provides detailed information on the systems and offers an ideal way for the system manager to become familiar with the equipment and software under his control.

- **Opportunity for savings or consolidation**—Various projects might have delivered Sun systems that were purchased from a number of resellers or third-party suppliers—often the package includes a maintenance agreement for the system supplied. During this exercise, there might be an opportunity to consolidate these systems under a single support agreement, providing the potential for negotiating a better deal with the maintenance provider. Examining the support agreements in place could also highlight possible duplication, where coverage is being provided twice by separate suppliers, or a system that is no longer in production might still be fully supported!

- **Assessment of cover**—During an exercise of this kind, the system manager could discover that a critical system is not covered by any maintenance agreement, or that the current agreement is grossly insufficient for the role being carried out by the system. There undoubtedly would be severe repercussions if a system failed and was not covered by any maintenance agreement—the system manager would bear the brunt of the criticism, too, even though he might know nothing about it. This scenario could occur quite easily, for example, if a major new system was delivered as part of a project; it is likely that the project manager would take responsibility for the first year of maintenance, prior to handing it over to the system manager as an operational system. In this case, the renewal of the agreement could be easily overlooked, and this exercise would identify the anomaly.

Genuine Support or Middleman

Some third-party companies offering support for Sun systems require customers to contact their own response centers instead of the Sun response center when reporting a fault. In some cases, the third party may not be able to solve the problem, necessitating a call to Sun for a solution. Beware that this can seriously affect your response receive due to the added delay.

Hardware and Operating Systems

The support and maintenance of the hardware and operating system software are normally part of the same contract with the same vendor (such as Sun Microsystems), who provides support and maintenance packages depending on the level of support required. The system manager should review the agreements in place to see if any circumstances have changed or if any systems have an inappropriate level of support attached to them.

As an example, consider a large organization running a 24×7 computer operation with, say, 20 servers and 400 workstations. The previous system manager might have automatically taken support and maintenance agreements on a 24×7 basis for all the systems and associated workstations. The level of support might be entirely inappropriate if only 150 workstations are actually used on a 24-hour basis, mainly because the heaviest usage occurs during normal business hours when there are extra sales staff, marketing staff, and administration support staff. Additionally, the marketing server and several application servers might not be needed all the time. In this case, the opportunity for significant savings exists if the system manager asks a simple question:

"What do we actually *need* to be available 24 hours a day, 7 days a week?"

The answer could be that the 250 workstations and 5 servers are not even used out of normal business hours, so their support and maintenance level could be adjusted accordingly.

Sun Microsystems provides a program of support called "SunSpectrum" that is designed to provide comprehensive hardware and software support for all kinds of customers. There are four major options—the main distinguishing features are described here:

- **Platinum**—This option is the full, mission-critical support plan, providing 24×7 onsite hardware service as well as a 2-hour response time. A business requiring a faster response can also have a site resident engineer. This option includes full 24×7 telephone support to the Sun response center, with mission-critical escalation and assistance with planning software releases and patch management. The platinum support agreement provides the highest level of support for hardware and software.

- **Gold**—This option provides support for business-critical systems where 24×7 continuous cover is not required. The default is 8–8 (12-hour coverage) Monday through Friday, although this can be extended if required. The response time for this option is four hours—again, it can be enhanced if a faster response is needed. The gold option provides 24×7 telephone support to the Sun response center with priority response.

- **Silver**—This basic level of support provides 8–5 (business hours support) from Monday through Friday, with a four-hour response time. As with the other options, the coverage can be extended and the response time can be expedited. The silver option includes telephone support to the Sun response center during business hours. It is designed for businesses requiring basic hardware and software support, without the need for critical assistance.

- **Bronze**—The bronze option is designed to accommodate businesses that carry out their own hardware repairs or those that have a system in a remote location not covered by Sun onsite service. Technical support is also available via the Sun response center.

All these SunSpectrum options provide software upgrades at no additional cost, as well as 24×7 online access to technical information and software patches through Sunsolve.

One further option for support complements the SunSpectrum program: the Sunclient support option. Basically, this option is designed for noncritical workstations or Javastations. Two alternatives exist within this support option: to opt for either next business day response or a central maintenance option in which the customer waits until there are five faulty workstations and then calls for an engineer. This option represents considerable savings and provides a realistic alternative for non–business-critical workstations. It allows a company to focus the highest level of support where it is needed.

Considerable savings can be had if workstations not required to be available all the time are downgraded to, for instance, the Sunclient level of support. It is important to note that even though there is a cost savings being made, there is no corresponding reduction in the service being provided—it is merely removing unnecessary support.

A further aspect of maintenance agreements to consider is that when systems are replaced or upgraded, the corresponding support agreement is frequently not amended. The system manager might find that his department is still paying for systems that are no longer in production.

Finally, test and development systems need to be addressed. The required level of service would normally be less than that of the production systems because these systems are less critical to the operation. It is rare to find a test or training system on 24×7 maintenance cover because it would not be deemed business-critical. If support is required, it can usually wait until the next working day, making it a potential candidate for the Sunclient support option or, at best, the SunSpectrum silver support level.

Real-Life Example

At one site I was supporting a number of systems, both Sun systems and a non-Sun legacy system. A review of the support arrangements for the systems revealed the following:

- Three standalone Sun workstations were being supported by two different third-party suppliers at a total cost of about $7,000 per year. The large Sun servers were all supported under a Sun Microsystems gold maintenance contract.

- A standalone workstation with an attached multitape autoloader, being used for business-critical daily backups, was not present in any support agreement.

- The legacy system had previously been two systems, but one had been decommissioned and the serviceable components had been moved to the remaining system, resulting in a single, more powerful system. The support agreement itemized every component down to processor and memory board level—it ran to five pages when printed. The decommissioned system had been removed from the support agreement, but there were several entries in the agreement for components that were no longer present in the system cabinet.

As a result of the review of the maintenance agreements, the following modifications were made:

- The three Sun workstations were incorporated into the main Sun support agreement but did not warrant the gold support. They were reduced to silver support, saving $5,000 per year.
- The standalone (backups) workstation was added to the main system support agreement at a cost of $2,500 per year because it was carrying out a business-critical function.
- A revised list of components that were actually present in the legacy system cabinet was faxed to the supplier, resulting in a $12,000 reduction in cost per year.

A saving of $14,500 might be considered fairly small for a large company, but the whole exercise actually took only a few hours and demonstrates the potential savings when examining a much larger network. In addition, the potential loss that the business might have suffered as a result of failure of the standalone system running the critical backups—and a subsequent lack of support—could have been significantly greater.

Third-Party Applications

A large company might make use of several third-party products such as case tools, statistical packages, CAD applications, and so on. They all offer technical and maintenance support agreements, some of which can prove to be extremely costly.

The system manager must decide which of these are necessary and justified. With an existing product, the justification can be made by examining how many problems in the last year required a call to the product supplier's help desk—and, more important, whether the call actually resolved the problem satisfactorily. The system manager ultimately must decide whether to have support available all the time or to pay for each separate instance that support is required. The latter option can be more cost-effective if a very small number of support calls were made. A large percentage of problems are often related to configuration and compatibility issues; the majority of these can be resolved by the system administrator(s), although the quality of the product documentation is also a factor to be taken into account.

A new system manager might discover that the previous manager always opted for the full technical support option, representing a significant cost but not always at the best value. For example, a thorough review of third-party application maintenance agreements could reveal that an agreement is still in place for a software product that is no longer in use. The maintenance agreements need regular reviews to ensure that the business is receiving the required level of service while providing value for money.

Documenting the Systems

This section considers system documentation, the reasons for having it, and the kind of information that it should contain to be of any value. This task is frequently overlooked or viewed as a trivial, time-consuming background project that remains at the bottom of the priority list to be done when there's time.

System documentation, in this context, is the information that describes the entire system, its hardware and software configuration, its business function, and its relationship to other systems on the network. This documentation needs to contain information about how the disks are partitioned, any modifications that might have been made to the operating environment, or patches that were installed. These are just a few examples, of course—many more are discussed in the following subsections.

The system manager is responsible for the provision of the IT service, which includes the systems under his control. Therefore, he is also responsible for ensuring that he has a complete inventory of those responsibilities and their relevance to the rest of the business.

The Importance of Good Documentation

System documentation is an extremely important part of system management. It has ramifications for other business functions within the company if it is not present or if it is out-of-date, for the following reasons:

- System documentation is the one place where all the details of the systems can be found, without needing to assemble pieces of information from a variety of sources. When the job has been done thoroughly, this is also the only place where the system manager can be sure to find a complete and comprehensive description of the systems under his control.

- The disaster recovery plan could refer to a good set of system documentation. This removes the need for duplication of effort and hence the increased risk of error. If the documentation is accurate and kept up-to-date, it is the ideal place to obtain the information that would be needed if disaster were to strike the company's computer systems.

- The system documentation has a part to play in fault resolution and recovery. Suppose that a system has crashed and completely corrupted a system disk volume containing a number of partitions. The information is held in the original Solaris installation log file /var/sadm/system/install_log, but getting to it is more difficult if the disk containing /var has just crashed or if the system won't boot. Moreover, this log file will not contain details of any disk volumes that were subsequently added to the system or any repartitioning that might have been carried out. Similarly, with a failed system and a call to the Sun response center, the system engineer would normally ask for details of kernel modifications and patches installed on the system, to aid resolution of the problem. Having all this information on hand can greatly speed up fault resolution by eliminating unnecessary delays. In a mission-critical environment, this becomes even more important.

- Documentation demonstrates professionalism. For example, a project manager designing a replacement for one of the existing systems under the system manager's control might require information about the system being replaced. With good documentation, this information can be provided in seconds, probably electronically if stored on the LAN as well as in hard copy.

- When planning upgrades, the documentation provides comprehensive information that could highlight potential problems or conflicts.

System Information

The purpose of system documentation is to provide information about a specific system or group of systems. It is a functional document aimed at a technical audience. If disaster strikes the computer systems, a nontechnical disaster coordinator could, in the absence of the system manager, pass the system document to a Sun supplier, who would then have sufficient information to be able to organize a replacement system of the same (or equivalent) configuration. Similarly, if a major system failed, the current kernel parameters or the partition information for a failed disk volume could be easily located to assist in the system recovery.

Figure 8.1 shows an example technical data sheet. This provides a good system summary and some generic information about the system.

SYSTEM INFORMATION - "COVERDB"	
Technical Data	
System type:	Sun Enterprise 250
Architecture:	sun4u
Memory:	1024 MB
Processor:	2 X UltraSPARC-II (400 MHz)
Operating System:	Solaris 2.6 - 5/98 (SunOS 5.6)
Kernel:	Generic_105181-19
Ethernet Address:	8:0:20:00:00:00
Ethernet Interface:	hme0 [named in/etc/hostname.hme0 as coverdb]
Netmask:	255.255.255.0 [ffffff00]
Broadcast Address:	210.127.8.255
IP Addresses:	
Sun Enterprise 250	210.127.8.4
SCSI Targets:	
Controller 0, Target 0	Internal disk - (9 Gigabytes.)
Controller 0, Target 8	Internal disk - (9 Gigabytes.)
Controller 0, Target 9	Internal disk - (9 Gigabytes.)
Controller 0, Target 10	Internal disk - (9 Gigabytes.)
Controller 0, Target 11	Internal disk - (9 Gigabytes.)
Controller 0, Target 12	Internal disk - (9 Gigabytes.)
Controller 0, Target 4	HP DDS3 4mm Archive (Dat Tape)
Controller 0, Target 6	CD-ROM
Hardware Serial Numbers	
Sun Enterprise 250	SN 000M0FF0

Figure 8.1   The technical data sheet yields important information about the system and its generic configuration.

The next three subsections identify the type of information that needs to be included in the system documentation to ensure that it contains a comprehensive description of the system, its configuration, and the commands that can be used to obtain the required data.

System Hardware and Device Configuration

A list of the hardware installed in the system is critical to the documentation, especially if faced with a disaster in which the computer could be completely destroyed. The same is true of device configuration information.

The following information normally is found in the system hardware and device configuration section of the documentation:

- **Output from the `prtdiag` and `sysdef` commands**—These commands display the current system definition, including all hardware, pseudo and system devices, loadable modules, and the values of some tunable kernel parameters.

- **Physical disk partition information**—This is the only place where the disk partitioning information will be held, apart from the system itself. See Listing 8.1 for a sample output from the `format` and `prtvtoc` commands.

- **Storage subsystems**—Include any information about RAID configurations or Solstice Disksuite metadevice usage. Even though this is technically a software issue, it is concerned with configuring the underlying hardware and should be included here.

- **Special devices**—This includes any information about other devices that require special consideration, such as the use of a third-party autoloading tape stacker.

Listing 8.1 shows the relevant part of the `format` command to list the disks attached to the system, as well as the output from running `prtvtoc` on two of the disk volumes. The advantage of using `prtvtoc` over `format` for this particular information is that it shows the mount point on which the partition is currently mounted (which `format` does not) and gives details about the geometry of the disk.

Listing 8.1 **Annotated Output from the Commands** *format* **and** *prtvtoc* **Showing Physical Disk Partition Information and the Current Mount Points.**

```
#format
AVAILABLE DISK SELECTIONS:
0. c0t0d0 <SUN9.0G cyl 4924 alt 2 hd 27 sec 133>
   /pci@1f,4000/scsi@3/sd@0,0
1. c0t8d0 <SUN9.0G cyl 4924 alt 2 hd 27 sec 133>
        /pci@1f,4000/scsi@3/sd@8,0
      2. c0t9d0 <SUN9.0G cyl 4924 alt 2 hd 27 sec 133>
         /pci@1f,4000/scsi@3/sd@9,0
      3. c0t10d0 <SUN9.0G cyl 4924 alt 2 hd 27 sec 133>
         /pci@1f,4000/scsi@3/sd@a,0
```

continues

Listing 8.1 **Continued**

```
#prtvtoc /dev/dsk/c0t0d0s2
* /dev/dsk/c0t0d0s2 partition map
*
* Dimensions:
*     512 bytes/sector
*     133 sectors/track
*      27 tracks/cylinder
*    3591 sectors/cylinder
*    4926 cylinders
*    4924 accessible cylinders
*
* Flags:
*   1: unmountable
*  10: read-only
*
*                            First      Sector     Last
* Partition  Tag  Flags      Sector     Count      Sector   Mount Directory
         0    2    00             0     254961     254960   /
         1    3    01        254961     610470     865430
         2    5    00             0   17682084   17682083
         3    4    00       2420334    4197879    6618212   /var
         4    4    00       6618213    4197879   10816091   /opt
         5    4    00      10816092    4668300   15484391   /application
         6    4    00        865431    1246077    2111507   /usr
         7    8    00       2111508     308826    2420333   /export/home
#


#prtvtoc /dev/dsk/c0t9d0s2
* /dev/dsk/c0t9d0s2 partition map*
* Dimensions:
*     512 bytes/sector*
133 sectors/track
*      27 tracks/cylinder
*    3591 sectors/cylinder
*    4926 cylinders
*    4924 accessible cylinders
*
* Flags:
*   1: unmountable
*  10: read-only
*
*                          First      Sector     Last
* Partition  Tag  Flags    Sector     Count      Sector   Mount Directory
         2    5    01           0   17682084   17682083
         7    0    00           0   17682084   17682083   /data/tables
#
```

Software Configuration

This section contains information on how the system software has been configured. It is not enough to show the initial install detail here because it has most likely changed when system tuning was carried out or software was added, requiring the modification of specific parameters.

The following information normally is found in the system software configuration section of the documentation:

- **Solaris software option**—State here which option was used to install the operating environment, either core, end user, developer, or entire distribution. If required, use the output from the `pkginfo` command to include specific package information.

- **Name service**—Details about name service should be supplied here, including the domain name, if applicable, and the status—for example, NIS master or slave server.

- **Use of the system**—Include a few words to describe the purpose of the system. Examples include file server, database server, application server, boot server, backup server, and so on.

- **Kernel parameters**—Include the file /etc/system to show the kernel parameters that have been modified. (See Listing 8.2 for an example of a customized configuration file.) This provides the necessary information and makes the document easy to update for further modifications.

- **Configuration files**—Include details of files that might be changed as a result of software requirements or security implementations. Such files include /etc/inittab, which shows the initialization levels; /etc/nsswitch.conf, which shows the order in which key files are accessed; /etc/syslog.conf, for system logging parameters; and /etc/inetd.conf, for details of disabled services for security reasons. The startup files are located in /etc/rc* and the /etc/rc*.d directories, which will be modified if applications are added or services removed.

- **Remote dependencies**—Provide details of services provided to other systems or file systems that are mounted from other systems. The contents of files such as /etc/dfs/dfstab could be included to show all file systems that are shared, as well as the files /etc/auto_master and /etc/auto_home to show details of automounted file systems.

Listing 8.2   **The File /etc/system Displaying the Kernel Configuration Options in Use**

```
*ident   "@(#)system   1.1897/06/27 SMI" /* SVR4 1.5 */
** SYSTEM SPECIFICATION FILE*
*
#Oracle Parameters
set shmsys:shminfo_shmmax=130023424
set shmsys:shminfo_shmmin=1
set shmsys:shminfo_shmmni=300
set shmsys:shminfo_shmseg=10
set semsys:seminfo_semmns=1200
set semsys:seminfo_semmni=300
set semsys:seminfo_semmsl=1000

#Set the maxusers parameter to 128 to increase the size of the task table.
set maxusers=128
#Increase the number of descriptors
set rlim_fd_cur=1024
set rlim_fd_max=1024
```

Patch Status

An essential part of the current system configuration is the capability to quickly and easily identify the patches that have been applied to the operating environment and to application software such as Sparc compilers.

The output from the command `showrev -p` displays information about all patches that are currently applied to the system. The command `patchadd -p` also produces information about patches that are installed. The output from these commands is useful because it contains the following information:

- **Patch**—The identifier and version of the patch. For example, 106542–08 represents patch 106542 and version 08.
- **Obsoletes**—The patches that have been superceded by installing the patch.
- **Requires**—Any prerequisites that this patch depends on. These patches must already be installed, or the patch installation will abort.
- **Incompatibles**—Any patches that conflict with this patch.
- **Packages**—The software packages that are affected by the installation of the patch.

An example of the type of information produced is shown in Listing 8.3.

Listing 8.3   **The Output from the Command *showrev -p* on an Intel Platform Running Solaris 7**

```
#showrev -p
Patch: 106542-08 Obsoletes: 106833-03, 106914-04, 106977-01, 107440-01, 107032-01,
107118-05, 107447-01 Requires: 107545-02 Incompatibles:  Packages: SUNWkvm,
SUNWcsu, SUNWcsr, SUNWcsl, SUNWcar, SUNWesu, SUNWarc, SUNWatfsr, SUNWdpl, SUNWhea,
SUNWipc, SUNWtoo, SUNWpcmci, SUNWpcmcu, SUNWscpu, SUNWtnfc, SUNWvolr
Patch: 107545-03 Obsoletes:  Requires:  Incompatibles:  Packages: SUNWcsu, SUNWcsr
```

```
Patch: 106794-03 Obsoletes:    Requires:   Incompatibles:  Packages: SUNWcsu, SUNWhea
Patch: 107452-02 Obsoletes:    Requires: 107118-03 Incompatibles:  Packages: SUNWcsu
Patch: 107455-03 Obsoletes:    Requires:   Incompatibles:  Packages: SUNWcsu
Patch: 107793-01 Obsoletes:    Requires:   Incompatibles:  Packages: SUNWcsu
Patch: 108302-01 Obsoletes:    Requires:   Incompatibles:  Packages: SUNWcsu
Patch: 108483-01 Obsoletes:    Requires:   Incompatibles:  Packages: SUNWcsu
Patch: 107457-01 Obsoletes:    Requires:   Incompatibles:  Packages: SUNWcsr
Patch: 106945-02 Obsoletes:    Requires:   Incompatibles:  Packages: SUNWcsr
Patch: 107894-04 Obsoletes: 108123-01, 108238-01 Requires:  Incompatibles:
Packages: SUNWtltk
Patch: 108375-01 Obsoletes: 107882-10 Requires:  Incompatibles:  Packages:
SUNWdtbas, SUNWdtdte, SUNWdtinc, SUNWdtmad
Patch: 106935-03 Obsoletes:    Requires:   Incompatibles:  Packages: SUNWdtbas
Patch: 108220-01 Obsoletes:    Requires:   Incompatibles:  Packages: SUNWdtbas
Patch: 107588-01 Obsoletes:    Requires:   Incompatibles:  Packages: SUNWaccu
Patch: 106979-09 Obsoletes:    Requires: 107457-01 Incompatibles:  Packages:
SUNWadmap, SUNWadmc
Patch: 108663-01 Obsoletes:    Requires:   Incompatibles:  Packages: SUNWadmfw
Patch: 107888-08 Obsoletes: 107002-01 Requires:  Incompatibles:  Packages:
SUNWdtdte, SUNWdtdst, SUNWdtma
Patch: 107181-12 Obsoletes:    Requires:   Incompatibles:  Packages: SUNWdtdte
Patch: 107023-05 Obsoletes:    Requires: 108375-01 Incompatibles:  Packages:
SUNWdtdmn, SUNWdtdst, SUNWdtma
Patch: 108222-01 Obsoletes:    Requires:   Incompatibles:  Packages: SUNWdtdmn
Patch: 106737-03 Obsoletes:    Requires:   Incompatibles:  Packages: SUNWoldst
Patch: 106953-01 Obsoletes:    Requires:   Incompatibles:  Packages: SUNWbnuu
Patch: 107039-01 Obsoletes:    Requires:   Incompatibles:  Packages: SUNWdoc
Patch: 107886-06 Obsoletes: 107220-02 Requires: 106935-03 Incompatibles:
Packages: SUNWdticn, SUNWdtdst, SUNWdthev, SUNWdtma
Patch: 107201-11 Obsoletes:    Requires: 108375-01, 107888-08 Incompatibles:
Packages: SUNWdtdst, SUNWdtma
Patch: 108344-02 Obsoletes:    Requires: 108375-01 Incompatibles:  Packages:
SUNWdtezt
Patch: 106328-06 Obsoletes:    Requires:   Incompatibles:  Packages: SUNWlibC
Patch: 107339-01 Obsoletes:    Requires:   Incompatibles:  Packages: SUNWkcsrt,
SUNWkcspg
Patch: 106961-01 Obsoletes:    Requires:   Incompatibles:  Packages: SUNWman
Patch: 107116-03 Obsoletes:    Requires:   Incompatibles:  Packages: SUNWpcu, SUNWpsu
Patch: 107637-03 Obsoletes:    Requires:   Incompatibles:  Packages: SUNWxi18n,
SUNWxim
Patch: 107685-01 Obsoletes:    Requires:   Incompatibles:  Packages: SUNWsndmu
Patch: 107973-01 Obsoletes:    Requires:   Incompatibles:  Packages: SUNWsutl
Patch: 107260-01 Obsoletes:    Requires:   Incompatibles:  Packages: SUNWvolu
#
```

This information can be invaluable if the system crashes or needs to be reinstalled from scratch. In the former instance, the relevant page of documentation can be sent by fax or email to the Sun response center very quickly, greatly assisting the fault-resolution process.

Application Information

In addition to the system configuration information, there is a requirement to document the application software installed on a specific system or group of systems. This information is of value because it is frequently the only record that describes what is installed on the whole system. Of course, each application should have its own documentation, but this applies to the whole system, which might run several applications. The information contained within the documentation is useful in a number of situations, such as considering disaster recovery initiatives, capacity planning for future upgrades, or determining the number of licenses for renewal purposes.

Usually, this type of documentation is split into two categories: applications that are developed and maintained within the company (known as in-house software) and applications that are purchased from a third-party supplier—that is, commercial software or outsourced developments. The categories are discussed separately in the following two subsections.

In-House Applications

For application software that is developed and maintained within the company, the following information should be recorded about each application:

- The name of the application and a basic description of its components and function within the business—for example: "This is an Oracle forms/reports-based application that queries and updates the main customer database."

- Any software dependencies that exist for the application—for example, the assumption that the Oracle Developer runtime product is already installed so that forms and reports can be run.

- The users of the application—for example, sales, accounts, marketing. An indication of how many users actually make use of the application should also be included.

- The current version of the software that is installed.

- The installed location of the software on the system and the amount of disk space required. Include the location of any installation media and documentation.

- Contact details of the development section and, if different, the application support authority.

Third-Party Applications

Third-party application software is usually subject to a formal maintenance and support agreement with the supplier of the software. The following information should be present for each application listed:

- The name of the application package and details of the vendor and supplier (if they are different).

- A brief description of what the package does, as well as what department(s) make use of it.

- The version number of the software installed on the system, along with also details of any patches that the supplier has delivered (and are installed).

- Details of any existing support and maintenance agreement for the software, including the level of support, the renewal date, the number of licenses purchased, and how to contact the support authority, together with any account numbers/serial numbers that might be necessary to obtain support.

- The installed location of the software on the system and the amount of disk space required. Also include the location of the installation media and supporting documentation.

Relational Database Information

Relational database management systems (RDBMS) warrant their own section in the system documentation because of their importance to the business. They frequently hold business-critical information such as customer data, sales or marketing information, and personnel data. For this reason alone, each database that resides on the system should be clearly identified and documented.

A further reason for documenting separately the existence of a database on the system is that it might be maintained by the "database administration (DBA) section," a section that is often separate from the system administrators and one that also might administer a number of different databases on different systems. Ideally, the two sections should be co-located, but this is not always the case. If the DBA section maintains its own documentation for the database, the central system documentation will be incomplete, and multiple sources will be needed to get the complete picture—that's a far from ideal situation. A better solution should ensure that the DBA section maintains this part of the document so that the entire system documentation remains in a single reference document.

The information contained within the document needs to include the following details:

- The RDBMS product and version installed on the system, together with any patches that have been subsequently applied to the product

- Details of support and maintenance agreements, including contact numbers for the DBA section as well as the supplier (such as Oracle), and any account numbers/serial numbers that might be required to obtain support in the absence of a DBA

- A brief description of the database instance and its function within the company

- The location of the installation media and supporting documentation

- Information about the size of the database and location on the system of its components, such as tablespaces, redo logs, archive logs, and so on

Beware of Raw Disk Usage

Most, if not all, RDBMS products allow the storage of the database either in a file system, as with any other file, or with raw disk (bypassing the UNIX I/O buffering). The advantage of using raw disk is that there is a performance gain through direct communication with the disk. The downside is that it requires a greater administration overhead, and it is not visible to the unfamiliar person, unlike the presence of a file system, for example.

Raw disk partitions that are used as part of a relational database are not mounted like file systems. They are only defined in the database configuration file, usually by a symbolic link to the raw disk device in question. Volume management software, such as that supplied by Veritas, is often used to manage the disk allocation on systems configured for use with relational databases. A good idea is to store a list of managed volumes and mirrors on a regular basis using the command vxprint, for example, which is part of the Veritas volume management software.

If the raw disk option is being used, it must be clearly identified, as the following example demonstrates.

Suppose that a system administrator is hired who has not previously used a relational database environment. If he is requested to create a new file system, he might look at the format command to see the disks available to him and then he might use the prtvtoc command to see how a disk is partitioned and to see any mount points associated with the partitions. After checking the file /etc/vfstab to check for any file systems not mounted, the system administrator could assume that a partition that is not referenced is actually free for use, when in reality it is being used by the database—the problem is that it isn't documented clearly. If this system administrator ran the newfs command on the partition to create the file system, the previous contents would be lost and the database would be trashed.

The impact of this scenario, although avoidable, is potentially severe:

- The database will have to be recovered, and there is the potential for loss of business.

- The cause of the problem will not be immediately clear, creating a delay while it is investigated.

- The system administrator won't come clean because he is not aware of having done anything wrong!

Show Database Instances and Their Purpose

The main reason for documenting existing database instances is that there might be a requirement to re-create the instance if a serious failure or disaster occurs. If the database uses UNIX file systems for the storage of the database, then the recovery can be carried out using the normal file system restore from the latest backup. However, if raw disk is being used, then recovery is more complicated and the database instance must be created and initialized before a restore can be carried out. A further reason for documenting this information is that it is useful for familiarizing a new department staff member with the configuration. The documentation should contain the following information for each instance running on the system:

- The database name. This is the unique name by which the instance is identified. For example, in Oracle, it is the `ORACLE_SID` variable; in Informix, it is the `DBSERVERNAME` parameter in the tbconfig file.

- A brief description of the database, what it is used for, who uses it, and how many people use it (approximately).

- The type of storage used. This could be a file system, raw disk, or possibly a combination of both.

- Database creation and configuration information. Most of the required information can be derived from the configuration file and from a query of some of the system tables, showing the tablespaces, their size, and the location of the data files, for example.

Keeping It Up-to-Date

Probably the most important aspect of documenting the systems in use is to keep everything up-to-date. Documentation is of any real value only if it contains information about the current state of the systems. This is the most frequently omitted part of documentation because it is thought to be complete once the document has been created rather than being an ongoing task requiring regular attention. This task is also often seen as being "boring" when there are so many more interesting things to do, so it finds itself at the bottom of the priority pile—as a result, the documentation quickly becomes outdated and loses any value it had. One way of making the documentation easier to update is to include the output of Solaris commands, such as the one used in the earlier section "Patch Status." If a new patch is installed, the documentation can be quickly and simply updated to reflect the change by running the command and "pasting" the output—this also makes the updating more likely to be done altogether.

> **Presentation or Content**
>
> Including command output can affect the presentation quality of the document. Although it is important to present the system documentation professionally, the content and ease of update should be the overriding priority.

The system manager must ensure that the system documentation is regularly updated, either each week or, at the most, each month. The best policy, of course, is to update the document as part of carrying out a change, while it is still fresh in the mind of the system administrator. It may not always be practical to do this, but the longer the interval is between updates, the greater the risk of omission or errors becomes.

Configuration Management

Configuration management is normally associated with the development process, in which vast amounts of source code, documentation, and test packs are stored in a repository. It provides a control mechanism for all changes that are subsequently made, as well as a facility to revert to previous versions of code, if necessary.

In reality, though, it isn't just the development section that can make use of configuration management—a number of other uses could be of value to the system manager. Some of these are listed here:

- System administration scripts
- System documentation
- Important system configuration files

The Need for Configuration Control

With business-critical systems and applications, it is imperative that some control mechanism exists to manage changes made to systems (particularly live production systems), even though any changes should have been thoroughly tested on nonproduction systems before implementation.

The use of a configuration control package such as the Source Code Control System (SCCS), bundled with the Solaris operating environment, provides the facility to track changes made to a program or file. Equally important, however, a configuration control package provides a history, a documented evolution of how the program or file became what it is now and the changes made along the way. If inline documentation has also been present, normally in the form of comments, this will include an explanation of why a specific change was made or a reference to the request that initiated the change.

Keeping Track of Changes

Using SCCS as an example, a new version of a file is created and managed each time it is updated. This new version is stored in a specified subdirectory—by default, it is named SCCS. Each file present in the directory is prefixed with s., so the script called sys_monitor.ksh, for example, would be stored as s.sys_monitor.ksh within SCCS.

Consider a real-life Solaris example. Whenever an important system file is changed (such as /etc/system, which contains kernel configuration information), it is recommended practice to make a copy of the file, as an obvious precaution. A common scenario is to copy the file to, say, /etc/system.bak. When a subsequent change is made, the history is lost because the file is overwritten. By storing the versions of the file in a control system such as SCCS, the history is preserved and can easily be referred to. SCCS maintains a check-in and check-out control so that if a file is retrieved for editing, it is said to be checked out, similar to a rental system. As a result, no one else can change the file until it is checked in again.

It Could Affect Others

If no form of configuration management is used, a new system manager or new member of staff joining the system administration team will have difficulty seeing how and why previous changes were made to either configuration files or administration shell scripts, for example. Configuration management provides a fully traceable history that can be used for familiarization purposes and for investigating future problems.

This is also an important aspect to consider if files or scripts are being shared with other departments—the disaster recovery documentation is a good example. In this instance, the correct version of the documentation can easily be identified to ensure that all parties are using the current version.

Finally, the documentation for a specific system should highlight the facilities available on the system, who uses them, and approximately how many users there are. This information can be used to see at a glance the effect on the business if this system is taken out of service or fails for any reason. The documentation also can provide useful input when attempting to prioritize systems by their importance to the business functions.

Big Brother's Watching

The system manager and the administrator have considerable power over the Solaris systems. The only elements that they might not be able to see are those that have been privately encrypted; anything else is readily accessible. The superuser account (root) has unlimited access to all directories and files on the system—hence the title of this section. These privileges are not exclusive to UNIX or Solaris—the same is true of VMS, Novell NetWare, and so on—but they are necessary for effective system management and problem resolution.

This section takes a look at some of the information that the system manager can obtain about who's been doing what, when a user was last logged in and for how long, what commands were executed, and so on. In reality, though, a system manager often doesn't have the need or the time to go searching for a specific user's command history of activity—although it could be done to investigate possible abuse of the system. This is normally used to gather statistical information, for example, to see how many times the StarOffice package was used last month compared with the month before, or to determine whether a particular software package is being used at all.

The following subsections discuss the use of the system accounting software to obtain and collate the kind of management information that is required. They also examine the whodo command, which provides a snapshot of the commands being executed at the time.

Using the System Accounting Software to Your Advantage

The accounting software is capable of much more than just providing financial information based on computer usage. In fact, the concept of billing for computer time is fast becoming outdated, unless the company is using an external bureau for its computing needs. Most system managers charge customers an agreed fee, say, for a year; the fee is based on the cost of providing the service rather than how much CPU time is utilized.

The system manager can make better use of the data collated by the software and use the information derived from this data to see, for example, which software packages are actually being used and how much. This kind of information is invaluable for assessing license renewals or levels of support required.

Enabling the Accounting Software

The system accounting software is not enabled by default when the Solaris operating environment is installed. A number of steps must be performed to initiate the accounting software:

1. Become superuser (root).

2. The packages SUNWaccr and SUNWaccu must be installed before the accounting software can be used. Check the status using the pkginfo command. If these packages are not installed, add them using the pkgadd command or the admintool facility.

3. Install the script /etc/init.d/acct as the startup script for Run Level 2 so that the accounting software is activated when the system is restarted. This is achieved by creating a link in the /etc/rc2.d directory, as shown here:

```
#ln /etc/init.d/acct /etc/rc2.d/S22acct
```

4. Install the script /etc/init.d/acct as the stop script for Run Level 0 so that the accounting software is shut down cleanly when the system is stopped. This is achieved by creating a second link, this time in the /etc/rc0.d directory, as shown here:

```
#ln /etc/init.d/acct /etc/rc0.d/K22acct
```

5. Modify the crontab file for user adm to install the automatic management scripts. The following lines should be added to the crontab:

```
0 * * * * /usr/lib/acct/ckpacct
30 2 * * * /usr/lib/acct/runacct 2> /var/adm/acct/nite/fd2log
30 7 1 * * /usr/lib/acct/monacct
```

These entries are suggested defaults and can be amended, if required.

6. Modify the crontab file for user root to automatically run the command dodisk, the disk accounting program. The following line should be added to the crontab:

```
30 22 * * 4 /usr/lib/acct/dodisk
```

This entry is a suggested default and can be amended, if required.

7. Edit the file /etc/acct/holidays if it is to be used. Each line contains the date of a public holiday. These days will not be treated as normal working days by the accounting software.

8. The system accounting software will be started automatically the next time the system is restarted. Alternatively, it can be started immediately by running the following command as user root:

```
#/etc/rc2.d/S22acct start
```

Where Is the Data Kept?

The system accounting software stores all its data in the /var/adm directory structure. In larger systems, it is still fairly common to have /var as a separate file system to protect the root file system (/) from becoming full. The importance of doing this has reduced considerably due to the high disk capacities available today, although some companies still do this as part of their configuration policy.

The main accounting file is /var/adm/pacct. This contains the active process accounting information. It is reset each day when the runacct program is run automatically via cron.

The directory /var/adm/acct also contains three further subdirectories, fiscal, nite, and sum. These subdirectories contain the following information:

- **fiscal**—Reports by fiscal period. This is normally a monthly period, but it can be configured to suit the company's own reporting period. The reports are created when the monacct program is run automatically via cron.

- **nite**—Daily binary summary files, a daily processed accounting record, and disk accounting information. These files are created daily when the runacct program is run automatically via cron.

- **sum**—Cumulative summary accounting files and daily reports. These are merged when the monthly fiscal report is generated.

Some of the reports produced by the various accounting programs are available in ASCII text format and therefore are readable by any editor or can be used as part of a more general report on system activity. Other files are held in accounting data format designed to be accessed using programs such as acctcom, acctcms, and acctprc, located in the /usr/lib/acct directory. These programs extract processing and command information, the output of which also can be saved to ASCII files for further analysis.

Common Usage Statistics

The system manager needs statistical information about the activity on the system for a variety of reasons. The best place to get this information is from the accounting report located in the fiscal directory. This is an ASCII format report that can be easily manipulated and searched, using either an editor or a shell script. A number of fiscal reports can be searched to provide information on trends. Figure 8.2 shows a graph created by using the output from three fiscal reports to display the trend in usage for the shells and the StarOffice suite as well as the sudo command.

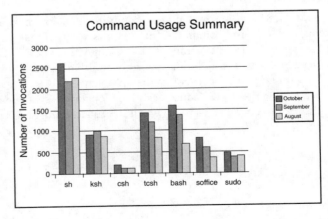

Figure 8.2   The graphical representation of the data makes it easy to see the upward trend in the usage of the selected commands.

Using *acctcom*

The `acctcom` command is used to display a summary of process accounting records. This command displays information only about processes that have already terminated. The `ps` or `whodo` commands can be used to obtain information about current processes.

For example, to obtain a detailed listing of commands that have been executed today by user `jephilc`, the program acctcom is used. This program, by default, reads the current accounting file /var/adm/pacct and produces a list of command information as shown in Listing 8.4.

Listing 8.4 **The Output from the `acctcom` Command Showing the Command Usage for a Specific User**

```
#acctcom -u jephilc
ACCOUNTING RECORDS FROM:  Mon Oct 30 10:45:58 2000
COMMAND                        START    END       REAL    CPU     MEAN
NAME       USER     TTYNAME    TIME     TIME     (SECS)  (SECS) SIZE(K)
touch      jephilc  ?          10:50:14 10:50:14   0.07    0.01   584.00
cat        jephilc  ?          10:50:14 10:50:34  20.10    0.02   650.00
head       jephilc  ?          10:50:34 10:50:34   0.06    0.01   704.00
touch      jephilc  ?          10:50:34 10:50:34   0.02    0.01   748.00
ksh        jephilc  ?          10:50:38 10:50:38   0.11    0.02  1528.00
dtfile     jephilc  ?          11:09:40 11:09:40   0.01    0.01  2672.00
sh         jephilc  ?          10:25:42 11:12:06 2784.64   0.03  1690.67
dtterm     jephilc  ?          10:25:40 11:12:07 2787.20   2.65  2816.00
sh         jephilc  ?          11:12:13 11:18:45  392.24   0.02  2272.00
dtterm     jephilc  ?          11:12:13 11:18:46  393.04   0.94  3366.13
sqlplus    jephilc  pts/22     14:56:45 15:08:42  717.44   0.07  3113.14
Xsupport   jephilc  pts/22     15:59:48 16:04:32  284.80   0.13  3819.69
ls         jephilc  pts/22     16:22:07 16:22:07   0.01    0.01  1416.00
cp         jephilc  pts/22     16:22:13 16:22:13   0.02    0.01  1024.00
more       jephilc  pts/22     16:22:22 16:22:22   0.01    0.01  1368.00
soffice    jephilc  pts/22     16:22:51 16:25:48  177.76   0.11  3350.55
sh         jephilc  ?          11:18:50 22:21:31 39761.92  0.06  1065.33
sh         jephilc  ?          22:21:38 22:34:04  746.24   0.02  2414.00
dtterm     jephilc  ?          22:21:36 22:34:04  748.16   0.71  3303.21
sdtimage   jephilc  ?          23:15:50 23:17:57  127.76   1.34  4468.54
sh         jephilc  ?          09:05:34 23:26:24 51650.56  0.08   948.00
dtterm     jephilc  ?          09:05:31 23:27:02 51691.52  2.51  1844.02
ls         jephilc  pts/4      23:34:25 23:34:25   0.01    0.01   780.00
more       jephilc  pts/4      23:34:32 23:34:32   0.01    0.01  1016.00
#
```

This example shows the command usage for a specific user. When executed for all users, this command is particularly useful for diagnosing bottlenecks in the system because it is fairly easy to establish exactly what commands were being executed at the time the system suffered from poor performance.

Is Anyone Using This Expensive Package?

One of the best uses of the accounting software that I have personally come across is using the software to determine whether a particular software product is being used and, if so, to what extent. It could be that the product was very expensive to purchase, was requested as a high priority, and demanded full technical support. However, on running the relevant query, the system manager can interrogate a number of monthly reports and find out exactly how many invocations of that piece of software have actually occurred. Sometimes it turns out that the software hasn't been used for months, yet the system manager has been paying for full technical support—and even when it was used, it was only by one user, who has since left the company.

This scenario is not typical, but it demonstrates the need for the system manager to keep a "watching brief" on the usage of software products. The information obtained from such analysis can prove extremely useful when deciding on future support and licensing requirements, and it can be instrumental in providing the justification for whichever decision is taken.

Using the *whodo* Command

The whodo command also provides information on commands, but this command details processes that are currently running. The output from the command is easier to read than the output of ps: It provides a snapshot of what is currently being executed, as opposed to commands such as acctcom that list historical information about commands that have previously run (and completed).

The whodo command, in conjunction with the ps command, is also useful for investigating why a system might be suffering from poor response.

Summary

The system manager implements strategic management policies to try to anticipate potential problems and prevent them from occurring rather than simply dealing with them after the fact.

Support and maintenance agreements ensure that the systems under the system manager's control are adequately protected if a system fails. The system manager must also ensure that the level of support is right and must strike a delicate balance of providing value for money and protecting the interests of the business.

Documenting the systems is extremely important, especially if the documentation is to be used as part of a disaster recovery plan. The information provided must be up-to-date if it is to be of any real value and also must be comprehensive enough to cover all aspects of the systems under the system manager's control.

A form of configuration management, such as SCCS, strengthens the integrity of the systems by providing a fully documented history of changes made to configuration files, administration scripts, or system documentation.

The system accounting software is an excellent tool for monitoring the activity on the systems. The information it provides can be used to assist with future planning and license renewal, and to identify trends in command usage, to name but a few uses.

9

Tactical Management

THE SYSTEM MANAGER'S PRIMARY RESPONSIBILITY is not solely to provide an IT service, but also to maintain it in an efficient, reliable, and cost-effective manner. The precise level of service provision and user expectations is normally the subject of a service level agreement (SLA) between the IT department and the user requesting the service. Discussed in Chapter 3, "Delivering the Goods," SLAs clearly define the operating parameters and any mutually acceptable tolerances.

This chapter discusses the tactical aspect of managing a Solaris environment, the necessary tasks and procedures that will ensure the achievement of any SLA targets. It is not solely about the provision of the service; it's also about maintaining that service in an efficient and reliable manner. The tactical management aspect involves the daily supervision of the Solaris environment, including routine operational management, monitoring and analysis of system log information, and monitoring of the performance of the systems, taking remedial action where necessary. The first section in this chapter investigates the daily procedures that need to be carried out to provide a fully administered environment. The system manager is not a system administrator, but he is responsible for these procedures and must ensure that the necessary actions are being taken to guarantee (as far as is reasonably possible) the continuity of service at or above the required level.

Management of outages is also an important aspect. Scheduled outages need to be coordinated efficiently, and unscheduled outages require a mechanism for keeping the customer informed—that's not so easy when there's no system!

If configured correctly, the system logging process provides essential information for monitoring the systems effectively. This chapter also identifies the level of logging delivered by default when the Solaris operating environment is installed. A surprising number of installations just use the default values without investigating what else could be done. A brief description of the user account maintenance procedure is included, as is information on how making use of user groups can help the system manager to make multiple configuration changes very easily.

The subject of performance monitoring is considered here because the system manager is responsible for the continued provision of an acceptable service. This chapter discusses some of the symptoms to look for when analyzing performance and the tools that can be used.

The final section in this chapter investigates some useful commands that can help the system manager, particularly combinations of frequently used commands to obtain specific information. Some other commands relevant to the manipulation of text files and data are discussed as well. These commands are frequently forgotten, but they can save a lot of time with large amounts of data, something the system manager is likely to have to use when compiling periodic reports.

Daily Procedures

The system manager has a primary responsibility for providing a continued level of service. Therefore, he must ensure that certain essential administration tasks are carried out. Some of these tasks need to be done only once a day, for example, while others must be carried out at regular intervals throughout the day. The purpose of this section is to identify the things that need to be done to provide the best possible service to the customers.

Some system managers like to use a checklist approach in which the system administrator manually completes a list of required actions and enters a confirmation either on a hard copy or into a file on the system. This approach is perfect for junior system administrators in the process of learning how to do the job, but it is less appropriate for a senior system administrator, who might resent the implication that he is not trusted to do his job properly. The system manager must make a judgment call on how this is to be handled. My own preference is to use the mandatory checklist only for junior administrators in the first few months because it reinforces and reminds them of the tasks that need to be carried out, and it helps with their own development.

It is worth restating here that the system manager does not expect to have to do the system administrator's job, but he does have to possess a good knowledge of what is involved in keeping the systems running. Of course, the system manager also is responsible for the administrator from a personnel perspective as well as a technical one and will no doubt have to assess his performance at least on an annual basis. Unless he knows what his staff is doing (or is meant to be doing), it is difficult to accurately assess performance.

What Must Be Done?

The following is a list of the tasks that must be carried out. The system manager, together with the system administrator(s), should review the daily procedures on a regular basis to ensure that everything that needs to be done is being done. To some, this may seem like stating the obvious, and sometimes it is. However, the system manager is ultimately responsible, and with companies relying so heavily on the continued availability and performance of the IT systems, he must be sure that they are being monitored in a professional and efficient manner:

- **Check the systems**—The first thing that must be done is to determine the current status of all the systems, ensuring that they are all available and operating correctly. This task is the highest priority because a system that is down or in a hung state will seriously affect the business. A network management utility likely will be running in larger organizations, but this may not capture a struggling or underperforming system. The system messages file /var/adm/messages should be examined on each system to see if any system errors have occurred. This check is invaluable because it can highlight the beginning of a problem, such as a memory module giving intermittent (and correctable) errors. In this instance, the module can be replaced before the error has any detrimental effect on the performance or availability of the system.

  Of course, most organizations running high-availability environments make use of a monitoring or management tool, such as Solstice Site or Domain Manager (discussed in Chapter 14, "Network Management Tools"), or, for smaller, less critical environments, a monitoring application such as Big Brother (discussed in Chapter 13, "Network Monitoring"). However, these applications still need to be monitored and occasionally modified to reflect changes in procedures or the environment. The downside, if there is one, is that too much reliance on automation products can gradually diminish personal skills due to absence of use. It doesn't hurt to do it manually once in a while—one day it might be necessary!

- **Deal with any help desk trouble tickets**—See if any incidents have occurred that you should be aware of. This includes general incidents, such as network problems, that could adversely affect the systems and the processing being carried out on them.

- **Check application logs**—An inspection of any application logs, especially for custom applications, is required to see if any errors have occurred. Tools such as Expect and Analog are freely available in the public domain. These can scan output or very large log files in a fraction of the time it would normally take. These tools also can flag any messages that might be of interest or that require addressing.

- **Examine the processes**—This check looks particularly for "runaway processes"—that is, processes that are constantly using up system resources and that have been disconnected from owning processes. A good example of these can be found in organizations where terminal emulation sessions are used, or client/server database applications. Runaway processes occur most frequently when a user simply turns off a machine at the end of the workday instead of logging out in the proper manner. The processes consume vast amounts of system resources and eventually slow the system to an unacceptable level. The top command is commonly used to monitor the state of processes on the system; it's particularly useful in this instance because of the refreshing display that highlights processes of this nature.

- **Check the backup logs**—When it has been established that the systems are functioning correctly, check the backup logs to make sure that there aren't any errors that could affect the integrity of the backup. This task, although of very high importance, is normally done after the system status has been verified because the previous checks are relevant to the real-time operation of the system, whereas the backups have already run and involve historical information.

- **Examine security logs**—Examine files such as /var/adm/sulog, /var/adm/loginlog, and sudolog if you're using sudo. These files will report any instances of attempts to gain access to the superuser account, repeated attempts at login in which the password was not entered correctly, and all instances when the sudo utility was used—both successfully and unsuccessfully.

- **Monitor disk space**—Keep a regular watch on disk space utilization. This can cause problems when a process encounters a failure and continually writes to a log file. An entire disk can be filled up very quickly, sometimes in minutes. Again, a monitoring tool such as Big Brother can detect this and page out the administrator. A management tool can also be configured to take some predefined action in an attempt to rectify the situation.

- **Monitor performance**—Performance utilities such as vmstat and iostat should be run regularly to check that no performance issues could affect the business's capability to carry out its function. Performance monitoring is discussed in more detail later in this chapter in the section "Performance Monitoring."

This list is not exhaustive: Different organizations will have other priorities, depending on the nature of the business being carried out. However, this list does give a good general appreciation of the kind of things that must be done.

Managing Outages

System and network outages can seriously affect availability targets normally set as part of a service level agreement. The system manager must try to be as realistic as possible when agreeing to an acceptable level of availability, taking into account any scheduled maintenance outages that might be essential to maintain the computing environment. These outages may not actually be on the systems themselves, but they could be periodic maintenance on air conditioning units or the uninterruptible power supply (UPS), for example. On these occasions, it is sometimes necessary to shut down all the systems, although this can often be avoided when there is sufficient redundancy to allow the operation to continue when part of the environment is disabled.

Scheduled Outages

Undoubtedly times will arise when a scheduled outage is needed, usually for a major upgrade or for work on the power supply. It is the responsibility of the system manager to coordinate the outage of any system under his control and to ensure that any disruption to the operation of the business is kept to an absolute minimum. If there is a "quiet" time, such as during the middle of the night or on weekends, the system manager should take advantage of these where possible.

The most important issue, though, is to keep the user community informed of any scheduled outages so that users also can plan their activities around it. To this end, three facilities are available on Solaris systems—the "Message of the Day" file, email, and message broadcasting:

- **The Message of the Day file (MOTD)**—Whenever a user logs in to a Solaris system, the contents of this file are displayed on the screen. Place notification of any upcoming scheduled outages clearly in this file so that users are kept fully informed. Conversely, if the outage is cancelled for any reason, the file should be updated to reflect the amended situation. This file can be edited using any normal editor, such as vi, and can be found in the /etc directory as file motd.

- **Email**—Using email to inform users of forthcoming scheduled outages is less than ideal because there is no guarantee that every user will open the email that has been sent. Thus, some users might never know that there is to be an outage. Email presents just another means of contacting the user community.

- **Message broadcasting**—In this instance, a message is sent to every user logged in to the system through the use of the wall command. The message flashes on the user's screen and causes an audible beep. This kind of message is normally used immediately before an outage, to give the logged-in users the opportunity to save their work and log out. Typically, a message might be sent 30 minutes before an outage, reminding everyone that the outage will shortly commence. Further messages 10 minutes and 5 minutes before the outage remind the users that they should be getting ready to log out. Finally, a message is sent informing users that the system is going down.

Unscheduled Outages

When the system is unavailable due to an unscheduled fault, it is difficult (if not impossible) to inform the user community of resolution progress or an estimated time of return to normal operation.

To combat this situation, many organizations employ other methods of providing essential information at such times:

- **Telephone answering machine**—This option is suitable for smaller organizations where users can telephone a specific number to obtain information about the current status of the systems. The IT staff is responsible for keeping the answering machine recorded information up-to-date. If a serious outage occurs, the message should be updated every 5 or 10 minutes, even if there is nothing to report—this demonstrates a professional approach to keeping everyone informed.

- **Help desk updates**—Inform the help desk that the problem has occurred, and keep the staff updated on progress and estimated time of recovery. This will avoid multiple trouble tickets being raised for the same problem.

- **Do a voice broadcast**—Many companies have a voice broadcast system used for announcements. This facility can be used to convey information to all users in the same building regarding a system outage. Regular updates keep the user community informed of any progress or expected resolution time.

- **Use a tickertape system**—Larger organizations frequently make use of tickertape systems, which can be centrally controlled and administered. This system can convey messages to alert users to an incident, and the messages can be quickly updated to reflect an amended status. These types of systems are also useful for informing users of virus attacks, especially through email attachments. The advantage is that the message can be left on for extended periods, reminding users of the threat.

Of course, most users tend to have a PC running a corporate email system and probably could be informed of a Solaris system outage via this method. This list definitely would apply if some users relied totally on the Solaris systems to carry out their business.

System Logging (syslogd)

Solaris, along with the majority of other flavors of UNIX, uses the syslogd process for its main system logging. It traps various events and forwards the system messages to a specified location, which can be a screen or a file, or even to a remote system, as dictated by the configuration file /etc/syslog.conf. The default configuration file is shown in Listing 9.1.

Listing 9.1 **The Default System Logging Configuration File Supplied with the Solaris Operating Environment**

```
#ident  "@(#)syslog.conf     1.5    99/02/03 SMI"   /* SunOS 5.0 */
#
# Copyright (c) 1991-1999 by Sun Microsystems, Inc.
# All rights reserved.
#
# syslog configuration file.
#
# This file is processed by m4 so be careful to quote (`') names
# that match m4 reserved words.  Also, within ifdef's, arguments
# containing commas must be quoted.
#
*.err;kern.notice;auth.notice                   /dev/sysmsg
*.err;kern.debug;daemon.notice;mail.crit        /var/adm/messages

*.alert;kern.err;daemon.err                      operator
*.alert                                          root

*.emerg                                          *

# if a non-loghost machine chooses to have authentication messages
# sent to the loghost machine, un-comment out the following line:
#auth.notice              ifdef(`LOGHOST', /var/log/authlog, @loghost)

mail.debug                ifdef(`LOGHOST', /var/log/syslog, @loghost)

#
# non-loghost machines will use the following lines to cause "user"
# log messages to be logged locally.
#
ifdef(`LOGHOST', ,
user.err                                         /dev/sysmsg
user.err                                         /var/adm/messages
user.alert                                       `root, operator'
user.emerg                                       *
)
```

The system manager is responsible for ensuring that all system messages receive the attention they require, depending on their priority. The default configuration file logs a number of messages to the system console (/dev/sysmsg) and to the messages file in the directory /var/adm. Others are forwarded via email to the root and operator user accounts.

A large number of companies let the standard system logging configuration run in its default form and do not amend it to suit their specific requirements. There are potential disadvantages of logging too much information to the system console:

- A "headless" system (one with no console) will never display the messages.
- The message might scroll off the screen and be lost before anyone sees it.
- There may not be anyone watching the console to be able to take immediate action.
- The message may not be stored elsewhere so that it can be reviewed later.

With a busy system, some discrimination of priorities is necessary; otherwise, the main messages file can become large very quickly. One approach is to configure the system logging by feature—that is, for example, to log all messages relating to mail to a different log file, such as /var/log/mail.log; to log kernel-related messages to /var/log/kernel.log; to log authentication messages to /var/log/auth.log; and so on. This method of system logging can make monitoring the events more manageable while still logging only the highest-priority events in the system messages file.

Syslog message levels are defined in a series of levels. The following list details the levels in order from the highest level to the lowest.

Level	Code	Description
LOG_EMERG	0	Kernel panic
LOG_ALERT	1	A condition requiring immediate attention
LOG_CRIT	2	A critical condition
LOG_ERR	3	An error
LOG_WARNING	4	A warning message
LOG_NOTICE	5	Not a serious error, but one that might require attention
LOG_INFO	6	Information message
LOG_DEBUG	7	Used for debugging

It is important to note that when a level is inserted into the configuration file, messages for the selected level and higher will be forwarded to the location specified.

Which Files Are Involved?

The syslog process comprises a number of files, apart from the syslogd daemon. The following list describes each of them and the purposes they fulfill:

- **/etc/syslog.conf**—The configuration file where the rules are defined, as well as the locations and method of message delivery.

- **/var/log/syslog** —The data file containing data gathered by the syslog process. There will also be syslog.[0–7] files containing older data. The files are recycled every eight weeks.

- **/var/adm/messages**—The data file containing system messages, often from the syslog process, and also attempts to become superuser and system startup messages.

- **/usr/lib/newsyslog**—An automatic job that is run by cron to cycle the syslog data files.

- **/etc/init.d/syslog**—The startup and shutdown script that is executed each time the system is shut down or rebooted.

User Accounts

It is important for the system manager to understand how the user account mechanism functions under the Solaris operating environment. It is also important that the files associated with it are suitably protected and backed up. Poor management of these files can leave the system wide open for an unauthorized intruder. If there is a system security policy governing user access to the system, it is the responsibility of the system manager to ensure that it is being implemented in line with this document. This policy should include details about usernames, the password aging strategy, expiration of accounts, and so on. Armed with sufficient information about the user account management files, the system manager is better able to verify compliance with the security procedures.

The following subsections describe the files related to the administration of user accounts, tell how to lock a specific account, and, finally, give an example of how proper use of groups can be used to the system manager's advantage.

Which Files Are Involved?

Three files are used as part of account management: /etc/passwd, /etc/shadow, and /etc/group. Collectively, they identify a user, the groups that user belongs to, and details about password management. Listing 9.2 shows an example of each of these files.

Listing 9.2 **Examples of the Files /etc/passwd, /etc/shadow, and /etc/group**

```
#cat /etc/passwd
root:x:0:1:Super-User:/:/sbin/sh
daemon:x:1:1::/:
bin:x:2:2::/usr/bin:
sys:x:3:3::/:
adm:x:4:4:Admin:/var/adm:
lp:x:71:8:Line Printer Admin:/usr/spool/lp:
uucp:x:5:5:uucp Admin:/usr/lib/uucp:
nuucp:x:9:9:uucp Admin:/var/spool/uucppublic:/usr/lib/uucp/uucico
listen:x:37:4:Network Admin:/usr/net/nls:
nobody:x:60001:60001:Nobody:/:
noaccess:x:60002:60002:No Access User:/:
nobody4:x:65534:65534:SunOS 4.x Nobody:/:
oracle:x:500:500:Oracle:/u01/app/oracle:/bin/ksh
logger:x:511:1:Log Files:/home/logfiles:/opt/bin/bash
amanda:x:513:1:AMANDA Backup Utility:/home/amanda:/usr/bin/ksh
backup:x:515:1:Backup User:/home/backup:/usr/bin/ksh
john:x:120:14:John Philcox:/export/home/john:/usr/bin/ksh
#
# cat /etc/shadow
root:7mZuQjRKy8syU:11208::::::
daemon:NP:6445::::::
bin:NP:6445::::::
sys:NP:6445::::::
adm:NP:6445::::::
lp:NP:6445::::::
uucp:NP:6445::::::
nuucp:NP:6445::::::
listen:*LK*:::::::
nobody:NP:6445::::::
noaccess:NP:6445::::::
nobody4:NP:6445::::::
oracle:rAXbO74IDUBE.:11018::::::
logger:cY1S4X8uhZESY:11212::::::
amanda:*LK*:::::::
backup:*LK*:::::::
john:kyQC3jrIC8EtY:11267::::::
#
#cat /etc/group
root::0:root
other::1:
bin::2:root,bin,daemon
sys::3:root,bin,sys,adm,backup,amanda
adm::4:root,adm,daemon
uucp::5:root,uucp
mail::6:root
tty::7:root,tty,adm
lp::8:root,lp,adm
nuucp::9:root,nuucp
staff::10:
daemon::12:root,daemon
sysadmin::14:john
```

```
nobody::60001:
noaccess::60002:
nogroup::65534:
dba::100:oracle,john
amanda::105:
```

The most important of the three files is /etc/shadow because it contains the encrypted password for the user, including the superuser account. The file permissions should be the absolute minimum—that is, read permission for the superuser only. The shadow file also contains details of password aging. The passwd and shadow files should not be edited manually—use admintool or vipw to make consistent changes.

Locking an Account

When a user leaves the company, that account should be removed from the system to prevent unauthorized access. This is not always done immediately, however, because the files and directories belonging to the user are often archived before being deleted. If this is the case, it is good practice to lock the account during the intervening period so that only the superuser can access it. An account is locked by replacing the encrypted password field of the /etc/shadow entry for the specified user with *LK*. Use vipw to do this rather than editing the file manually. In Listing 9.2, the users backup and amanda are both locked.

If the system manager finds any user accounts with no password assigned (these can be easily found by running login -p as user root), then these should be locked at the earliest opportunity. Some organizations run an automatic task that removes any user accounts with no password, requiring the offending user to reapply for a user ID.

Making Better Use of Groups

It is not uncommon for organizations to create users who all have a primary group of Staff instead of assigning them to, say, Sales or Human Resources. The security implications should be sufficient to justify the proper use of primary groups, but they often aren't. The manipulation of groups can be an effective administration tool, particularly in large applications where users log in using captive accounts to access a specific software application or database. In this instance, they will not have access to a command-line prompt (the shell), and they will all execute a common startup file to initiate the application. By using the primary group, it becomes easy to move large numbers of users to, for example, a new version of the software, leaving the remainder on the current version. The startup file simply tests which group the user belongs to and takes a defined action, such as the command to start the application. Changing the user's primary group automatically changes the command that is run when that user next logs in to the system.

Performance Monitoring

The system manager is responsible not only for the provision of an IT service to customers, but also for the maintenance of an acceptable level of performance. To this end, the system manager must ensure that the systems under his control are not suffering from poor performance or substandard response times.

Performance monitoring is normally carried out by the system administrator, but the system manager needs to have a good appreciation of what is involved and the tools that are available to obtain the required information. This is especially important because the system manager will be compiling the periodic reports that undoubtedly will form part of an ongoing SLA.

Regular monitoring of the systems builds a crucial library of information, highlighting trends of both usage and performance. For example, the data that is gathered could provide an early warning indicator of increased usage or load on the systems, perhaps necessitating a hardware upgrade or even a replacement system. The important point is that, armed with this information, the system manager should not face any surprises; any additional processing power or other resource that might be needed can be planned for and implemented before it becomes a performance issue.

The other side of performance monitoring is to investigate problems as they occur, to try to identify bottlenecks that could be affecting the overall performance of the system, or to gather evidence that the loading is not evenly balanced—this is especially visible with disks. Frequently, a problem may manifest itself in some way but actually be caused by something else. This is one reason why the activity of monitoring is so useful: The process of elimination helps to narrow down the true cause of the problem.

The next subsections describe the kind of problems likely to be encountered, as well as the tools provided with the standard Solaris release. These sections also discuss some utilities and tools that are available both commercially and in the public domain.

What Are You Looking For?

Monitoring the performance of the system generally involves looking for areas of weakness or contention. Bottlenecks can slow down the rest of the system; for example, a badly balanced disk setup that is overloaded with requests and is causing the processor to regularly wait for data. The monitoring process also can provide evidence that the current resources are starting to struggle with the load being placed upon them. The system manager can use this information as evidence that an upgrade is required (possibly due to increased usage by the customer) and also to justify why the consumer department should pay for it to be able to maintain the required level of service.

Solaris Utilities

Solaris provides a comprehensive set of tools to allow monitoring of the system's performance. These are discussed in the following paragraphs to show the type of information that can be obtained and to tell what to actually look for to ascertain whether there is a performance problem. The final utility in this section, top, is available in the public domain and is now included with the standard release of the Solaris operating environment (as of Solaris 8). It is extremely useful for seeing the processes that are utilizing most of the system resources.

vmstat

The vmstat utility is listed as a tool for reporting virtual memory statistics, but it does much more than that. It also gives a good overall picture of how the system is performing. Listing 9.3 shows the output from the vmstat command.

Listing 9.3 **Output from the vmstat Command Using an Interval Period of 3 Seconds**

```
#vmstat 3
 procs      memory            page            disk          faults      cpu
 r b w   swap  free  re  mf pi  po  fr  de sr s0 s6 s7 s8   in   sy   cs us sy id
 0 0 0   1184 96992   0   6 11   9  12   0  0  2  0  0  2  260 1253  429 64  8 29
 6 0 0 2873928 33128   0   0  5  18  18   0  0 23  0  0 66 1754 4880 1806 81 19  0
 3 0 0 2873928 33136   0   0  0   2   2   0  0 26  0  0 33 1281 5937 1523 83 17  0
 3 0 0 2873928 33128   0   2  2   2   2   0  0 15  0  0 15  988 6416 1523 83 16  0
 1 0 0 2873928 33128   1   0  8  18  18   0  0 16  0  0 23 1229 5428 1755 77 22  0
 2 0 0 2873928 33128   0   2  2   2   2   0  0 28  0  0  6  966 6366 1342 84 16  0
 2 1 0 2873928 33136   0   0  5   8   8   0  0 29  0  0 30 1405 6175 1925 81 18  1
 2 0 0 2873928 33128  15   0 525 312 312  0  0 31  0  0 35 1452 3331 2005 76 20  4
 1 2 0 2873928 32744  15   1  8 594 594  0  0  9  0  0 77 1838 3356 2047 74 23  3
 2 0 0 2873928 33128   4   0  8  45  45   0  0 24  0  0 19 1178 3077 1616 80 20  1
 1 0 0 2873928 33120  14   1  8 128 128  0  0 28  0  0 14  975 3099 1439 70 23  6
 1 1 0 2873928 33120   5   0 16  66  66   0  0 27  0  0 32 1386 3764 1953 74 22  4
 2 1 0 2873928 33128   3   0  2  90  90   0  0 34  0  0 81 1984 2961 1820 78 18  3
 2 0 0 2873928 33128   2   0  2  24  24   0  0  2  0  0 26 1255 3518 1944 78 21  0
 2 1 0 2873928 33128   3   0  5  58  58   0  0 30  0  0 74 1804 2810 1656 75 23  2
 2 0 0 2873928 33184  10   0 592 77  77   0  0  8  0  0 32 1129 2972 1490 80 20  1
 3 0 0 2873928 33176   1   0 202 10  10   0  0 31  0  0 26 1305 3315 1825 71 26  3
 1 0 0 2873928 33128   1   0  2  13  13   0  0 27  0  0 14  952 3063 1366 68 24  8
 2 0 0 2873928 33128   0   0  2   8   8   0  0 12  0  0 40 1529 3514 2060 73 24  4
 2 2 0 2873928 33120   5   0 13 261 261  0  0 30  0  0 83 2260 3466 2180 71 18 11
```

Ignore the first entry here because it is a summary of all activity since the system was last rebooted. The information provided in this entry is meaningless.

This system is heavily loaded and could benefit from additional processor power, as shown by the combination of the number of runnable processes in the "r" column, coupled with the fact that the CPU is running almost constantly at near 100% busy, with very little idle time. Additionally, disk balancing is not ideal, with s0 and s8 bearing most of the work while s7 has no activity at all. There are also some blocked processes, identified by the "b" column. This indicates that the process had to wait for I/O, probably from disk. The output in this listing also shows that there is no shortage of physical memory—otherwise, the scan rate (sr) column would be showing high numbers (more than 200–300).

The page-in and page-out columns (pi and po) would be high (maybe several thousand) if the system were being used as an NFS server. These show both file system I/O activity and virtual memory activity.

The vmstat command shows at a glance the overall status of the various components. For fuller details of processor usage on systems containing more than one processor, use mpstat. Detailed disk information can be found using the iostat command; further statistics about the swap space can be displayed with the swap command. These commands are discussed next.

mpstat

The mpstat command produces a tabular report for each processor in a multiprocessor environment, providing useful information on how the CPUs are performing, how busy they are, whether the load is evenly balanced among them, and also how much time is spent waiting for other resources. Listing 9.4 displays a sample output from running the mpstat command.

Listing 9.4 **Output from the *mpstat* Command Using an Interval Period of 5 Seconds**

```
#mpstat 5
CPU minf mjf xcal  intr ithr  csw icsw migr smtx  srw syscl  usr sys  wt idl
  0    2   0    8    39    3  159   55    6    2    0   450   67   7   1  26
  1    2   0   14   275   52  170   56    6    2    0   522   58   8   2  32
CPU minf mjf xcal  intr ithr  csw icsw migr smtx  srw syscl  usr sys  wt idl
  0   23   0    3   306   49 1264  553   29    7    0  2204   86  13   0   1
  1   51   0   16   543   26 1208  581   29    7    0  2036   82  18   0   1
CPU minf mjf xcal  intr ithr  csw icsw migr smtx  srw syscl  usr sys  wt idl
  0    0   0    2    88   32  637  274   13    4    0  1791   83  17   0   0
  1    0   0    6   279   17  193   91   13    5    0   388   92   8   0   0
CPU minf mjf xcal  intr ithr  csw icsw migr smtx  srw syscl  usr sys  wt idl
  0    0   0    1    77    1  269  105   32    5    0   506   89   4   0   7
  1    0   0    5   297   58  573  226   33    4    0  1123   67   5   0  28
CPU minf mjf xcal  intr ithr  csw icsw migr smtx  srw syscl  usr sys  wt idl
  0    0   0    1    85    2  213   95   24    2    0   778   73  19   0   8
  1    0   0    7   267   36  907  404   23    3    0  2003   89   9   1   2
CPU minf mjf xcal  intr ithr  csw icsw migr smtx  srw syscl  usr sys  wt idl
  0    0   0    4    74    3  622  258   26    3    0  1253   94   4   0   2
  1    0   0    6   291   27  314  112   27    2    0   611   53  15   0  32
CPU minf mjf xcal  intr ithr  csw icsw migr smtx  srw syscl  usr sys  wt idl
  0    0   0    1    16    2   23   14    3    0    0    27   99   1   0   0
  1    0   0    7   217   16   28    7    2    0    0   611   34  15   0  52
```

CPU	minf	mjf	xcal	intr	ithr	csw	icsw	migr	smtx	srw	syscl	usr	sys	wt	idl
0	0	0	5	16	6	68	9	7	0	0	81	60	2	1	37
1	0	0	7	233	30	53	8	5	0	0	385	53	8	1	39
CPU	minf	mjf	xcal	intr	ithr	csw	icsw	migr	smtx	srw	syscl	usr	sys	wt	idl
0	0	0	1	53	2	158	51	5	0	0	161	79	2	0	19
1	0	0	8	262	33	170	37	6	0	0	517	41	12	0	47
CPU	minf	mjf	xcal	intr	ithr	csw	icsw	migr	smtx	srw	syscl	usr	sys	wt	idl
0	0	0	2	16	1	29	15	4	0	0	25	91	2	0	8
1	0	0	6	223	22	25	8	3	0	0	680	43	17	0	40
CPU	minf	mjf	xcal	intr	ithr	csw	icsw	migr	smtx	srw	syscl	usr	sys	wt	idl
0	2	0	6	38	3	213	71	7	0	0	307	61	4	0	35
1	0	0	7	253	18	237	84	5	0	0	366	49	6	0	46
CPU	minf	mjf	xcal	intr	ithr	csw	icsw	migr	smtx	srw	syscl	usr	sys	wt	idl
0	0	0	1	18	1	27	16	2	0	0	23	99	1	0	0
1	0	0	5	212	11	21	8	4	0	0	979	52	27	0	21
CPU	minf	mjf	xcal	intr	ithr	csw	icsw	migr	smtx	srw	syscl	usr	sys	wt	idl
0	0	0	6	16	6	48	10	4	0	0	59	83	0	1	15
1	0	0	7	238	36	76	2	5	0	0	96	11	3	1	85
CPU	minf	mjf	xcal	intr	ithr	csw	icsw	migr	smtx	srw	syscl	usr	sys	wt	idl
0	0	0	1	75	1	142	73	6	1	0	177	97	3	0	0
1	0	0	7	271	18	138	64	5	1	0	875	52	17	0	31

As with `vmstat`, the first entry is a summary of all activity since the system was last rebooted. The information in this entry is meaningless and should be ignored.

The columns of real interest are described here:

- `intr`—The number of interrupts on each of the processors. An unbalanced number of interrupts is caused by placement of the SBUS cards on the system board. If the differences are high (by more than, say, 2000), consider redistributing the SBUS cards.

- `usr`—The amount of processor time being given to the user process. A normally functioning system would expect this to be around 85% of the usage. The example output in Listing 9.4 shows that the processors are functioning correctly.

- `wt`—How much time the processor(s) had to wait while I/O was carried out, normally a read from disk. If this figure is high, maybe 40–50, then the system is definitely I/O-bound. The example output shows only an occasional wait for I/O, which poses no threat to performance.

iostat

The `iostat` command reports statistics on terminal, disk, and tape I/O activity (as well as CPU utilization), although its main use is to monitor disk performance. It can be used to identify a badly balanced disk configuration, and it provides sufficient options to examine the performance of a single disk partition. Listing 9.5 displays the `iostat` command with extended statistics for each disk volume.

Listing 9.5 **Sample Output from the *iostat* Command Using an Interval Period of 5 Seconds and the Flags *-xn***

```
#iostat -xn 5
extended device statistics
   r/s  w/s   kr/s   kw/s wait actv wsvc_t asvc_t  %w  %b device
   0.0  4.0   0.0   30.7 0.0  0.0    0.0    9.7   0   4 c0t0d0
   0.0  0.0   0.0    0.0 0.0  0.0    0.0    0.0   0   0 c0t6d0
   0.0  0.0   0.0    0.0 0.0  0.0    0.0    0.0   0   0 c0t8d0
   1.8 49.7  16.0  397.6 0.0  0.4    0.0    8.5   0  34 c0t9d0
   0.0 74.5   0.0  595.7 0.0  0.5    0.0    6.3   0  44 c0t10d0
   2.0 66.3  22.4  530.2 0.0  0.7    0.0   11.0   0  56 c0t11d0
   0.0  0.0   0.0    0.0 0.0  0.0    0.0    0.0   0   0 rmt/0
extended device statistics
   r/s  w/s   kr/s   kw/s wait actv wsvc_t asvc_t  %w  %b device
   0.0 14.2   0.0   67.4 0.0  0.1    0.0    6.8   0  10 c0t0d0
   0.0  0.0   0.0    0.0 0.0  0.0    0.0    0.0   0   0 c0t6d0
   0.0  0.0   0.0    0.0 0.0  0.0    0.0    0.0   0   0 c0t8d0
   0.6 32.0   4.8  256.0 0.0  0.2    0.0    6.7   0  20 c0t9d0
   0.0 73.8   0.0  590.4 0.0  0.4    0.0    5.9   0  42 c0t10d0
   0.6 68.2   4.8  545.6 0.0  0.9    0.0   13.2   0  64 c0t11d0
   0.0  0.0   0.0    0.0 0.0  0.0    0.0    0.0   0   0 rmt/0
extended device statistics
   r/s  w/s   kr/s   kw/s wait actv wsvc_t asvc_t  %w  %b device
   0.0 23.6   0.0  111.8 0.0  0.2    0.0    7.0   0  16 c0t0d0
   0.0  0.0   0.0    0.0 0.0  0.0    0.0    0.0   0   0 c0t6d0
   0.0  0.0   0.0    0.0 0.0  0.0    0.0    0.0   0   0 c0t8d0
   1.8 52.2  14.4  417.5 0.0  0.4    0.0    6.9   0  34 c0t9d0
   0.0 34.6   0.0  276.7 0.0  0.2    0.0    5.9   0  20 c0t10d0
   1.6 89.2  22.4  713.4 0.0  1.5    0.0   16.1   0  85 c0t11d0
   0.0  0.0   0.0    0.0 0.0  0.0    0.0    0.0   0   0 rmt/0
```

As with vmstat and mpstat, the first entry is a summary of all activity since the system was last rebooted. The information in this entry is meaningless and should be ignored.

The information provided by iostat clearly shows disk volumes that are being used excessively and those that are not being used at all. The columns of interest are described here:

- **wait**—The number of requests waiting in the O/S to get to the disk. If this figure is greater than 0, it should be treated as a warning that there might be a performance issue, particularly if the disk is in a disk array.

- **actv**—The number of requests pending in the disk volume itself. There is likely a performance problem if this figure is high (15–20) and the disk is already very busy.

- **%b**—How busy the disk volume is, displayed as a percentage. Normally this figure should be less than 65%; disk device c0t11d0 has a value of 85%, which constitutes excessive usage, especially when compared to the other disk volumes.

- **svc_t**—The time taken to service a request, in milliseconds. The value shown in this column includes any time that a request might spend waiting in the queue. When this value is high (greater than 100), it can point to a performance problem if the disk is already busy.

Listing 9.6 shows a more detailed picture for disk volumes, displaying the usage information for each partition of each disk.

Listing 9.6 **Sample Output from the *iostat* Command Using an Interval Period of 5 Seconds and the Flags *-xnp* to Show Greater Detail for Each Physical Disk Volume**

```
#iostat -xnp 5
extended device statistics
   r/s  w/s    kr/s   kw/s wait actv wsvc_t asvc_t  %w  %b device
   3.5 14.4    29.1   92.1  0.0  0.2    0.0   12.9   0  10 c0t0d0
   0.0  0.1     0.2    0.3  0.0  0.0    0.0   42.2   0   0 c0t0d0s0
   0.1  1.9     0.4   10.3  0.0  0.0    0.1   17.8   0   2 c0t0d0s1
   0.0  0.0     0.0    0.0  0.0  0.0    0.0    0.0   0   0 c0t0d0s2
   0.0  0.0     0.0    0.1  0.0  0.0    0.0    9.0   0   0 c0t0d0s3
   0.3  8.9     2.5   46.1  0.0  0.1    0.0   14.3   0   6 c0t0d0s5
   0.4  0.0     2.5    0.1  0.0  0.0    0.0    5.4   0   0 c0t0d0s6
   2.6  3.5    23.5   35.1  0.0  0.1    0.0    9.3   0   4 c0t0d0s7
   0.0  0.0     0.0    0.0  0.0  0.0    0.0    0.0   0   0 c0t6d0
   1.6  2.2    17.0   18.4  0.0  0.0    0.0    5.8   0   2 c0t8d0
   0.5  0.3     6.9    2.3  0.0  0.0    0.0    5.2   0   0 c0t8d0s0
   0.0  0.0     0.0    0.0  0.0  0.0    0.0    0.0   0   0 c0t8d0s2
   0.6  1.9     6.4   15.8  0.0  0.0    0.0    6.1   0   1 c0t8d0s5
   0.0  0.0     0.0    0.0  0.0  0.0    0.0    5.2   0   0 c0t8d0s6
   0.5  0.0     3.7    0.3  0.0  0.0    0.0    5.2   0   0 c0t8d0s7
   0.0  0.1     0.9    0.9  0.0  0.0    0.0    5.5   0   0 c0t9d0
   0.0  0.1     0.5    0.5  0.0  0.0    0.0    5.5   0   0 c0t9d0s0
   0.0  0.0     0.0    0.0  0.0  0.0    0.0    0.0   0   0 c0t9d0s1
   0.0  0.0     0.0    0.0  0.0  0.0    0.0    0.0   0   0 c0t9d0s2
   0.0  0.0     0.0    0.0  0.0  0.0    0.0    0.0   0   0 c0t9d0s6
   0.3  1.9    14.7   14.8  0.0  0.0    0.0    5.5   0   1 c0t9d0s7
   0.0  0.1     0.9    0.9  0.0  0.0    0.0    5.5   0   0 c0t10d0
   0.0  0.1     0.5    0.5  0.0  0.0    0.0    5.5   0   0 c0t10d0s0
   0.0  0.0     0.0    0.0  0.0  0.0    0.0    0.0   0   0 c0t10d0s1
   0.0  0.0     0.0    0.0  0.0  0.0    0.0    0.0   0   0 c0t10d0s2
   0.0  0.0     0.0    0.0  0.0  0.0    0.0    0.0   0   0 c0t10d0s6
   0.3  2.0    15.7   15.9  0.0  0.0    0.0    5.5   0   1 c0t10d0s7
   0.0  0.1     0.9    0.9  0.0  0.0    0.0    5.5   0   0 c0t11d0
   0.0  0.1     0.5    0.5  0.0  0.0    0.0    5.5   0   0 c0t11d0s0
   0.0  0.0     0.0    0.0  0.0  0.0    0.0    0.0   0   0 c0t11d0s1
   0.0  0.0     0.0    0.0  0.0  0.0    0.0    0.0   0   0 c0t11d0s2
   0.0  0.0     0.0    0.0  0.0  0.0    0.0    0.0   0   0 c0t11d0s6
   0.3  2.0    16.1   16.2  0.0  0.0    0.0    5.5   0   1 c0t11d0s7
   0.0  0.1     0.9    0.9  0.0  0.0    0.0    5.5   0   0 c0t12d0
   0.0  0.1     0.5    0.5  0.0  0.0    0.0    5.5   0   0 c0t12d0s0
   0.0  0.0     0.0    0.0  0.0  0.0    0.0    0.0   0   0 c0t12d0s1
```

continues

Listing 9.6 **Continued**

0.0	0.0	0.0	0.0	0.0	0.0	0.0	0.0	0	0	c0t12d0s2
0.0	0.0	0.0	0.0	0.0	0.0	0.0	0.0	0	0	c0t12d0s6
0.3	2.1	16.4	16.6	0.0	0.0	0.0	5.5	0	1	c0t12d0s7
0.0	0.6	0.1	37.4	0.0	0.0	0.0	35.1	0	2	rmt/0

The initial information displayed in Listing 9.5 could identify a disk volume that might be the cause of a performance problem, but the information in Listing 9.6 can isolate the problem to a particular disk partition or file system being used to excess. The result is usually that the disk is too slow and needs to be replaced with a faster one, or that the file systems resident on the disk need to be split across multiple disks to achieve a performance gain. This problem would not normally point to a disk controller being at fault unless all disk volumes and partitions being serviced by a particular controller displayed the same symptoms.

sar

sar, which stands for "System Activity Report," is used to collect cumulative activity information and optionally to gather the information into files for subsequent analysis.

By default, automatic collection of this information is disabled. To enable it, carry out the following steps:

1. Uncomment the crontab entries for user sys. This is the cron user to use for performance collection activities.

2. Uncomment the lines in the file /etc/init.d/perf.

3. Run the script /etc/init.d/perf manually, or wait until the next system reboot to activate the performance collection-gathering process.

The data is collected and stored in daily files in the directory /var/adm/sa. The data is stored in files named saxx, where xx is a number representing the day of the month.

An example of sar output monitoring CPU activity is shown in Listing 9.7.

Listing 9.7 **Sample Output from the *sar* Command Using the Flag *-u* to Show CPU Activity with a Time Interval of 5 Seconds**

```
SunOS systemA 5.7 Generic_106541-12 sun4u    11/20/00

15:29:02    %usr    %sys    %wio    %idle
15:29:07     80      20      0        0
15:29:12     78      22      0        0
15:29:17     79      21      0        0
15:29:22     80      20      0        0
15:29:27     83      17      0        0

Average      80      20      0        0
```

The `sar` command provides information on many system resources and, because it is stored in daily files, can be used to good effect for historical analysis. Consult the sar manual page for a full description of the facilities available with this command.

perfmeter

The performance meter, or perfmeter, is a graphical display of system performance. It allows monitoring of performance on remote hosts as well as the local system, but it provides less detail than the commands already discussed in this section. The data can be displayed either as a strip chart or as multiple dials. Figures 9.1 and 9.2 show an example of each type of display, with all the available options selected.

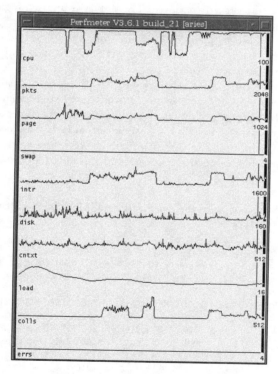

Figure 9.1   The strip chart displays cumulative results and is extremely useful in identifying peaks of activity over a given period of time.

Figure 9.2 The hour hand of the dials represents the average figure over a 20-second period, while the minute hand shows the average over a 2-second period.

top

This utility is bundled with versions of Solaris from version 8 onward and is also freely available in the public domain. It displays information about the processes currently utilizing the most of the system's resources. The display is updated regularly at an interval that is configurable by the user.

The top command can be downloaded from a number of sites on the World Wide Web, including http://www.sunfreeware.com. It is easily installed and comes either as a precompiled delivery or with source code, along with supporting documentation. It is most useful for analyzing performance problems as they are in progress so that it can be seen in a real-time display exactly which processes are being executed and how much of the CPU is currently allocated to a particular process. The top command also shows summary information, such as the current system load, the amount of swap space and physical memory in use (and how much is free), how many processes are on the system and what their respective states are, and also how CPU utilization is being divided.

Listing 9.8   **A Snapshot from the *top* Command Showing the Processes Using the Most of the Resources**

```
load averages:  0.63,  0.61,  0.64                             18:58:46
103 processes: 95 sleeping, 1 running, 4 zombie, 3 on cpu
CPU states: 43.4% idle, 25.0% user, 27.2% kernel,  4.4% iowait,  0.0% swap
Memory: 2048M real, 317M free, 517M swap in use, 3198M swap free

PID USERNAME THR PRI NICE  SIZE   RES STATE   TIME   CPU COMMAND
15132 nobody    1  58    0   49M   40M sleep   0:09  7.34% oracle
 6811 oracle    1   1    0   48M   37M sleep   0:21  1.88% oracle
29672 john      1  11    0   19M   12M cpu1    0:03  1.56% sqlplus
29673 john      1  11    0   48M   37M cpu1    0:02  1.47% oracle
15128 oracle    1  58    0   20M   12M sleep   0:01  0.84% svrmgrl
 6658 nobody    7  12    0   24M   21M sleep   0:15  0.80% jre
15879 john      1   0    0 2208K 1592K cpu0    0:00  0.72% top
    1 root      1  38    0  752K  304K sleep   5:36  0.42% init
15970 root      1   0    0 1080K  840K sleep   0:00  0.13% mkbb.sh
 2949 oracle    1  58    0   60M   52M sleep   3:57  0.11% oracle
16104 root      1   0    0 1080K  664K sleep   0:00  0.11% mkbb.sh
 1395 oracle   60  58    0   50M   36M sleep   0:48  0.09% oracle
28718 nobody    1  58    0   49M   40M sleep   0:10  0.08% oracle
```

Useful Commands

Solaris contains a huge number of commands, all of which are useful in their own right and most of which are more relevant to the system administrator than the system manager. As such, these commands are very well documented in system administration texts, so they are not discussed here. The objective of this section is to show a few commands and combinations to make the system manager's job easier. This particularly applies to the management and manipulation of data files, predominately those used as logging facilities for different processes or applications. These files can easily become numerous if a new log file is created each time the process is run, or large, if logging data is constantly being appended to a log file, for example.

Combinations of Popular Commands

Commands are combined using the pipe (|) so that the output from one command becomes the input to the next, and so on. The equivalent of an entire shell script often can be written on the command line using this facility. Consider the following example, which can be used to move large numbers of files and directories in one simple action.

To move the entire contents of /data into a new location, called /newdata, the following single command line will copy the whole directory structure:

```
cd /data; tar cf - * | (cd /newdata; tar xf -)
```

The command breaks down as follows:

1. Move to the source directory (/data).
2. Execute the `tar` command to archive all files in the current directory and write this to the standard output (this is normally the screen).
3. The output is piped into the next command, which is actually two commands because of the parentheses. This first changes to the destination directory (/newdata) and then extracts the archive that was just created into the current directory. The parentheses ensure that the two commands are handled together.

The most frequently used combinations involve the commands `grep`, `awk`, and `sed`. These commands have extensive documentation—entire volumes are dedicated to the workings of `sed` and `awk`, so these commands are not discussed here in any detail.

Consider the following command example, though, to see the sort of command that can be easily executed.

The command itself spans two lines and extracts the process ID (pid) of the top process and then uses it as a parameter to the command `ptree`, which displays the process tree, including all parent processes as well as children processes. This can be very useful when trying to identify (and kill) the calling program of a hung process.

```
aries> treepid=`ps -ef |grep top|grep -v grep| awk '{print $2}'`; \
export treepid; /usr/proc/bin/ptree $treepid
166    /usr/sbin/inetd -s
  28964 in.telnetd
    28966 -ksh
      882   top
aries>
```

find

The `find` command is arguably one of the most powerful commands available in Solaris. A popular use for it, however, is in maintenance of file systems, where `find` is used to delete, say, all files matching a certain pattern or residing in a specific file system that are more than a specified number of days old.

For example, `find` could be used in the deletion of all core files (dump files generated by a process or application failure). This is a popular one because you might have a problem with a particular application being used by 100 different users. Each time the failure is encountered, a core file would be created in the users' current directory, potentially creating 100 different core files in 100 different directories. The system administrator would require only one example to analyze or pass to the developers. Because these files can be quite sizeable (several megabytes), they can soon consume considerable amounts of disk space. The command to delete all core files more than seven days old throughout the system is shown here, although it would normally be run as a cron job on a daily basis (probably overnight).

As the superuser (root):

```
#find / -name core -mtime +7 -exec rm -f {} \;
#
```

Notice that there is no output as a result—in this case, `find` just goes away and carries out the operation. The only sign that it has finished is the return of the shell prompt.

The system manager can use the `find` command for other purposes, maybe to run a periodic check for files belonging to user root and having world write permission allowed. This combination presents a security risk and should be discouraged, so if the `find` command does locate any matching files, it can automatically remove the world writeable bit to make it more secure and then can log the name of the file. The command to do this and save the output (and any error messages) into a log file is shown here:

```
#find / -type f -user root -perm -o+w -print -exec chmod o-w {} \;
>>/var/adm/rootsec.log 2>&1
#
```

fold

The `fold` command imposes a line length for a file, which is specified by the user and, rather than truncating, folds the data onto subsequent lines. This command is particularly useful when a data file is to be printed but has a greater line length than the printer. For example, the system manager might have a data file from a process that needs to be printed that has 155 columns per line. The printer outputs onto A4 paper in portrait format and therefore can print only 80 columns per line. In this instance, the printer normally would truncate each line to 80 characters and would discard the remaining columns. Using `fold`, however, retains the extra 75 characters of data and "folds" them onto the next line, thereby printing the entire file and also keeping the data in a contiguous format.

As shown in Figure 9.3, the window displays only the portion of the line that is currently visible. The scrollbar at the bottom of the window would have to be used to view the remainder of the line. If this document were printed on an 80-column printer, then this is all that would appear; any extra columns would be lost.

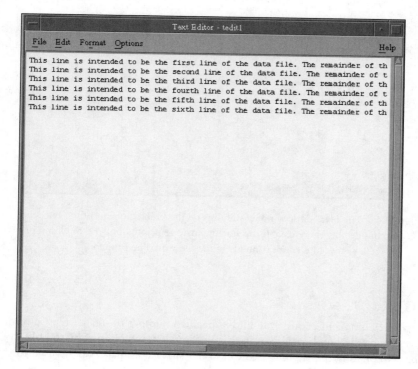

Figure 9.3   Here, a data file (tedit1) is being viewed using the text editor application, available with the CDE windowing environment.

The `fold` command inserts a newline character after the specified number of columns have been reached, creating an extra line containing the remainder of the data. Figure 9.4 shows the same data file after running this `fold` command and saving it to a new file (tedit2):

```
#fold -w 80 tedit1 >>tedit2
```

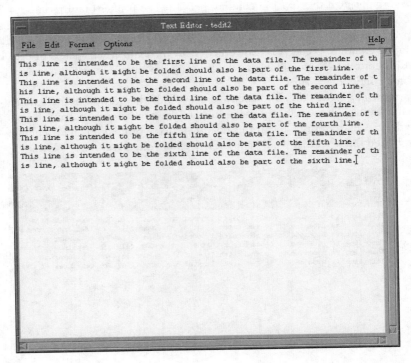

Figure 9.4 The text editor window still displays the visible portion of the line, but there is now considerably more data. If this document were printed on an 80-column printer, the entire contents of the file would be printed.

split

The `split` command chops a file into a specified number of smaller files, according to either size or the number of lines in the file. Sometimes a file will be too big to be manually edited using, say, the vi editor, so the `split` command can be used to produce a number of smaller files that are easier to view.

Another, probably more useful, way of using `split` is for recycling cumulative log files. Suppose that a log file is appended to on a regular basis and becomes large. Although it might be tempting to just delete the file every now and then and start again with a new log file, it might be a better solution to retain, say, the latest (most recent) 10% of the file. In this way, the latest log information is not discarded until the next time the file is split. By doing this, the file size (and number of lines) is reduced by 90%, reclaiming disk space and retaining potentially valuable information.

As an example, suppose that the file logfile is used as a cumulative log for a specific application process. Over a period of a week, its size grows to just under 500,000 lines. An automatic cron job could be initiated to remove 90% of the file, keeping the latest 10% for another week so that the information is available if it is required.

The following command will create 10 files, each containing 10% of the cumulative log file:

```
split -l `expr \`wc -l logfile| awk '{print $1}'\` / 10` logfile log_
```

This command basically takes a line count of the file logfile, divides it by 10, and uses the answer as the argument to the split command. It creates the 10 files log_aa to log_aj. Listing 9.9 shows the line count for the file logfile, followed by the line counts for the 10 derived files.

Listing 9.9 **Sample Output Demonstrating That a File Can Be Split Equally**

```
$ wc -l logfile
  494280 logfile
$ wc -l log_*
   49428 log_aa
   49428 log_ab
   49428 log_ac
   49428 log_ad
   49428 log_ae
   49428 log_af
   49428 log_ag
   49428 log_ah
   49428 log_ai
   49428 log_aj
  494280 total
```

The only thing left to do is to rename the file log_aj to logfile, replacing the original large file and delete log_a*—that is, the remaining nine files that were created as a result of running the split command.

unix2dos and dos2unix

These two commands are used when transferring files between the Solaris environment and the PC environment. The dos2unix command converts a file from DOS format to an ISO ASCII format so that it can be read correctly in the Solaris environment. The unix2dos command does the conversion the other way so that a file can be read correctly in the DOS environment. The only limitation with these commands is that the filename(s) must be in accordance with the environment in which the command is run—that is, 8.3 format if run from the DOS environment.

As an example, suppose that the Oracle listener configuration file tnsnames.ora is to be copied to the Solaris environment from a PC rather than creating a new one. Figure 9.5 shows the file being edited with the vi editor after it has simply been transferred using FTP without any conversion.

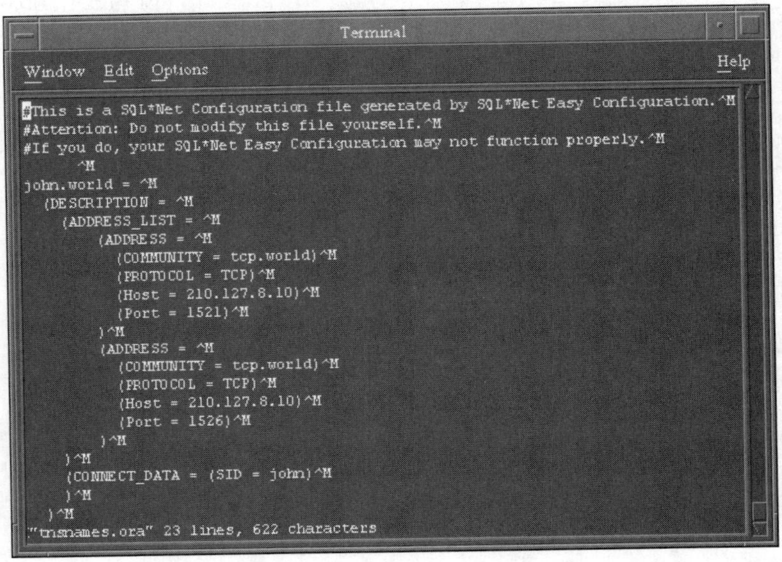

Figure 9.5   The vi editor window displays the extra return characters that the DOS format includes, depicted by ^M at the end of each line.

To process this file correctly, the following `dos2unix` command was run:

```
#dos2unix tnsnames.ora tnsnames.ora
#
```

In this case, I chose to overwrite the file with the properly formatted version of the file, although any output filename can be chosen. Figure 9.6 shows the converted file being edited with the vi editor after the conversion has taken place.

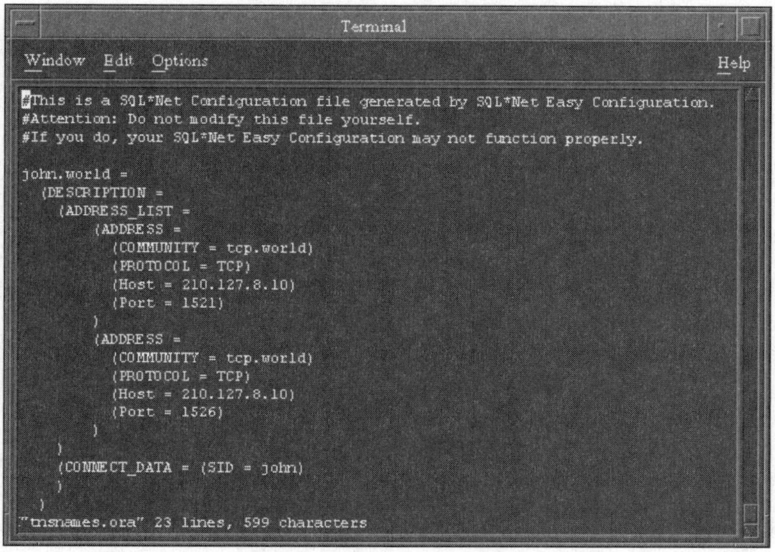

Figure 9.6   The extra characters have been stripped away,
and the file will now process correctly.

head and tail

The head and tail commands display either the top or the bottom of a file, respectively. For example, the head command is useful when a data file contains a header on
the first line detailing maybe a total record count. In this case, the following command
will select only the first line:

```
#head -1 datafile
00987764
#
```

In this case, the total record count value can be used as a validation check to ensure
that the entire file was read and that the number of records matched the expected
total.

By default, head reads the first 10 lines of the specified file if no value is entered.

The tail command works in a similar way to the head command, except that it is
used to examine the lines at the end of a file. By default, tail shows the last 10 lines if
no numeric value is entered. The tail command is often used to look at the last line
of a log file, for example, to see if the processing has completed so that the next task
can be initiated. This is frequently used when data files are received on an ad-hoc basis
rather than at scheduled intervals.

An extremely useful feature of `tail` is the `-f` flag, which shows any lines that are subsequently added to the end of a file. This is particularly useful when monitoring a process that is writing to a log file because all entries will be displayed on the screen as they are written to the log file.

od (Octal Dump)

The `od` command has value for the system manager (and administrators) because it can be used to display nonprintable characters. This is especially useful when filenames contain such characters and cannot be easily deleted. Consider the following example, in which the filename consists only of five <tab> characters. The `od` command with the `-c` switch displays the characters clearly so that the file can now be deleted.

Listing 9.10 shows the five tabs file being identified and subsequently deleted.

Listing 9.10 **An Annotated Screen Session Using the _od_ Command**

```
# ls
                                       <<< Here's the file, but it contains
nonprintable characters
# ls | od -c
0000000  \t  \t  \t  \t  \t  \n <<< od has identified the characters
0000006
# rm \        \        \        \        \           <<< The file can now be
explicitly deleted
# ls
#                                      <<< All gone
```

Filenames such as those listed are normally a result of some typing error and cause minor inconvenience, but a file of this kind might have been left by an unauthorized guest—it is not obviously detected and would not be automatically deleted by routine housekeeping processes.

Some companies have a policy to alias the `rm` command to include the `-i` flag so that a prompt is always issued before a file is deleted. This method can also be used to delete files containing nonprintable characters.

A further way of removing unwanted or invalid characters is to use the `tr` command to translate these characters into something that is readable. This command is popularly used to force user responses into upper case, for example.

Summary

The tactical aspect of the system manager's responsibility involves ensuring that an acceptable, efficient, and professional IT service is provided to the user community and that it then is maintained. The system manager must ensure that essential administration tasks are carried out. For junior administrators, a checklist approach is often useful because it ensures that the job gets done and also assists with the administrators' learning and familiarization.

Outages are becoming fewer as high availability is becoming a top priority for a large number of businesses. The system manager must be able to keep his customers informed of any outage status, whether due to a scheduled upgrade or a major, unexpected interruption to service. Tickertape systems and voice announcement facilities can be used to good effect when the normal means of communication are unavailable.

Performance monitoring is a large part of the system manager's responsibility. He must be able to identify potential bottlenecks and resolve them quickly to minimize the effect. Regular monitoring using Solaris tools such as vmstat, mpstat, iostat, and sar, for example, ensures that sufficient data is available for analysis as well as for periodic reports.

10

Working with PCs

ONE OF THE TASKS FACING SYSTEM MANAGERS today is how to get the best out of the computer hardware as well as reduce the overall cost of ownership—while at the same time continuing to provide a reliable, efficient service to the customer. Offices and computer rooms are often overrun with vast numbers of PCs acting as Windows servers to the office environment, making it not only difficult to support and administer, but extremely costly as well. Coupled with this problem is the dilemma that PCs need regular upgrading or replacing to keep up with new versions of software that are constantly demanding more resources.

The PC is here to stay, and Windows NT has definitely made a significant impression on the desktop market. For quite some time, Sun Microsystems has been working toward the integration of PC functionality with the high performance range of Solaris workstations and servers.

The evidence that PC integration is becoming more of a strategic issue is demonstrated by the significant improvements that have been made in recent years and the investment that companies such as Sun have made in this field.

The Microsoft range of Windows operating systems certainly provides a popular desktop environment, but the hardware lacks the reliability or scalability that can be provided with a Solaris-based Sun workstation or server. To this end, Sun and other companies have marketed products to interact with, and support, the services offered by these operating systems.

Many organizations are also looking at ways of consolidating the desktop space, finding it unacceptable for users to need both a PC and a UNIX workstation on their desks to carry out their daily duties. The advent of products such as KEA!X, from Attachmate, solves this problem, allowing the full CDE graphical environment to be run as a window on an existing Microsoft Windows desktop.

This chapter looks at a number of products that can either be purchased or downloaded from the public domain and contribute to the success of merging UNIX and PC environments. The first section looks at interoperability products that allow significant integration between the two. The second section discusses PC connectivity products, such as X Window System software that runs on a PC, as well as some terminal emulation products.

The final section looks at the StarOffice suite of software that is freely available from Sun Microsystems and is being used in an increasing number of establishments. This section also discusses Sun's innovative program to deliver office software via the Web: the Webtop solution.

PC Integration Products

For some time, Sun Microsystems has pioneered the integration of the PC and Solaris environment, starting with the Windows Application Binary Interface (WABI), SoftWindows, and SunPC. Things have moved on significantly in recent years, with major innovations allowing a much more comprehensive integration—in some cases, the potential exists to completely replace PC servers altogether with Solaris systems to provide the same services, but with greatly increased performance, scalability, and reliability.

This section takes a look at some of the products that provide interoperability between the PC and Solaris environments. This is something the system manager should be actively implementing to provide the optimum service and range of facilities to his customers while also taking full advantage of the high availability and performance that Sun computer systems deliver as standard.

Sun PCi II Coprocessor Card

The Sun PCi Coprocessor card effectively puts a powerful PC into the Sun workstation, but it also has the advantage of utilizing the Solaris workstation resources. The card currently supports a 600MHz processor and up to 512MB of memory, which is dedicated to the performance of PC applications.

Using the Coprocessor card, users can run Microsoft Windows applications on the Sun workstation alongside the Solaris environment applications. An advantage of configuring the system in this way is that the PCi card takes full advantage of the reliable and robust Sun workstation. It can also share the Sun workstation's network interface if network ports are at a premium. Or it can use its own network port—the card comes with a separate network connector, if required.

The PCi Coprocessor card will run Microsoft Windows NT, 98SE, and 2000 applications while using the same monitor, keyboard, and mouse as the workstation. It also shares files and data with the workstation, permitting copy and paste facilities between the Solaris environment and the PC environment. In addition, the card shares the removable media devices, such as the floppy disk and CD-ROM drive.

The Sun PCi Coprocessor card is a serious option for offices that have standardized on the PC environment yet still require the use of dedicated Sun workstations on the desktop. In these cases, the user can save valuable desktop space, receive seamless integration between the two environments, and still run complex, resource-intensive PC applications.

PC Launcher

PC Launcher is used in conjunction with the Sun PCi Coprocessor card discussed in the previous section and is supplied on the Solaris Supplement CD-ROM from Solaris 7 onward.

The software delivers Sun PCi users the additional functionality to view, edit, and print numerous types of PC files and attachments by automatically launching the Windows application associated with the file, similar to the current practice on the native Windows platform.

PC Launcher provides users with the following facilities:

- Built-in support to identify icons for many Windows applications, such as Microsoft Word, Excel, and PowerPoint, as well as Lotus, WordPerfect, Corel, and bitmap graphics (BMP) among others.

- Support for Windows shortcuts from the Solaris desktop. The user can keep all PC application shortcuts on the Solaris CDE front panel and workspace.

- Automatic identification of PC file type attachments, launching the PC Launcher, the relevant PC application, and the PC file itself.

- Support for users to copy and paste text from Windows applications into any Solaris application.

- Easy access to PC-file type attachments in CDE Mail and File Manager, including the drag-and-drop capability for any file on the CDE front panel.

- The capability to define additional file types for other Windows applications using standard CDE tools.

Coupled with the Sun PCi Coprocessor card, the PC Launcher software delivers a comprehensive PC environment, but without the need for a separate PC system.

PC File Viewer

PC File Viewer is delivered as part of Solaris 7 and later releases (and Solaris 2.6 Hardware 5/98). It can be downloaded free from the Sun Microsystems Web site (http://www.sun.com) for users of early Solaris 2.6 releases. The software is available only for SPARC-based Solaris environments.

PC File Viewer provides the user with the facility to view a large number of popular types of PC files or attachments, similar to the PC Launcher software described in the previous section. In this case, however, there is no need to have the original application installed on the Sun workstation. Using PC File Viewer, email attachments can be read easily, even though they might have been created using a PC application such as Microsoft Word, Excel, PowerPoint, Lotus 1-2-3, Corel, or AutoCAD.

Text from PC files viewed using PC File Viewer can be copied and pasted into Solaris applications such as Text Editor, Mail, or FrameMaker. A file viewed with this software is displayed in exactly the same way as when it was originally created. The software also displays WYSIWYG format and color.

The real use for this software is to enable Solaris users on Sun workstations to receive files and email attachments, for example, in a PC application format and instantly open them—without needing the original PC application to be installed. Previously, these files were not readable and often needed to be manually transferred to a PC to be opened, which was highly inefficient and wasted resources.

Solaris PC Netlink

The PC Netlink software for Solaris is probably the biggest interoperability innovation to be delivered. This software enables Solaris SPARC-based systems to behave like Windows NT4 servers and to replace them as domain controllers. Formerly known as Project Cascade, PC Netlink brings reliability and scalability to Windows NT networks, something sorely missing from the PC environment.

Companies that have standardized on the Windows NT platform for the office network have faced problems accommodating exponential growth and still providing a reliable, available platform on which to deliver the services required by the customer. PC Netlink solves both of these problems by running the Windows NT network services on SPARC-based Solaris systems, which deliver high availability and are fully scalable. PC Netlink runs on the full range of Enterprise servers, from the Ultra 5 to the Enterprise 10000.

System managers fighting to control the proliferation of Windows NT servers can replace large numbers of PC-based servers with a single Solaris-based SPARC server. This reduces the maintenance and administration costs significantly because PC Netlink servers can be administered using standard Windows NT tools, just like the PC server; thus, no change to the current operating procedures is required.

PC Netlink software provides the following native services:

- Primary and backup domain controller, NT Directory Services (NTDS)
- Network file and print services
- Security and authentication
- Support for NT file system (CIFS/SMB)
- Windows NT naming services
- Support for all major client types (Windows 2000, 95, 98, 3.11, and NT workstation).
- Support for up to 2,000 concurrent users
- Compliance with the service pack

Windows Support

Support for the Windows family of products includes clients only—not, for example, native Windows 2000 environments. Therefore, facilities such as Active Directory, which were introduced as part of Windows 2000 server, are not supported.

Figure 10.1 shows how a Solaris SPARC-based server can be integrated into the office network.

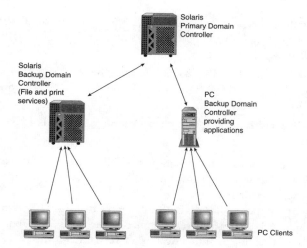

Figure 10.1 Consolidation of Windows NT servers onto the Solaris platform reduces the total cost of ownership, simplifies management, and provides a fully scalable and reliable NT network.

Even though PC Netlink supports all major clients, it does not actually run any Windows NT applications, although it can store and serve them to the clients. This is because the actual application runs on the client itself, not on the server.

With consolidation and total cost of ownership being very popular goals in the IT business arena, this product offers a realistic opportunity to achieve both of these objectives in one go. In addition, it offers increased reliability and the capability to accommodate the demanding growth factors that companies everywhere are experiencing.

Totalnet Advanced Server

Totalnet Advanced Server (TAS) is an interoperability product available from Syntax, Inc. (http://www.syntax.com), that enables diverse operating systems to successfully share file, print, and application resources across both local and wide area networks.

The software runs on a UNIX operating environment, such as Solaris, and creates a common file system, enabling it to act as a file, print, and application server for Windows 2000/NT/95/98, NetWare, Macintosh, and other UNIX variants. It enables users to create and store files in their native environment, and also to take full advantage of the power and reliability of a Solaris Enterprise system, for example.

TAS enables interoperability among these diverse environments through three realms, each defining the combination of specific operating systems and transport protocols:

- **CIFS Realm**—LAN Manager, Windows NT, Windows 2000, Windows 95/98, and IBM OS/2 clients running NetBIOS over TCP/IP or NetBIOS over NetBEUI transports

- **NetWare Realm**—NetWare clients running the IPX/SPX transport, supporting NETX, VLM, Windows 200, Windows 95/98, Windows NT, and NetWare clients

- **AppleTalk Realm**—Macintosh clients running AppleTalk or TCP/IP transports

The TAS file system that is created is common to all realms, enabling seamless integration regardless of the originating platform. A user (with correct permissions) can access files from anywhere on the network.

Another feature supplied with the TAS software is that the TAS server can be configured as a Windows NT logon server, eliminating the need for Windows 2000 and Windows NT servers acting as authentication servers. One of the goals of the TAS environment is to provide single signon facilities on a network containing multiple file system types and authentication mechanisms, as well as a simple account management function.

Samba

Samba is freely available in the public domain and can be downloaded from the Samba Web site (`http://www.samba.org`) or from other sites offering public domain software for Solaris systems (such as `http://www.sunfreeware.com`). Samba is free and comes with the source code.

Samba runs on a UNIX platform, such as Solaris, but it communicates with Windows clients as if it were a native. The Solaris system running Samba is integrated into the Windows network neighborhood, providing file and print services to Windows clients that do not know that they are being delivered by a Solaris system—that is, the services are transparent to the client. Samba is based on the SMB protocol and Common Internet File System (CIFS).

In many ways, Samba is similar in functionality to Solaris PC Netlink, but Samba cannot (yet) completely imitate (and even replace) a Windows NT domain controller—PC Netlink can already accomplish this.

Briefly, Samba provides the following facilities:

- **File and print**—The Samba SMB daemon (smbd) manages these facilities, making the UNIX system appear as a PC file server.

- **Authentication and authorization**—Also managed by the smbd daemon are share mode and user mode authentication and authorization. The facility enables passwords to be applied to network shares, such as printers. Depending on the mode, either a single password is used by all users permitted to use the shared resource (share mode), or a user has a username and password, individually administered by the system administrator.

- **Name resolution**—This can take one of two forms. In broadcast, the client broadcasts the hostname of the required system and waits for the IP address to be returned. Broadcast name resolution, however, is limited to the local network. The second kind of name resolution is point-to-point, using a NetBIOS Name Service (NBNS) server. Clients in this configuration send the NetBIOS names along with their corresponding IP address to the NBNS server, where it is stored in a simple database. The server then answers name resolution requests. The utility nmblookup exists to interrogate a server. NBNS is very similar to DNS but is less secure because there are fewer controls that check for authorized clients.

- **Browsing—service announcement**—Browsing in this context is different from Web browsing. It is a "browsable" list of file and print services being made available by computers on the network.

- **The Samba client**—smbclient is an FTP-style interface used to access PC resources, such as files or printers from UNIX and NetWare systems, among others.

- **tar**—Samba includes a tar extension to the client software so that PC systems can be backed up on the Solaris host.

- **Administration tool**—The Samba Web Administration Tool (SWAT) enables the administrator to use a Web browser to configure Samba remotely.

Samba is used to integrate and merge with existing Windows networks and resources. This is different from the Solaris PC Netlink, which can also replace Windows NT domain controllers, although it is an eventual objective of the Samba team.

Citrix Metaframe for Solaris

The recently announced version of Citrix Metaframe for UNIX enables Solaris applications to be delivered to virtually any device. The software supports Solaris 2.6 for SPARC and Solaris 7 and 8 on both SPARC and Intel platforms. The product provides seamless integration of applications onto the local desktop, enabling the user to resize the windows and also to switch easily between local and remote applications, as if they were all running on the local system.

When used in conjunction with Citrix Metaframe for Windows, this version of Citrix Metaframe can deliver virtually any application to virtually any device, including Windows 2000, 9x, 3.x, and NT, as well as DOS, OS/2, Macintosh, wireless devices and handhelds, terminals, and network computers, to name a few.

One added piece of functionality that is extremely useful for users of UNIX and PC-based applications is that Metaframe grants the user full access to local resources, such as the Clipboard. This makes it easy to copy and paste graphics and text between both local applications and remote applications deployed using Citrix's Independent Computing Architecture (ICA). Using this, the entire application processing is carried out on the server, reducing the bandwidth requirement and eliminating the problems found in other terminal emulation products.

For organizations using multi-platform environments and a wide variety of devices, Citrix Metaframe not only provides much greater seamless access to the UNIX applications running on powerful and reliable Solaris systems, but it also provides simplified administration. All this enables the system manager to take full advantage of the scalability, processing power, and reliability of Solaris while also increasing his potential customer base.

PC Connectivity Products

Products that enable a PC to connect to hosts running a different operating system have been available for many years in a variety of forms. Telnet and X Window System connections have eliminated the need for a separate dedicated console or monitor on the desktop, when both PC and non-PC environments are needed.

Although these products are not full PC-integration software packages like the ones described in the previous section, they can still greatly assist the system manager in the rationalization and consolidation of resources becoming increasingly popular in IT departments.

This section discusses a PC X Window System product that can seamlessly integrate the Solaris CDE environment as a window session on the PC desktop. This enables the user to run graphical applications remotely on the Solaris host, taking advantage of the processing power and reliability, while still being controlled entirely from the PC—the output appears on the PC monitor, and the input comes from the PC's mouse and keyboard. This section also discusses a similar product called Virtual Network Computing (VNC), which is freely available, and explores a few of the terminal emulation products that allow a Telnet-style connection to a Solaris system to initiate a shell session.

KEA!X Server Software

KEA!X is a software product supplied by Attachmate. It provides the facility to manage X Window System applications alongside existing PC applications, all on the Windows desktop. Functionality such as this completely eliminates the need for any dedicated X Terminals or graphical monitors. KEA!X is fully compliant with the X11R6 release of the X Window System.

When KEA!X is first started on the PC, it broadcasts a startup request to all servers running the X Window Display Manager (XDM). Any hosts that respond are identified in a list box, and the user can choose which host to connect to. Figure 10.2 shows the initial list box.

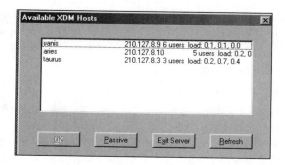

Figure 10.2 The choice of available hosts enables the user to select a host that is not being heavily used, spreading the load among the hosts.

When the user selects a host to connect to, the Solaris CDE desktop software starts and the CDE login window is displayed, exactly as it would if the user were logged in to a Sun workstation with a dedicated graphical monitor. Figure 10.3 shows the CDE login screen.

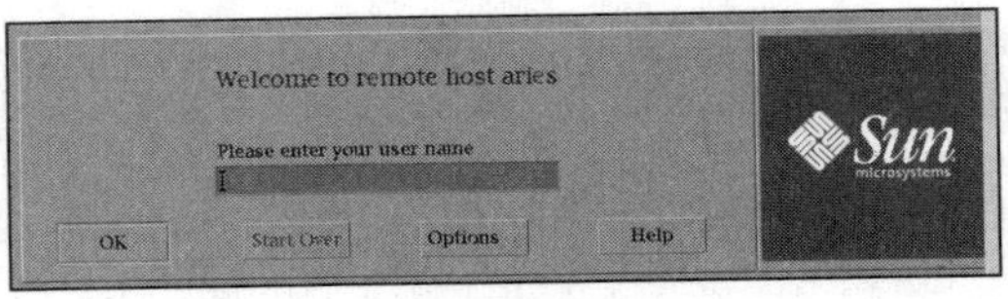

Figure 10.3 The Solaris CDE environment behaves exactly as if it were connected to a local graphical monitor or a dedicated X Terminal.

KEA!X offers the following features:

- The choice of either single- or multiple-window mode, enabling the user to view X applications in a single root window or in individual windows under the control of another window manager, such as Windows 98
- The capability to use Microsoft Windows as the window manager, giving the X applications the look and feel of the Microsoft Windows environment
- Multiple instances of the X server can be run, each with a different window manager
- The capability to run X applications alongside the current Windows applications, permitting copy and paste functionality between the two
- The capability to take advantage of the Windows 95/98 and Windows NT operating systems because of its 32-bit technology
- The capability to be fully user-configurable
- User-defined keyboard mappings
- The facility to permit the screen, or a selected rectangle, to be copied to a printer or a file
- The option to choose which network adapter to use to initiate the connection, when more than one is present (for example, Ethernet and dial-up)
- Support for up to 32-bit color, ensuring compatibility with the various levels of video graphic adapters

This list is not exhaustive, but it provides a good indication of how flexible and useful products such as KEA!X can be in the world of interoperability. The X Suite from WRQ provides similar PC X server facilities.

Virtual Network Computing (VNC)

VNC is a freely available product provided by AT&T Laboratories that enables a user to view a desktop environment from virtually anywhere and from a variety of machine architectures. The effect is quite similar to that gained by using an X Window System server on a PC (with KEA!X, discussed in the previous section). However, there are some important differences to note:

- The viewer application that runs on the PC stores no state information. This means, for example, a user could start editing a document and type a few lines, then disconnect and travel halfway around the world—and then reconnect and resume editing the document as if it had never been left.

- With a PC X server, all remote applications die if the PC crashes for some reason. With VNC, they continue running. The user merely reconnects again to resume the viewer.

- The viewer application is very small (about 150K) and fits onto a floppy disk, making it easily transportable.

- The software is free. It can be downloaded from `http://www.uk.research.att.com/vnc` which offers both source code and documentation.

- A number of viewer applications can view the same desktop simultaneously.

Figure 10.4 shows a viewer connection using a standard X Window System desktop environment.

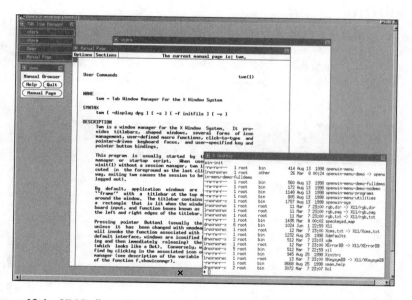

Figure 10.4   VNC allows the same desktop to be accessed from a variety of platforms.

Terminal Emulation

Terminal emulation software products do not provide any integrated functionality. Instead, they provide connectivity to a Solaris system using a Telnet client. They are configurable in that they can emulate different types of terminals, such as VT100, VT320, and so on. The user also can customize the keyboard mappings, which can be useful for bespoke applications.

Several companies produce terminal emulation software, such as WRQ with Reflection, Attachmate with EXTA! TN, and Netmanage with Rumba. A further Telnet client is Tera Term, which is freely available in the public domain. It can be downloaded via `http://www.tucows.com`, for example, where the appropriate platform can be selected. This client also has an extension module, TTSSH. When added to the Tera Term installation, TTSSH interacts fully with the secure shell daemon running on the Solaris host, providing secure Telnet access without losing any of the Tera Term functionality. The TTSSH module supports only SSHv1. The Tera Term source is freely available, as is the source for the TTSSH extension.

StarOffice

Sun Microsystems has produced an integrated suite of office software that is beginning to rival the major providers, Microsoft and Corel. What's more, it's free.

The software is already available for Solaris, Linux, OS/2, and the Windows platforms. Figure 10.5 shows the initial screen when StarOffice is started in the Solaris CDE environment.

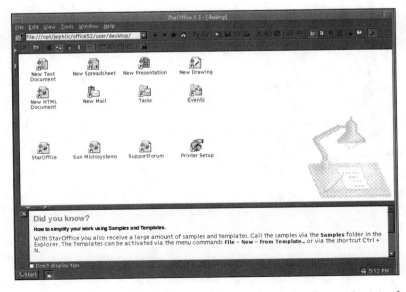

Figure 10.5 The StarOffice desktop provides easy access to all the office productivity facilities.

StarOffice delivers a special feature that Microsoft Office and Corel WordPerfect Office 2000 don't: real Windows/UNIX cross-platform compatibility.

Multiplatform enterprises can benefit from using StarOffice because it uses a platform-independent file format. This means, for example, that documents created on a Linux platform can be transferred accurately to the Solaris or Windows version without modification or conversion. A number of larger educational establishments are now standardizing on the StarOffice suite—not just because it is free from licensing restrictions and doesn't cost anything, but because it works and is compatible with the major vendors' offerings.

StarOffice has a Start bar that closely resembles the Windows Start bar. Figure 10.6 shows the Start menu.

Loading Star Office

The only downside to StarOffice noted has been the time it takes to start up: about 10 seconds, on average. This is because the software is so tightly integrated that the startup loads about 10–12 applications. Sun is seriously considering unbundling the major applications so that the package will behave more like Microsoft Office, with only the relevant application loaded. This will definitely improve its performance when loading.

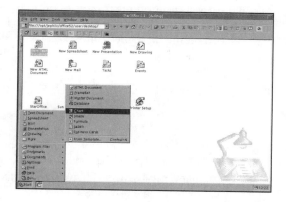

Figure 10.6   The Start bar, menus, and toolbars are all fully user-configurable and help to maintain the suite's look and feel across multiple platforms.

StarOffice Writer, the word processor, comprises some specialized tools: AutoPilot, Sun's version of a wizard, and AutoFunction, real-time spelling, error correction, and auto-completion make good examples. Documents can be saved in a variety of formats, including Word 97, Word 2000, and WordPerfect 8.

The presentation program, StarOffice Impress, aids in the production of high-quality presentation slides, and, like the other products, provides the facility to save in a number of formats, such as Microsoft PowerPoint. Figure 10.7 demonstrates this.

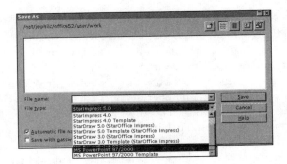

Figure 10.7 The variety of compatible formats make the documents and presentation files truly portable.

There is an increasing wave of support for the StarOffice suite, a fact demonstrated by more than 1 million downloads from the Web site. System managers are considering it a serious alternative to the Microsoft Office and Corel WordPerfect Office suites. Considerable financial savings can be achieved because the software is free and because the suite provides resource savings that would normally be spent managing the licenses. Those savings could be well spent on other projects or upgrades.

Following the StarOffice suite is Sun's latest initiative, StarPortal. This includes a product known as Webtop, based on the StarOffice suite, except that the local host does not have any applications to install or maintain, the applications (including the data) all reside on the network. Portal computing certainly will be the next major step forward as it begins to seriously threaten the domination of the Windows model.

Summary

System managers are under constant pressure to do more with the resources they already have and to rationalize and consolidate. The products available today to integrate the Solaris and PC environments greatly help achieve these objectives.

The Sun PCi coprocessor card effectively co-locates a powerful PC within the Sun system hardware, allowing it to take advantage of the Solaris system resources and eliminating the need for two separate systems on the desktop.

Solaris PC Netlink delivers sufficient Windows NT integration to replace NT servers completely with significantly fewer Solaris systems, thanks to the reliability and scalability that the Sun platform is renowned for.

Interoperability between UNIX and PC environments has been high on the Sun Microsystems agenda for several years. The StarOffice productivity suite of software is now considered to be a serious rival to the traditional Microsoft Windows environment.

11

Shells and Public Domain Software

LIKE ANY OTHER UNIX ENVIRONMENT, the Solaris operating environment contains at least one command interpreter called a *shell*. It isn't only an interpreter; it's also a command programming language. The shell is the main interface between the user and the system. The first section in this chapter identifies the shells that are packaged with the Solaris operating environment software, as well as the shells that can be obtained in the public domain. Another shell that is discussed, the secure shell, is an essential tool when extra security is required in a potentially vulnerable network environment.

A considerable amount of software also exists in the public domain, freely available and written by some of the best developers and technical experts in the field of UNIX. The second part of this chapter takes a look at some of the more popular public domain software applications, what they do, and where they can be obtained.

Shells

The shell is the means by which UNIX commands are executed, whether at the command line or from a file—the latter is known as a shell script or program. The system startup (and shutdown) procedures execute a number of shell scripts. The shell is an interactive programming language as well as a command interpreter; it enables the user to set variables and customize the environment. Choosing which shell to use often comes down to personal preference—you can use the one that you feel most comfortable with and that provides the functionality required.

This section identifies the shells that are available for use with the Solaris operating environment and discusses some of the differences between them. Entire books have been written on the use of the UNIX shells; some of these are referenced in the Appendix, "Resources." This section is intended only to identify and introduce the different shells.

Shells Bundled with the Solaris Environment

A number of shells actually are delivered with the Solaris operating environment, offering various features:

- **The Bourne shell (sh and jsh)**—This is the default shell and the only one that is always present in any version of UNIX. As the original UNIX shell, the Bourne shell is still used as the standard for system initialization scripts. Using the jsh option enables extra job control functionality, allowing jobs to be suspended or run as a background task, for example.

- **The C shell (csh)**—This shell is a Berkeley UNIX product. Its syntax resembles the C programming language much more than the Bourne shell. With SunOS 4.x based on BSD UNIX, the C shell was heavily used until SunOS 5.x, when Sun switched to System V-based UNIX. The C shell contained some extra features not present in the Bourne shell, including filename completion, in which a hot key could be pressed to instruct the shell to attempt to complete the name of the command or file being typed. Command aliases and command history were other functions available in this shell.

- **The Korn shell (ksh)**—The Korn shell has become the de facto standard for UNIX systems. It is now universally available and provides a far superior functionality than the Bourne shell. The Korn shell includes command-line editing, allowing the use of either vi- or Emacs-type editing syntax, command aliasing, filename completion, job control, and command history—virtually everything that the system administrator would need.

Don't lose the root shell

The standard shell for the superuser (root) resides in /sbin/sh. The sbin directory contains statically linked programs—that is, programs that already contain any library functions that might be required to execute the program. Therefore, they are self-sufficient, unlike dynamically linked programs that call library modules at runtime. Changing the default root shell to a dynamically linked shell might save a little bit of disk space, but it could also mean that the superuser cannot log on in case of a failure affecting the runtime libraries.

- **The desktop Korn shell (dtksh)**— This is a shell bundled with the Common Desktop Environment (CDE) software that provides an extended version of the Korn shell (ksh-93) with support for many X Window graphical functions. These functions were previously used in programs that required compilation and linking before they could run. The dtksh shell provides a very similar functionality that can run as a normal shell script—that is, it is interpreted rather than compiled.

- **The restricted shell (rsh)**—This is a more controlled version of the Bourne shell, and it is used to restrict the access of a user. With this shell, the user cannot change a directory or set the PATH variable. There can be no redirection of output, nor can any absolute pathnames be specified (starting with "/"). The restricted shell command should not be confused with the remote shell. Both are called rsh (the remote shell is also referred to as remsh), but they reside in different directories: the restricted shell in /usr/lib and the remote shell in /usr/bin.

Shells Available in the Public Domain

A number of shells have been written and made available in the public domain. These are mainly extensions to the existing shells with additional functionality added. Although there are many, three of the more popular ones are discussed here:

- **Bash**—Bash, which stands for "Bourne Again Shell," is a public domain shell written by the Free Software Foundation. It is intended to be a full implementation of the IEEE shell and tools standard, and it is provided as the default shell on most versions of Linux.

  Bash is fully compatible with the Bourne shell—Bourne shell scripts will run without modification under the Bash shell. It also incorporates useful features of the Korn shell (ksh) and the C shell (csh).

  In addition, Bash offers command-line editing without having to erase back to the point of error. Vi- or Emacs-style editing commands can be used, and Bash includes a command history feature as well as filename completion and a built-in help facility. This is by far the most popular of the public domain shells available.

- **tcsh**—This shell is an extended version of the Berkeley C shell. It is fully compatible with the C shell, but it includes additional functionality, such as a command-line editor, word completion, spelling correction, a command history recall mechanism, and built-in job control functions.

- **zsh**—This shell resembles most closely the Korn shell—specifically, ksh–88. As with the other public domain shells, it is an enhanced version. zsh incorporates some of its functionality from tcsh and includes other features to try to make users of the C shell feel more at home when using it. The zsh shell is highly configurable and, like the others mentioned, includes additional functionality for such things as job control, spelling correction, filename completion, command history, and command-line editing. zsh also can accommodate multiline commands (even files), allowing them to be edited as a single buffer.

These three shells are now delivered as standard with Solaris 8. Their basic functionality is extremely similar, with job control, word completion, a command-line editor, and the capability to recall a history of previously entered commands being common to all of them.

The Secure Shell

The secure shell provides the means to access systems securely, using encrypted communications between a client and a Solaris system based on their own SSH secure protocol. The secure shell daemon runs on the Solaris system and will accept a login request only from a "known host"—that is, a system with a registered encryption key. The secure shell is available from SSH Communications Security Corp. (http://www.ssh.com). This has become the de facto standard for users requiring remote logins.

Two versions of the secure protocol exist: SSH version 1 (SSH1) and SSH version 2 (SSH2). Both encrypt at different parts of the network packet. SSH2 uses only host keys to authenticate systems, whereas SSH1 uses server and host keys. The two protocols are incompatible, although they can both be run on the same system if SSH1 was installed before SSH2. The SSH2 protocol is a complete rewrite and is more secure. SSH2 also includes an easy-to-use secure file transfer facility, using the Secure File Transfer Protocol (SFTP).

Licensing of the two protocols has been a factor in deciding which one to use. SSH1 was originally free, although versions later than 1.2.12 apply restrictive licensing. A number of ISPs still work on SSH1 because it is free and has proven to be stable because it has been around longer. SSH2, on the other hand, is free only for nonprofit organizations, educational organizations, or entities using it purely for charity.

SSH is not only a shell, but it also provides a graphical environment when needed in a secure environment. The X Window System over SSH can be used when only secure connectivity is permitted.

Software in the Public Domain

An ever-increasing amount of Solaris-compatible software is becoming available in the public domain. The main differences between this kind of software and other commercial software are that this software is free and comes with the source code. Conversely, though, formal support often is not available with these products.

Historically, a significant number of system managers have prohibited the use of public domain software because of the "as is" nature of the software, the perceived risk of becoming infected with a virus, and the lack of formal support. This notion is slowly being eroded as the software's usefulness begins to be appreciated and because support for the majority of the packages is now available.

This section identifies some of the more popular public domain software application packages that are available for Solaris environments. Even though these packages are free, many books have been written about them; some of these are listed in the Appendix.

Apache

Apache is a commercial-grade, freely available HTTP (Web) server software package. It was created by volunteers from around the world who worked together to develop the server and its associated documentation. Like other freely available software applications, Apache comes with the source code. Apache runs not only on Solaris, but also on most versions of UNIX as well as Windows NT/9x, NetWare, and OS/2.

When you connect to a home page on the Internet, there is a good chance that the server providing the Web pages is running the Apache server—this is the most popular Web server in use. In addition to the Apache Web server, an Apache-SSL Web server is available; it implements the Secure Socket Layer (SSL) protocol and is widely used as a secure Web server. Like Apache, the Apache-SSL Web server is freely available both for commercial and noncommercial use.

Apache is a highly configurable and scalable product. It can run on the largest cluster of powerful computers or just a single PC. It is also modularized and can be easily extended using third-party modules. Alternatively, modules can be written using the Apache module API.

A final feature of Apache, one that frequently was requested by users of the product, is that Apache supports virtual hosts, also known as multihomed servers. This allows the server to distinguish among requests that have been made to different IP addresses or host names even though they are all mapped to the same physical host. A virtual host can be used to receive requests on different URLs, usually with the same IP address, so that different sets of documents are accessed depending on the URL entered (for example, viewing home pages for different clients or members of the company).

Virtual hosts can be either name-based, IP address based, or a mix of the two. Name-based virtual hosts are the preferred method, but they support only HTTP version 1.1 clients (the host names must be registered on the Web, however). A large number of organizations still use IP-based virtual hosts, though, because there remains a small proportion of clients that do not support HTTP 1.1. Because the Internet is running out of IP addresses, the full transition to name-based virtual hosts will be necessary in the coming years.

Apache has proven to be substantially faster and more stable than many other Web server products. It runs on sites that achieve millions of hits per day without suffering from performance or response time problems. Further information and the Apache software itself can be obtained from the Apache organization Web site, `http://www.apache.org`.

Also see the Appendix for details of further reading material on the Apache Web server, as well as some useful Web sites containing Apache documentation and frequently asked questions (FAQ) lists.

Perl

Perl is a programming language designed to make programming jobs easier. One of the features of Perl is that you don't have to know the language proficiently to write useful programs. The Perl programming language is freely available for commercial and noncommercial use, and has become extremely popular with system administrators and Web developers. It has a wide following throughout the world, with a number of Web sites, newsgroups, and FAQ lists providing a vast amount of help and information (see the Appendix for details of some of these locations and for some excellent recommended Perl reading material).

Although Perl is a programming language, the programs are interpreted rather than compiled, similar to UNIX shell scripts. But it's not just the language itself that has the appeal: There are also Perl modules that can be installed as "add-ons," the most popular one being CGI.pm. This module provides a simple interface for developing Common Gateway Interface (CGI) applications, primarily for use on the World Wide Web. Another extremely useful module is mod_perl, a module that embeds the Perl interpreter directly into the Web server, specifically Apache. This is not really a Perl module, but a module of Apache that provides full access to the Perl functionality from within Apache, something that many third-party suppliers have exploited to gain better performance on Web servers.

Many system administrators have switched from using shell scripts to using Perl because of the additional power that Perl provides, the ease of producing reusable code, and the comprehensive language facilities that are available without a full-blown compiler and linker.

Tcl/Tk

Tcl, which stands for Tool Command Language, is a scripting language that is freely available for download. It combines the advantages of a compiled language such as C with those of a scripting language (ease of learning, no need for compilation, and so on). Tcl reduces overall development time and is excellent for producing small, reliable, reusable pieces of software. The first application to have an embedded Tcl interpreter was a widely popular interactive dialog program named expect—and, incidentally, also freely available for download. Basically, expect is a Tcl interpreter with additional commands. For example, the spawn command creates a new process and a connection to the process so that other expect commands can access it. The interact command also enables a user to connect to a process interactively.

Tk is a graphical toolkit that was developed for Tcl. This made it easy for developers to write X Window System application software. Both Tcl and Tk are normally provided together as a single collection. Tcl runs on Solaris and most other variants of UNIX, as well as Microsoft Windows and Macintosh platforms.

Having mentioned the Perl programming language in the previous section, it's important to mention that there is a Perl/Tk extension used to write Perl programs with a graphical user interface (GUI). This is a port of the Tk application for use with Perl, and it makes it very easy to draw windows; populate them with buttons, menus, check boxes, and similar items; and have certain functions performed based on different user input.

GCC

Until 1999, GCC was an acronym for the GNU C Compiler, but it was changed to the GNU Compiler Collection because it no longer relates directly to the C compiler. It now also relates to C++, Objective C, Chill, Fortran, and Java.

As of Solaris 2.0, the Solaris operating environment no longer provides a bundled C compiler with its media release.

The public domain software that is freely available along with its source code requires a compiler to build the products for use on a computer system. The GNU C Compiler fulfills this requirement, delivering not only the compiler but also a comprehensive set of libraries. The GCC package can be downloaded as a prebuilt software package or in its source form for building on the local system. The latest version, for example, is always available from the Web site http://www.sunfreeware.com; it includes compilers for C, C++, Fortran, and Java.

You do need a C compiler to build GCC unless the pre-compiled version is downloaded. As an alternative, however, the mini-C compiler, which is found in the directory /usr/ucb, provides sufficient functionality to compile GCC.

Who Is GNU?

GNU stands for GNU's Not UNIX, an organization dedicated to the provision of free software, supported by the Free Software Foundation (FSF). This organization can be found on the Web at http://www.gnu.org.

Other Popular Tools

This section has attempted to provide information on a number of extremely popular freely available and useful public domain software packages. It is intended to be only a basic introduction, though, because most of the packages have at least one, if not several, books devoted specifically to their use and implementation. Several other products of note are briefly introduced here:

- **Python**—This is another interpreted and interactive programming language that is often compared with Perl, Tcl, and Java. Like the others, it has modules as well as an interface to Tk. Support newsgroups for Python and other useful information can be found on the Web.

- **Emacs**—If you don't like the vi editor, you will probably use Emacs instead. Emacs is an open source editor that is also available in an X Window System version, called Xemacs. Emacs is a popular editor used by developers because it contains modes for use when writing code in a common programming language such as C.

- **Joe**—This is a freely available ASCII screen text editor that users of PC editors will probably feel fairly comfortable with. It contains a number of extensions that emulate other editors.

- **Pine**—Pine, which stands for Program for Internet News and Email, is an email program and a tool for reading, sending, and managing electronic messages. It was primarily designed for novice users, but it is easily configurable to accommodate more experienced users.

Summary

The shell is the main interface between the user and the Solaris operating environment. It is also a fully interactive programming language. Solaris delivers the Bourne shell, the C shell, and the Korn shell as part of the standard release which, as of Solaris 8, also includes three public domain shells: Bash, tcsh, and zsh.

The *secure shell* (SSH) allows secure, encrypted communication between hosts on a network, a facility that is essential when the hosts are connected to the Internet and are potentially vulnerable to external attacks. SSH also enables users to make use of secure, graphical (X Window System) connections, making the increased security restrictions virtually transparent to the end user.

A large amount of extremely useful software is available in the public domain, which provides flexibility and variation to the facilities available to Solaris customers—the Apache Web server and Perl are prime examples. Both are used extensively throughout the UNIX world, with a large number of commercial software vendors providing software that is fully compatible with (or that actually uses) these software packages.

Management of the Solaris Network

12

Internet Protocol Version 6

THE INTERNET PROTOCOL (IP) ADDRESS is the common means by which data is transported between communications networks. It also identifies the particular computer (or, more specifically, the network interface) that is connected to the network. Every node (PC or workstation) that connects to the Internet requires a unique Internet Protocol (IP) address. For home users, the IP address is supplied by the Internet service provider (ISP).

With everyone using IP, the increase in the number of computers being connected to the Internet has given rise to a problem: Available unique addresses are in short supply. The current version of IP, version 4 (IPv4), has a limit of about 4 billion addresses. Various predictions by industry specialists indicate that the address range could be exhausted as early as 2002. Indeed, if subnetting and Network Address Translation (NAT) had not been used, the numbers might have already been exhausted. The impact of this is that any new computers or devices that require an IP address to connect to the Internet will not be capable of doing so.

A further problem is related to the use of Internet routers. Originally, IPv4, the current protocol, was designed for a relatively small network of mainly academics and engineers, primarily for file transfer operations. IP addresses were not allocated in a particularly structured or efficient manner, such as geographical location. This requires Internet routers to store details of many more routes than were originally intended. The routing information that is needed to cope with the diversity of addresses is becoming unmanageable.

The Internet Engineering Task Force (IETF) designed a new version of IP that provides, among other things, a vast increase in the number of available addresses that can be allocated. Sun Microsystems has been heavily involved with the design and development of IPv6 and is represented on virtually every major working group of the IETF. Sun was also the first vendor to release an IPv6 prototype to the Internet community.

This chapter describes the basic features of IPv6 and tells how it differs from the current IP structure. It also covers the steps that the system manager should be taking to prepare for the implementation of IPv6. Finally, it gives a brief discussion on how IPv6 affects the system manager and the business to which he is providing a service. It is assumed that the reader is familiar with the basic concept of IP addresses. For more in-depth information, an excellent reference book is identified in the Appendix, "Resources": *IPv6 Clearly Explained*, by Peter Loshin.

What Is IPv6?

Internet Protocol version 6 (IPv6) is an evolutionary step from the current version of IP, version 4. It previously was known as IPng, meaning "IP next generation." IPv6 has been designed to work alongside IPv4 so that the transition can be carried out in a piecemeal fashion, reducing the impact on the Internet community.

What Happened to IPv5?

IPv5 could not be designated for the next generation of IP because it had already been used for an experimental protocol called the Internet Stream Protocol Version 2 (ST2). It was never widely used, but because version 5 had already been allocated, the new version of IP had to be given its own unique identifying number—hence, version 6. ST2 is described in RFC 1819.

The actual IP addressing structure is discussed in the next section, "IPv6 Addressing." The remainder of this section looks at the features that the migration to IPv6 will provide:

- **Increased address space**—The current number of IP addresses available with IPv4 is about 4×10^9, or 4 billion, whereas IPv6 allows nearly 10^{39}—and that is without subnetting to create additional addresses. The number of addresses that can be allocated permits hundreds of computers per square meter of the Earth's surface, so it is intended to satisfy requirements for the foreseeable future.

- **Classless addresses**—Unlike IPv4, in which IP addresses are identified by their network class (A, B, or C), IPv6 addresses will not contain address classes. Obviously some addresses will be reserved for specific use, but the general concept of IP address classes will cease.

- **Better routing**—IPv6 will use classless Internet domain routing (CIDR) algorithms, which are more efficient in handling routes for large network environments. The longer IP address improves router efficiency by allowing grouping of addresses into hierarchies of network based on geographical location, (such as service provider or corporation, for example), something that IPv4 can not accommodate.

- **Increased security**—IPv6 will be capable of providing authentication, a method of ensuring that a received packet has actually come from the origin provided in the packet's source address, and, more important, that it has not been altered (spoofed) during transmission. IPv6 also allows the data to be encrypted, something that IPv4 cannot do. Additionally, groups of managers can agree to use certain procedures, such as encryption keys, and then create what has been termed "security associations" for the secure exchange of data.

- **Accommodation of non-IP address formats**—The longer IP address structure will provide sufficient space to allow translations of non-IP address formats, such as IPX or Ethernet, into IPv6 addresses. For example, an Ethernet address that is 48 bits long is too long to map directly into an IPv4 address, which is 32 bits long. With IPv6 being 128 bits long, direct mapping is now possible.

- **More efficient broadcasting**—IPv6 introduces limited broadcasting to only those hosts that request to receive the data. This differs from the current IP broadcast method, whereby the packet is sent to every host on the network. This is especially important in the use of multimedia, for example, in which video or real-time data (which can be very large) can be transmitted efficiently using guaranteed bandwidth.

■ **Address discovery**—With the current IPv4 protocol, every host must be manually configured with its own address information or must rely on a DHCP
server. IPv6 allows automatic address discovery using the IPv6 Stateless Address
Autoconfiguration Protocol, by which a computer can "discover" its own IPv6
address. The protocol uses the unique Media Access Control (MAC) 48-bit
address to form an interface identifier. For example, if a system has an Ethernet
interface, then the 48-bit address is formed into a 64-bit interface ID. The
Neighbor Discovery (ND) protocol then checks that there is not a duplicate on
the subnet—there shouldn't be because Ethernet addresses should be unique.
Having obtained a unique address, a message is sent out to see if there is a local
router capable of supporting IPv6. This allows two or more hosts on a network
to operate with no router present; it allows automatic configuration of their
IPv6 addresses and does not rely on any other server, such as a DHCP server.

This list highlights the major differences between IPv4 and IPv6. See the Appendix
for links to a more detailed technical specification of the protocol and a more comprehensive list of the features.

The next section outlines the new format of the IPv6 address, as well as the
changes that have been made to the address notation.

IPv6 Addressing

The current IP addressing structure, based on version 4 of the protocol, consists of a
32-bit address, made up of four groups of 8 bits. The address comprises a network
address and a host address, depending on which class of network the address refers to.
Figure 12.1 shows the current IP address structure:

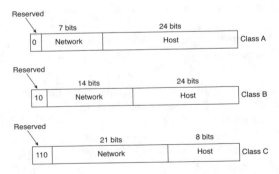

Figure 12.1   The mapping of network and host addresses
clearly shows the class structure in the 32-bit IPv4 protocol.

The current IP address is written as four decimal numbers separated by periods (.). An example of an IPv4 address is 210.127.36.133. This is a randomly chosen Class C address. The network number is 210.127.36, and the actual computer is host number 133 on that network; the network is subnetted on the expected boundary, which is ff:ff:ff:00.

IP addresses based on version 6 of the protocol consist of a 128-bit address made up of eight groups of 16 bits. As mentioned in the previous section, there are no classes, and the address is written as eight hexadecimal numbers separated by colons (:). The preferred format for writing IPv6 addresses is shown here: x:x:x:x:x:x:x:x.

Figure 12.2 shows the IPv6 address structure.

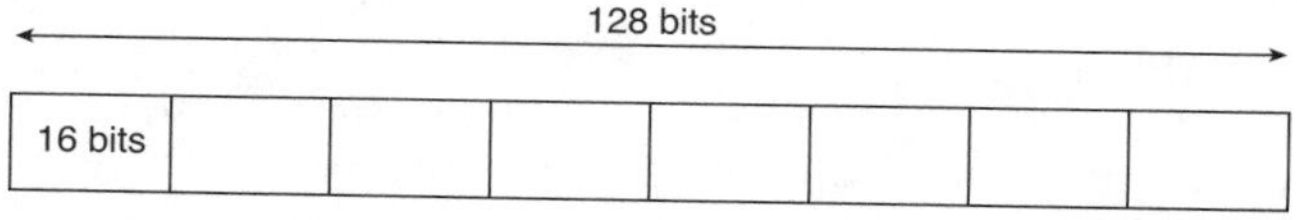

Figure 12.2   The 128 IPv6 address format shows that the entire structure is used to denote the address, without any network classes.

Because of the way in which some addresses are allocated, IPv6 addresses sometimes contain a number of empty (zero-filled) bits. The designers have taken this into account to make writing addresses easier by introducing a special syntax to denote "multiple groups of 16 bits filled with zeros." Thus, the following valid IPv6 addresses can be represented in two ways:

1040:FE3A:0:0:0:200:40C:8	OR	1040:FE3A::200:40C:8
0:0:0:0:0:0:0:A	OR	::A
FF02:0:0:0:0:0:0:2	OR	FF02::2

However, an IPv6 address could contain multiple blocks of 0, such as in 1080:0:0:0:4:0:0:2.

The use of the "::" to represent multiple groups of zeros can be used only once in an address, so the representation 1080::4::2 would be an invalid representation of the IPv6 address.

The IPv6 address structure also allows for a notation in which embedded IPv4 addresses can be written as part of a new IPv6 address. Consult the Appendix for more detailed information on the IPv6 address structure specification.

Getting Ready for IPv6

The Internet is growing at a phenomenal rate, probably much faster than many have anticipated. The enormous increase in Internet usage has come about mainly because of the e-commerce revolution and the desire of virtually every business to have a presence on the World Wide Web. There has also been a huge increase in the number of home users connecting to the Internet.

IPv6 is going to happen. It is not merely a suggestion that has been proposed, it is necessary to allow the Internet to continue to develop and to handle the future requirements of its users. As with the Y2K problem, there is no choice about whether to implement the changes; the only advantage over Y2K is that the date when everything happens is not fixed, so a phased transition can be applied to the whole scenario.

What You Should Be Doing Now

The system manager will not be directly responsible for the implementation of IPv6 within the organizational network—that task will be the responsibility of the network manager—but the system manager will be responsible for ensuring that all the systems under his control are IPv6-compatible. A further consideration that must be taken into account is the use of any distributed software applications. These also will require modification, in some cases, to interpret the new address structure.

The system manager should be actively pursuing the following:

- **Funding**—First and foremost, the system manager might have to secure additional funding to be able to carry out the transition of his systems and software to support IPv6.

- **Liaisons with the network manager**—The network manager will have all the information on when and how the company is planning to implement IPv6. The system manager cannot do very much if the routers can't handle the new addresses.

- **Vendor contacts**—The system manager must ensure that operating system vendors have included IPv6 support for their environments. This could be in the form of patches to the system software, or it might necessitate a system upgrade to a later version. Either way, the system manager will have to plan for the implementation.

- **Training**—The system manager should be identifying vendors that can supply relevant training for IP version 6. The training also needs to be assessed so that the members of staff can receive training before any implementation is in place.

- **Familiarity**—If a test network is set up within the company, the system manager should attempt to have a test system attached to it so that his staff can gain familiarity with the migration process and be better prepared for the actual transition when it happens.

Solaris 8 supports IPv6
Solaris 8 is the first version of the operating environment to fully support IP version 6.

- **Planning**—The system manager will have to plan the transition to IPv6 for all systems under his control. This includes replacement of current software and potentially the upgrade of the operating environment. Co-existence testing will be of particular importance, especially during the transition phase when the environment will contain a mixture of IPv4- and IPv6-aware systems.

- **Dissemination of information**—The system manager must ensure that the users are aware of what is being planned and of any possible effect that it might have on them. This might merely include details of the transition plan so that users know when the systems will be upgraded to support IPv6, or it might be that the users make network connections themselves, in which case more detailed information might be required.

Of course, it is not known exactly when the final change to IPv6 will occur or when IPv4 will cease to be used. It is safe to assume, however, that both IPv4 and IPv6 will co-exist for a number of years, making the transition a gradual one. Planning for a target date of, say, five years is probably reasonable.

Many vendors—including Sun, Cisco, and Microsoft—have implemented or are implementing a dual IP stack in which both protocols are supported. This allows applications to migrate one at a time to IPv6. The system manager should take his lead from the network manager, who will be responsible for the migration of the network infrastructure and who will also have access to the most recent information on developments. Meanwhile, any future upgrades, or new systems, should now include IPv6 as a standard requirement.

How Does This Affect You?

The transition to IPv6 has been designed so that it can be carried out in a piecemeal fashion, making it easier for companies to migrate while still supporting the current IP addressing structure. From an end-user perspective, the transition will be virtually transparent, with no noticeable effects on the functions carried out.

For the system manager, however, the transition will cost money, take time, and require careful planning (and a close liaison with the network manager). It also will require replacement software and retraining of staff members. Probably the most significant effect on the system manager will come during the actual period of transition, when some of the systems have been converted to IPv6 and some are still using IPv4. During this time, there will undoubtedly be "teething problems" requiring extra effort to ensure that the operation continues to run smoothly.

What Are Other Vendors Doing?

Cisco has produced a detailed IPv6 statement of direction paper, which can be found at the Web site `http://www.cisco.com`. IPv6 is being implemented in a three-phase plan for Cisco IOS software, starting in the fall of 2000. Microsoft also has released code for its IPv6 implementation to aid developers and testers in their migration plans. Most of the major vendors now support IPv6, particularly tunneling, which allows IPv6 packets to be transmitted over IPv4 networks.

The effect of IPv6, though, is not entirely negative. The system manager will gain some immediate benefits, such as more efficient network usage, increased security, and easier administration.

The alternative to converting to IPv6 is that a company eventually will be isolated and prohibited from participating in the future development and expansion of business on the Internet.

Summary

IPv6 is a necessary step forward to satisfy both the imminent exhaustion of available unique addresses with the current IP version 4, and the longer-term development of the Internet and global electronic computer communication. IPv6 increases the number of available addresses to such an extent that they will be sufficient to cater to the hundreds of computers or other devices per square meter of the Earth's surface.

In addition to providing an increased address space, IPv6 offers features such as increased security, classless addressing, more efficient use of broadcasting, guaranteed bandwidth, automatic address discovery, and the capability to accommodate non-IP address formats.

The system manager should be actively doing the following in preparation for the transition to IPv6:

- Seeking funding to allow the transition to go ahead
- Arranging suitable training for key staff members
- Having regular contact with the network manager to stay abreast of developments within his own environment
- Contacting vendors to ensure that their products either support IPv6 or will do so in the near future
- Making use of any test networks that might have been established to provide his department staff with the opportunity to become familiar with IPv6
- Ensuring that the users are kept informed of the planned developments and of any potential effect that it might have on them
- Planning for the transition to IPv6 and carrying out extensive co-existence testing

IPv6 is a certainty at some point in the future. A company that chooses not to migrate to IPv6 is one that does not intend to participate and benefit from the further development of the Internet.

Further references on IPv6 can found in the Appendix.

13

Network Monitoring

T HE SYSTEM MANAGER, ALTHOUGH NOT RESPONSIBLE for the network infrastructure and performance, must ensure that the systems he is responsible for can communicate at an acceptable speed with an acceptable response time. This might involve monitoring the throughput of data on a network interface, for example, or ensuring that other hosts are reachable—that is, they must respond to "Are you there?" messages, and also check the route taken to reach a remote host.

The term "network monitoring" for the Solaris system manager means checking the health of all the systems, to ensure that they can be "seen" on the network and that they are functioning correctly. Products such as Solstice Domain Manager, which is discussed in Chapter 14, "Network Management Tools," can be used as a monitoring tool, but it is primarily a network management product with the capability to take remedial action when a certain event occurs.

This chapter addresses the topic of network monitoring in a Solaris network environment. It takes a brief look at some factors that could affect network performance and security, such as subnetting and when it might be necessary. It also examines the difference between static and dynamic routing options. A section at the end of the chapter looks at troubleshooting some network problems, identifying some useful tools that can greatly assist with fault diagnosis and analysis. The first section discusses a network monitoring software package, Big Brother, outlining the type of functionality and reporting that can be utilized to determine how the systems on the network are performing.

Big Brother—A Network Monitoring Product

Big Brother is a network monitoring product that is freely available in the public domain. It can be obtained from the Big Brother Web site at http://www.bb4.com. Although the product itself is free, the writer(s) of the software offer formal support and licensing, if required. Big Brother comes complete with source code and access to extensive documentation, including Frequently Asked Question (FAQ) lists.

Big Brother is designed to allow anyone, but primarily administrators, to see how the systems and network are performing in near real time from any Web browser. It displays information as Web pages and is easy to read and understand. Figure 13.1 shows a typical top-level screen.

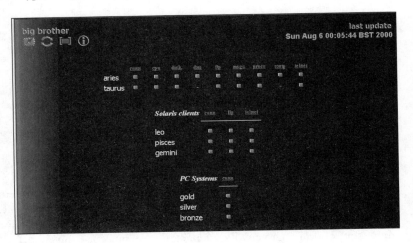

Figure 13.1 The clear nature of the displays and the ease of configuration make Big Brother an attractive option.

The display shows the systems being monitored down the left side and the tests for each system across the top. The user ends up seeing a matrix of color-coded dots on the screen, with green representing "no problems" and red representing "big problems." The background color of the status Web pages is also coded according to the most serious condition of any monitored element at that time.

Big Brother is a system and network monitoring package; it does not carry out any management, corrective action, or proactive maintenance. It highlights a problem and then the administrator fixes it. Big Brother is suitable for smaller installations; larger companies might use a more comprehensive monitoring and management product, such as Solstice Site/Domain Manager, which is discussed in detail in Chapter 14.

The software is downloaded and installed on a designated Big Brother server, which needs to be running Web server software, such as Apache, for hosting the Web pages. It includes support for testing FTP, HTTP, HTTPS, SMTP, POP3, DNS, Telnet,

IMAP, NNTP, and SSH servers as the default, but other tests can easily be added. The Big Brother software polls systems at regular intervals and retrieves information about its current status. An optional element is available to install Big Brother client software on other systems to be able to monitor disk space, CPU usage, and system messages. These clients send (push) the information to the Big Brother server at regular intervals instead of making the server poll (pull) the data. The Big Brother server can also check that specified processes are present and running. Figure 13.2 shows the disk space monitoring display for a client system.

Figure 13.2   The reporting tolerances can be easily set for each file system being monitored.

Big Brother supports additional plug-ins, which can be written in any language. Users have contributed hundreds of extra plug-ins for a variety of purposes, including monitoring the CPU temperature on Solaris systems, checking Oracle or Sybase databases, and so on. A full list of the plug-ins available for download can be found on the World Wide Web at http://www.deadcat.net.

The product is flexible in that all alarms and warnings are completely configurable so that they can be modified to suit the particular needs of a business. Also, external scripts can be written and included, for example, to monitor and report on bespoke or in-house applications software.

Big Brother includes a notification mechanism that is, again, fully configurable. It can automatically send paging requests and can be configured to notify based on a variety of criteria. Acknowledgement and escalation procedures are also built into the product.

As another feature of Big Brother, the product supports historical reporting, which can be used to determine whether SLAs are being met or to analyze the cause of a problem after the event. Figure 13.3 demonstrates a CPU usage event report.

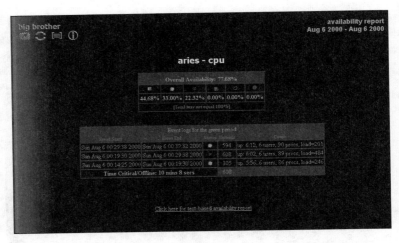

Figure 13.3 The background color provides an insight into the severity of the event, and the report shows additional information.

Network Capacity

As the speed of computer systems increases exponentially each year, the network itself rather than the processing power of the systems is in danger of becoming a bottleneck. Gigabit and fiber networks have helped to redress the balance, but it is still necessary to monitor the usage of the network—or segments of it—to establish whether it is capable of supporting the demand being placed upon it.

Most company computer networks can be divided into three general structures: the corporate backbone or wide area network (WAN), the campus backbone, and local area network (LAN) connections. These three structures require different levels of service and are discussed in this section.

- **Corporate backbone**—A large number of companies tend to use the fastest (and most expensive) network hardware for the corporate *backbone*—that is, the main spine running through the company's IT infrastructure, much like a freeway connecting several cities. This backbone is used primarily to interconnect departments (or sites) and to provide services affecting the entire company, such as domain name services, firewalls, and the main routing infrastructure. A network capacity of 100Mbps is the minimum for a large organization, although this may prove to be insufficient and too slow to provide an acceptable level of service.

- **Campus backbone**—This part of the network typically contains servers providing services to specific departments. A network capacity of 100Mbps is normally required because the kind of services being provided at this level include email servers, file servers, and application servers. Demand is likely to be high but is more localized than that required of the corporate backbone. This level of the network can be likened to the major roads leading from the freeway to the various towns.

- **LAN connections**—In the road analogy, this level represents the streets that lead to individual houses. The bandwidth requirement is again more localized, so demand is reduced. Connections to individual hosts normally carry less traffic than at the higher levels, where the services being provided are more generic and are applicable to many hosts. A 10Mbps network has typically been used to serve this level of the corporate network, but modern, busy offices find that it is quickly becoming insufficient for their needs. More companies are upgrading this network level to 100Mbps.

This list is intended to be a general overview of a company's network. On some occasions individual users might require a significant bandwidth—for example, the transmission of video data. In these instances, dedicated subnetworks can be installed to provide additional bandwidth. Devices such as the Sun QuadFast Ethernet card can be configured to act as a "large data pipe," allowing four separate 100Mbps connections into one 400Mbps connection. This can be doubled to 800Mbps if Sun Trunking software is used with compatible switch equipment.

Network Load

It is difficult and expensive to accurately determine the load being placed on a network, but a reasonable and useful estimate can be obtained by examining the number of "collisions" occurring on the network interface. By carrying out this exercise on a number of systems distributed around the network, a more accurate estimate can be calculated. In addition, this helps to identify network segments of particularly high (or low) usage.

A simple and effective way of gathering this information is to run the `netstat` command with the `-i` switch. Listing 13.1 contains some sample output.

Listing 13.1 **Sample Output from Using the Command *netstat -i* to Gather Network Interface Statistical Information**

```
taurus# netstat -i 3
```

input		le0 output			input	(Total)	output		
packets	errs	packets	errs	colls	packets	errs	packets	errs	colls
221981	5	302743	1	29087	283625	5	364387	1	29087
981	**0**	**2095**	**0**	**670**	**991**	**0**	**2105**	**0**	**670**
945	0	2025	0	847	953	0	2033	0	847
880	0	1901	0	1416	890	0	1911	0	1416
862	0	1862	0	1306	868	0	1868	0	1306
596	0	1249	0	857	606	0	1259	0	857
864	0	1872	0	417	872	0	1880	0	417
963	0	2083	0	588	971	0	2091	0	588
955	0	2050	0	535	963	0	2058	0	535
997	0	2114	0	532	1007	0	2124	0	532
928	0	2002	0	538	936	0	2010	0	538
1012	0	1980	0	505	1020	0	1988	0	505
947	0	2071	0	518	955	0	2079	0	518
935	0	2016	0	551	945	0	2026	0	551
978	0	2112	0	583	986	0	2120	0	583
934	0	2012	0	519	944	0	2022	0	519
986	0	2121	0	570	994	0	2129	0	570
923	0	2008	0	508	933	0	2018	0	508
944	0	2052	0	484	952	0	2060	0	484
975	0	2105	0	568	985	0	2115	0	568
432	0	986	0	295	440	0	994	0	295
350	0	824	0	235	358	0	832	0	235
360	0	850	0	251	368	0	858	0	251
371	0	877	0	231	381	0	887	0	231
360	0	853	0	247	368	0	861	0	247
373	0	879	0	260	383	0	889	0	260

```
taurus#
```

The sample output from Listing 13.1 is useful because it shows a heavily loaded network interface. The line in bold text displays a set of typical values that can be used to see the current collision rate at a glance.

The interface counted 2,095 output packets—that is, packets of data that were sent onto the network. Of those packets, 670 resulted in a collision—meaning that they never arrived and had to be retransmitted. To calculate an approximate collision rate (as a percentage), divide the number of collisions by the number of output packets and multiply by 100:

Collision rate = (670 ÷ 2095) × 100 = 31.9%

In this example, 31% of packets being transmitted onto the network are colliding with other packets and require retransmission. A network functioning normally should expect the collision rate to be 2% or less. A collision rate of between 2% and about 8–10% depicts a normal, busy network, but anything over 10% is a clear indication that the network (or at least the segment relating to the system being examined) is too heavily loaded and needs to be addressed.

The previous example describes a nonswitched Ethernet network, where collisions are often an issue to be addressed. Of course a Token Ring network, including FDDI, does not suffer in the same way that an Ethernet network does because the use of a token determines which (single) host can send traffic. In a switched network, the "switching" of traffic virtually eliminates the issue of collisions and is a solution to a heavy-loaded nonswitched Ethernet network, as is subnetting.

The next section describes subnetting, a method of segmenting the network to reduce the circulation of network traffic and thus reduce the collision rate. It also discusses some other benefits that subnetting provides.

Subnets

Subnetting involves segmenting an existing network into a number of smaller, separate networks. Subnetting might be considered to be a valid option for several reasons:

- **Collision rate**—If the number of collisions is high, as in Listing 13.1, then splitting the network into a number of subnetworks localizes the propagation of the majority of the network traffic.

- **Large numbers of hosts**—A large number of hosts exist on a particular network—say, greater than 25 or 30.

- **Performance**—Performance of network applications is degrading as more users access the network.

- **Isolating network power users**—Users of network-intensive applications can be provided with a dedicated subnetwork so that their usage does not adversely affect other users. A good example of this is in an engineering section, where graphical models are shared between a server and a small number of users.

- **Security**—The use of subnetworks is inherently more secure because network packets are restricted to the subnetted network segment instead of being propagated to the whole network. For example, a standard class C network, 210.127.8.0 supporting 255 hosts (with a network mask of 255.255.255.0), could be segmented, say, into 15 smaller networks, each of 14 hosts (by modifying the network mask to 255.255.255.240).

Benefits of Subnets

Splitting a network into several smaller subnetworks has a number of advantages:

- **Reduced traffic**—The amount of network traffic propagated to all hosts is reduced, improving the performance for the majority of users.

- **Fault diagnosis**—When diagnosing a network problem, it is easier to isolate smaller, existing portions of the network to assist with analysis and thus identify the cause of the problem. This also reduces the effect on the user community.

- **Testing**—The use of subnetworks allows small, manageable portions of the network to be used for testing and pilot implementations of applications, restricting the effect on other users. The subnetwork can be isolated from the "main" network quite easily to provide a standalone test facility when required.

- **IP address usage**—With the number of available IP addresses dwindling, subnetting can often make better use of existing IP address allocations.

- **Security**—Network traffic can be restricted to a small number of hosts on the subnetwork so that potentially sensitive information is not distributed too widely.

Of course, subnetting is not just a case of deciding what to do and then changing the network mask. Three basic steps are involved:

- The existing network must be physically split to mirror the required changes. This may involve the addition of network bridges or similar network devices.

- All affected nodes must be modified—that is, you must change the IP addresses and the network mask of each system that is changed to belong to the new subnetwork. There might also need to be modifications to DNS tables so that the addresses can be resolved by external connections.

- The new subnetwork needs to have a route supplied so that the hosts can communicate effectively with other networks or subnetworks.

Routing

Computer networks need to utilize some means of routing (or forwarding) mechanism so that communication can take place between two hosts, even though they may not be directly connected. Returning to the road analogy, routing loosely represents the use of maps. Take the example of traveling from Los Angeles, California, to a specific address in Las Vegas, Nevada. First, a map is needed to find out how to get to Las Vegas. Then, as the destination approaches, a more detailed map provides specific street information. Routing is similar in that, initially, the goal is to get to the corporate router on the required site. Other routers that are internal to the site direct the network packet to the correct network segment, and the packet arrives at the destination.

Companies usually have one router that acts as an external interface to the rest of the world through which all incoming and outgoing traffic will pass. The external router also must be capable of routing traffic internally within the company to deliver packets destined for specific hosts. Internal routing can be managed in two ways: static routing, in which packets are sent to a central point for distribution; or dynamic routing, in which the best route is determined at the time the packet is sent. Both of these routing methods are discussed next.

Static Routing

Static routing involves each host on the network sending all network traffic to a specified address for further distribution. This address is entered into the file /etc/defaultrouter. When the system is restarted, the address found in this file will be used as the default "route" for all network traffic. The network administrator must manually build routing tables on the router so that data can be delivered anywhere on the local network.

Static routing is used primarily on networks on which there is little or no change because it requires significant manual intervention when changes occur. For example, if the router address is changed, each host must have the file /etc/defaultrouter amended, and the network administrator must rebuild the routing tables to reflect the change.

A disadvantage of static routing is that it creates a single point of failure—that is, if the router fails, the network becomes unavailable because all the hosts have the address hard-coded in the /etc/defaultrouter file.

Static routing, however, can be considered more secure than dynamic routing. This is because the default route address is fixed so that all traffic follows a predefined route; the traffic cannot be deviated by an unauthorized system being attached to the network, as is possible using dynamic routing where routes are advertised on the network.

Dynamic Routing

In an environment in which the structure of the network changes frequently, dynamic routing provides the flexibility to adapt to the changes with little or no manual intervention.

Each host on the network runs a program that builds and maintains its own routing table. In Solaris, the program is the routing daemon—in.routed for internal routing, or the gateway daemon, in.gated, if both internal and external routing are used. The route to use for network traffic is determined at the time the request is sent and is made more flexible by the fact that the host will "ask" its network neighbor for a route if it doesn't "know" how to send to the required destination. However, dynamic routing is not recommended for leaf nodes of a network—that is, hosts not providing routing services for other systems. These nodes should use static routing so that the routers are not flooded with broadcasts from nonrouting hosts wanting to advertise their IP address.

Dynamic routing is considerably more processor-intensive than static routing. However, it also requires much less manual intervention and is inherently more reliable than static routing because there is no single point of failure (as long as more than one route can physically be used). For example, if a major router fails and becomes unavailable, the routing algorithm will try to determine an alternate route to use (unlike static routing, in which the route is fixed).

A potential disadvantage of dynamic routing is the advertising of routing information, a definite negative aspect for secure environments. It is possible, for example, for an unauthorized intruder to attach a host to the network and then to start acting as a router, advertising routes to destinations that don't exist, or capturing network traffic for malicious purposes. The dynamic nature of this routing method means that hosts might "learn" new routes from this bogus host. Static routing does not allow this to happen because of the fixed configuration of the central router.

Several dynamic routing protocols exist, generally split into two categories:

- **Interior gateway protocols (IGP), also known as intradomain routing protocols**—Communication is between two routers within the same organization. The most popular of these has been the Routing Information Protocol (RIP), but a newer one is Open Shortest Path First (OSPF).

- **Exterior gateway protocols (EGP), also known as interdomain routing protocols**—Communication is between routers from different organizations or networks. The most popular EGP has been the Exterior Gateway Protocol (EGP), although a newer one is the Border Gateway Protocol (BGP).

Troubleshooting Network Problems

Network problems can be manifested in a variety of scenarios. Some are very difficult to diagnose, while others become apparent very quickly. The system manager, although not normally responsible for the network, must know about network issues and how they can affect the systems that he is responsible for.

The majority of larger installations make use of network management software, such as Solstice Domain Manager (discussed in Chapter 14) in one form or another, so most of the problems that will be encountered should be dealt with by this software. However, to configure a network management product, a level of knowledge is required to understand exactly what events are being monitored and to determine the remedial action to take if it occurs.

This section looks at some of the basic troubleshooting tools used to determine the status of a system's network capability and also to diagnose network-related problems.

ifconfig

The `ifconfig` command is probably the first command to be run when diagnosing a network problem. From the information returned by the command, it is possible to verify that the network interface is functioning correctly, that the IP and broadcast addresses are correct, and that the network mask being used is also correct. Listing 13.2 contains the result from running the `ifconfig` command with the `-a` flag to show all network interfaces.

Listing 13.2 **Sample Output from the Command *ifconfig* *-a* Showing the Status of All Connected Network Interfaces**

```
taurus# ifconfig -a
lo0: flags=849<UP,LOOPBACK,RUNNING,MULTICAST> mtu 8232
        inet 127.0.0.1 netmask ffffff00
le0: flags=863<UP,BROADCAST,NOTRAILERS,RUNNING,MULTICAST> mtu 1500
        inet 210.127.8.3 netmask ffffff00 broadcast 210.127.8.255
        ether 8:0:20:a:a1:2a
taurus#
```

ping

The `ping` command is another extremely popular network monitoring tool. It is used for a number of purposes:

- To determine whether a known remote system can be contacted
- To see if a remote system is visible on the network and can respond to requests
- To see the round-trip time of sending a data packet to a remote host
- To establish the amount (if any) of packet loss being suffered on a communications link between two hosts

Listing 13.3 contains sample output from two different executions of the `ping` command. The first one merely establishes whether the remote host is responding to requests. The second sends a fixed-size data packet and records the time taken to send it, as well as overall statistics on round-trip times and packet loss.

Listing 13.3 **Two Options from the *ping* Command, One to Establish the Status of a Remote System and One to Determine Transmission Times and Reliability**

```
leo# ping taurus
taurus is alive
[ /export/home/john ]
leo#


leo# ping -s taurus
PING taurus: 56 data bytes
64 bytes from taurus (210.127.8.3): icmp_seq=0. time=15. ms
64 bytes from taurus (210.127.8.3): icmp_seq=1. time=6. ms
64 bytes from taurus (210.127.8.3): icmp_seq=2. time=5. ms
64 bytes from taurus (210.127.8.3): icmp_seq=3. time=5. ms
64 bytes from taurus (210.127.8.3): icmp_seq=4. time=6. ms
64 bytes from taurus (210.127.8.3): icmp_seq=5. time=5. ms
64 bytes from taurus (210.127.8.3): icmp_seq=6. time=6. ms
64 bytes from taurus (210.127.8.3): icmp_seq=7. time=6. ms
64 bytes from taurus (210.127.8.3): icmp_seq=8. time=5. ms
64 bytes from taurus (210.127.8.3): icmp_seq=9. time=5. ms
64 bytes from taurus (210.127.8.3): icmp_seq=10. time=5. ms
64 bytes from taurus (210.127.8.3): icmp_seq=11. time=6. ms
64 bytes from taurus (210.127.8.3): icmp_seq=12. time=5. ms
64 bytes from taurus (210.127.8.3): icmp_seq=13. time=5. ms
64 bytes from taurus (210.127.8.3): icmp_seq=14. time=5. ms
64 bytes from taurus (210.127.8.3): icmp_seq=15. time=7. ms
64 bytes from taurus (210.127.8.3): icmp_seq=16. time=5. ms
64 bytes from taurus (210.127.8.3): icmp_seq=17. time=5. ms
^C
— —taurus PING Statistics— —
18 packets transmitted, 18 packets received, 0% packet loss
round-trip (ms)  min/avg/max = 5/5/15
leo#
```

With the ever-increasing use of firewalls, it is possible that the network administrator might disable the protocol that ping uses—that is, the Internet Control Message Protocol (ICMP). If this protocol is disabled, then any ping messages that pass through the firewall will fail, indicating (perhaps falsely) that a system is down.

netstat

The netstat command has a wide range of uses. It can be used to monitor the state of a network interface, to determine which network connections are established (or hung) with remote systems, to provide information based on specific network protocols, and also to display the internal routing table.

As an example, consider Listing 13.4, which contains the first of two samples of output from the netstat command. The output is from a Sun Enterprise 250 running

Solaris 2.6, where the import of an Oracle database was taking an unacceptable amount of time yet all network connections were working as expected. On running the `netstat -i` command, with an interval of 5 seconds, a high number of input errors were apparent.

Listing 13.4 **Sample Output from the Command *netstat -i* Showing the Abnormally High Number of Input Errors on the Network Interface**

```
leo# netstat -i 5
 input   hme0      output                input   (Total)  output
packets  errs     packets    errs  colls packets errs      packets errs    colls
44845867 25576336 3627474     204  122543 44952869 25576336 3734476  204    122543
     108       44       28       0     0      108       44       28    0        0
      99       48       25       0     0       99       48       25    0        0
     182       77       26       0     0      182       77       26    0        0
     154       86       26       0     0      154       86       26    0        0
     179      113       25       0     0      179      113       25    0        0
      89       42       27       0     0       89       42       27    0        0
     101       47       28       0     0      101       47       28    0        0
     111       38       26       0     0      111       38       26    0        0
     136       55       25       0     0      136       55       25    0        0
     150       59       35       0     1      150       59       35    0        1
leo#
```

Some searching on the Sunsolve database revealed a patch for the symptoms. That patch was duly installed and fixed the problem, as displayed in Listing 13.5, which shows the same network interface following the patch installation.

Listing 13.5 **Sample Output from the Command *netstat -i* Showing That the Problem Is Resolved**

```
leo# netstat -i 5
 input   hme0      output              input  (Total)  output
packets  errs     packets    errs colls packets errs    packets errs    colls
8623134     0     707459      103 37491 8633461   0     717786   103    37491
     138       0       21        0    0     138     0       21    0        0
      64       0       22        0    0      64     0       22    0        0
     106       0       21        0    0     106     0       21    0        0
      92       0       21        0    0      92     0       21    0        0
     150       0       24        0    0     150     0       24    0        0
      82       0       21        0    0      82     0       21    0        0
     128       0       21        0    0     128     0       21    0        0
     114       0       21        0    0     114     0       21    0        0
      93       0       21        0    0      93     0       21    0        0
     124       0       22        0    0     126     0       24    0        0
     109       0       29        0    0     111     0       31    0        0
leo#
```

This example was more interesting because it did not appear to be a network problem at all. Indeed, this indicated a performance issue because the import took much longer to complete than was expected.

traceroute

The traceroute command does exactly as you would expect: It traces the path taken to get from one host to another. It displays information about each of the "hops" along the way. This command is extremely useful when trying to determine why two hosts are incapable of communicating because it will indicate routers along the way that are not responding. Listing 13.6 shows an example of the traceroute command.

Listing 13.6   **The *traceroute* Command Showing the Path Taken to Reach a Remote Host**

```
leo# traceroute taurus
traceroute to taurus (210.127.8.3), 30 hops max, 40 byte packets
leo-router (209.127.8.1)  3 ms 2 ms  2 ms
bb1-gate-x (188.101.25.67)  22 ms 21 ms  18 ms
  3   bb2-gate-a (187.100.80.10)  32 ms 29 ms  17 ms
  4   bb5-area-xconn-alpha (192.150.100.68)  7 ms 5 ms  3 ms
  5   taurus-router (210.127.8.1)  6 ms 4 ms  3 ms
  6   taurus (210.127.8.3)  7 ms 5 ms  3 ms
leo#
```

snoop

The snoop command is a powerful network command that captures packets on a network interface. The captured packets can be displayed on the screen as they occur or can be saved to a file for later analysis. The snoop command requires superuser privilege to run because it puts the network interface into promiscuous mode so that all packets can be captured. Listing 13.7 demonstrates the type of information that can be gathered with this command. The example shows a simple Telnet connection being established by user john with his password of john1.

It is worth noting that snoop will capture all traffic on a nonswitched network, including traffic between other systems that might not have been requested. On a switched network, however, snoop will capture only packets on the system on which the command is being run and any systems communicating with it; network traffic from other systems will not be captured.

The command is extremely useful, however, particularly when trying to see if acknowledgements are being received from a remote host.

Listing 13.7 The *snoop* Command Can Even Capture Password Information That Is Transmitted Across the Network

```
34   0.04790          aries-> taurus       TELNET C port=60321
35   0.00006          taurus -> aries      TELNET R port=60321 \377\373\1\3
77\375\1login:
36   0.00045           aries-> taurus       TELNET C port=60321
37   0.00015          taurus -> aries      TELNET R port=60321
38   0.04937           aries-> taurus       TELNET C port=60321
39   0.60130           aries-> taurus       TELNET C port=60321 j
40   0.00021          taurus -> aries      TELNET R port=60321 j
41   0.04841           aries-> taurus       TELNET C port=60321
42   0.01563           aries-> taurus       TELNET C port=60321 o
43   0.00019          taurus -> aries      TELNET R port=60321 o
44   0.04418           aries-> taurus       TELNET C port=60321
45   0.11145           aries-> taurus       TELNET C port=60321 h
46   0.00013          taurus -> aries      TELNET R port=60321 h
47   0.04839           aries-> taurus       TELNET C port=60321
48   0.12778           aries-> taurus       TELNET C port=60321 n
49   0.00012          taurus -> aries      TELNET R port=60321 n
50   0.04208           aries-> taurus       TELNET C port=60321
51   0.31836           aries-> taurus       TELNET C port=60321
52   0.00021          taurus -> aries      TELNET R port=60321
53   0.04148           aries-> taurus       TELNET C port=60321
54   0.00004          taurus -> aries      TELNET R port=60321 Password:
55   0.04991           aries-> taurus       TELNET C port=60321
56   0.53745           aries-> taurus       TELNET C port=60321 j
57   0.09865          taurus -> aries      TELNET R port=60321
58   0.00022           aries-> taurus       TELNET C port=60321 o
59   0.09976          taurus -> aries      TELNET R port=60321
60   0.03078           aries-> taurus       TELNET C port=60321 h
61   0.09923          taurus -> aries      TELNET R port=60321
62   0.07719           aries-> taurus       TELNET C port=60321 n
63   0.09280          taurus -> aries      TELNET R port=60321
64   0.09994          aries-> taurus       TELNET C port=60321 1
65   0.10005          taurus -> aries      TELNET R port=60321
66   0.12767          aries-> taurus       TELNET C port=60321
67   0.00041          taurus -> aries      TELNET R port=60321
68   0.04594          aries-> taurus       TELNET C port=60321
69   0.00007          taurus -> aries      TELNET R port=60321 Last login:
Wed Jan  3 19:05:21 from aries
70   0.04989          aries-> taurus       TELNET C port=60321
71   0.00005          taurus -> aries      TELNET R port=60321 Sun Microsys
tems Inc
72   0.04991          aries-> taurus       TELNET C port=60321
73   0.01966          taurus -> aries      TELNET R port=60321 [ /export/ho
me/john
```

lsof

All the commands mentioned previously in this section are bundled with the standard installation of the Solaris operating environment. This one, lsof, is freely available in the public domain and can be downloaded from a number of sites, such as `http://www.sunfreeware.com`.

The lsof command displays the files that are opened by processes running on the system. It is extremely useful when trying to determine why a file system cannot be unmounted. The information provided is often sufficient for the administrator to identify the offending process and take the appropriate action.

Listing 13.8 shows the number of open files owned by user john, who has simply logged on to the system.

Listing 13.8   **The *lsof* Command Shows How Many Files a User Opens Merely by Logging On and Running a Single Shell**

```
aries# lsof -u john
COMMAND        PID     USER    FD      TYPE    DEVICE   SIZE/OFF       NODE
NAME
ksh            16282   john    cwd     VDIR    32,56    1024   10176
/export/home/john
ksh            16282   john    txt     VREG    32,6     192764  36481
/usr/bin/ksh
ksh            16282   john    txt     VREG    32,6     1115940 23161
/usr/lib/libc.so.1
ksh            16282   john    txt     VREG    32,6     832236  22968
/usr/lib/libnsl.so.1
ksh            16282   john    txt     VREG    32,6     17252  18373
/usr/platform/sun4u/lib/libc_psr.so.1
ksh            16282   john    txt     VREG    32,6     19876  22890
/usr/lib/libmp.so.2
ksh            16282   john    txt     VREG    32,6     56988  22908
/usr/lib/libsocket.so.1
ksh            16282   john    txt     VREG    32,6     4600   23169
/usr/lib/libdl.so.1
ksh            16282   john    txt     VREG    32,6     183060  22768
/usr/lib/ld.so.1
ksh            16282   john    0u      VCHR    24,0     0t670181
135213/devices/pseudo/pts@0:0->ttcompat->ldterm->ptem->pts
ksh            16282   john    1u      VCHR    24,0     0t670181
135213/devices/pseudo/pts@0:0->ttcompat->ldterm->ptem->pts
ksh            16282   john    2u      VCHR    24,0     0t670181
135213/devices/pseudo/pts@0:0->ttcompat->ldterm->ptem->pts
ksh            16282   john    63u     VREG    32,56    4406   10192
/export/home/john/.sh_history
aries#
```

Summary

It is becoming harder to draw the line between system management and network management because there are frequent overlaps where the precise responsibility is very hard to determine. Although the system manager is not being responsible for the health of the network, he must put in place sufficient monitoring of his systems to ensure, as far as possible, that connectivity is maintained and the network response times are acceptable to his customers.

Big Brother is a system and network monitoring tool that is freely available, although it is normally sufficient only for relatively small networks. It is a useful product because it identifies problems and records information, but it does not have the capability to take remedial action if a threshold is exceeded. To do this, a more comprehensive management product, such as Solstice Domain Manager, is required.

The system manager needs to determine the network capacity and the current load before trying to add more nodes. He can provide firm evidence if a network segment appears to be overloaded and can meet with the network manager to resolve the problem, possibly by creating a number of subnetworks so that the network traffic is restricted to a smaller proportion of the hosts.

Troubleshooting is a significant part of the system manager's job. The system manager must possess sufficient knowledge about the systems and the network tools available to him. Basic commands such as `ifconfig`, `ping`, `netstat`, `traceroute`, and `snoop` are all provided as part of the Solaris operating environment. A further useful command is `lsof`, which is freely available in the public domain.

14

Network Management Tools

THE CONTINUING EXPANSION OF COMPUTER NETWORKS and the rapid growth of client/server computing has added another problem for today's companies to deal with: how to manage these complex and heterogeneous environments that can often number thousands of systems in different locations.

In this instance, network management does not encompass the actual management of the network infrastructure, such as hubs, switches, and so on. Instead, it deals with the systems that comprise the network, for which the system manager has responsibility. The management of the network itself is the responsibility of the network manager.

The task facing the system manager is more one of remote systems management, and choosing a suitable off-the-shelf product with which to achieve it can be a difficult and sometimes extremely expensive exercise. Several companies have resorted to writing their own "in-house" network management applications, but this has the disadvantage of being customized to their own specific network; it also carries the overhead of having to maintain and update it when new methods or network protocols are implemented.

The objective of this chapter is to highlight some of the products that are available and to provide insight into the type of use to which they can be put. It is not intended to be an in-depth guide of how to use any of them. However, as part of the discussion of Solstice Domain Manager, this chapter gives a more detailed example of SunNet Manager, which is incorporated as part of Solstice Domain Manager.

This chapter takes a look at some of the network products available from Sun Microsystems designed to manage a Solaris network, no matter how small or large it happens to be:

- The first section describes in detail the Solstice Domain and Site Manager products, along with Co-Operative Consoles. This includes detailing how they can be used together to effectively manage a Solaris-based network of computer systems.
- The second product, Solstice Bandwidth Manager, involves the allocation of guaranteed network bandwidth so that mission-critical activities can be carried out in accordance with the criteria specified by an SLA.
- The final Sun product, Solstice Adminsuite, is covered with a brief look at this collection of utilities that allows remote system administration for a number of Solaris systems.

The products listed here collectively deliver the necessary tools to provide the best quality of service to the customer while also being fully scalable to allow for future expansion or diversity.

Several other network management products available on the commercial market, such as HP Openview, CA Unicenter, Tivoli Netview, and BMC Patrol, would be suitable for multivendor environments. A brief description of these other products appears at the end of this chapter.

Benefits of Using Network Management Tools

Traditionally, networks of interconnected computer systems required someone to sit at a console, or a number of consoles, checking the status of each machine periodically. This was normally the system administrator or sometimes a computer operator. The advent of network management software means that the systems can be monitored from a single position. When set up correctly, there isn't really anything to monitor, unless the console receives an alarm. In this case, it normally warns the operator by either flashing an icon or sounding an audible alarm—it also writes to a log file.

Network management tools allow distributed systems to be managed from a centralized management console; for resilience, from multiple consoles acting as peers with the same privileges; or as a network management hierarchy.

The health of the entire network can be seen from a single screen, giving a global view of every computer system that the system manager is responsible for. This reduces the staff resources needed not only at the central site, but also at remote sites because management can be carried out remotely. This is especially valuable for out-of-business-hours management.

A major benefit of a network management tool is that the management console is automatically informed of any problems (called events) as the remote systems are being regularly polled to see if any thresholds have been exceeded or conditions have been met. With a large network, however, there might be numerous events, some of which require immediate attention. The event processing and notification software included with a network management product also includes a priority mechanism allowing important events to be highlighted and attended to first. The Solstice Domain Manager suite of software additionally provides the capability to launch a program or script when a specified event condition is encountered, for example, to take corrective action such as compressing or removing files if a disk partition becomes full or reaches a predefined capacity threshold.

Performance and statistical information can be gathered and displayed as text or in graphical form for later analysis and reporting. This provides useful data when trying to establish whether service level agreement targets have been achieved.

Sun Network Management Products

Since its inception, Sun Microsystems has been heavily involved with network computing. Therefore, it's no surprise that the company has produced the leader in network management software products, the Solstice Domain Manager suite, described in detail in this section.

The products being described in this section do not all merely show different ways of doing the same thing. They each have a separate purpose, as follows:

- Solstice Domain Manager manages the entire network of computer systems, whereas Solstice Site Manager carries out the same functions but on a smaller, single-site basis.

- The Solstice Bandwidth Manager product ensures that mission-critical applications are guaranteed the necessary network priority to meet processing deadlines.

- Solstice Adminsuite is a set of tools for carrying out system administration tasks on multiple Solaris systems.

When these Sun products are used together, they provide all the necessary functionality to monitor and manage a Solaris installation, from a small site to a large enterprise.

Solstice Site Manager

The Solstice Site Manager software product is built upon the proven SunNet Manager software and can effectively manage up to 100 separate nodes. It addresses the issue of managing smaller computing environments based on a single site. The product is fully scalable and runs the same application, database, and user interface on all Sun platforms, whether a small SPARCstation or a large ULTRA enterprise server.

A typical view as seen by the administrator is shown in Figure 14.1.

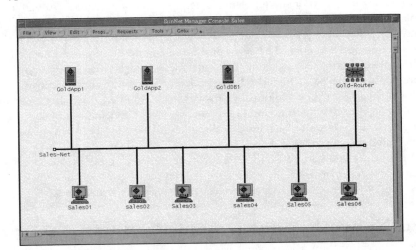

Figure 14.1 The flexible configuration enables views to be configured to suit the user.

Solstice Site Manager includes the entire functionality from SunNet Manager as well as a limited version of the Cooperative Consoles software. The following sections describe the capabilities of Solstice Site Manager.

Network Discovery and Layout Tools

This tool automatically finds devices on the network, enters the details in the database, and creates an icon on the top-level view. The information entered includes at least the IP address of the discovered device. However, it uses this to name the device, which is not always desirable; a hostname normally is used to identify a system on the display. When in the database, a discovered object can be managed by the software and made subject to data and event requests.

This facility is useful because it identifies any new (and possibly unauthorized) devices that have been connected to the network. It is also very network-intensive, so some care should be taken about when this utility is run to avoid affecting the user community.

The layout tool attempts to lay out the screen in a meaningful way, having discovered the visible devices on the network. The layout tool reads the information in the management database and automatically places the objects and connections in one of three layout styles:

- **Hierarchical**—The elements are organized into a hierarchy of subnetworks.
- **Circular**—This style organizes subnetworks into circles.
- **Symmetric**—The elements are laid out in a uniform symmetric distribution on the top-level screen.

Inherited from Children

A feature of the original SunNet Manager is that the status of managed objects is passed upward through the hierarchy of user-defined views. For example, a single workstation in the sales department, located in Building1 and displaying a problem, will be noticed on the console screen several levels higher, where the whole site is displayed only as a number of buildings. The administrator then traverses through the views, to the building and then the department within the building, and so on, to locate the troubled system and deal with the problem.

Request Management Software

Data requests and event requests are sent to managed remote nodes and are handled through the request management software. Data requests gather specific data, such as disk capacity information or processor usage, for later analysis, whereas event requests set tolerances to be monitored. An alarm is raised if a tolerance is exceeded; the action to be taken and the form of the alarm are entirely user-configurable. Figure 14.2 shows an event request being initiated.

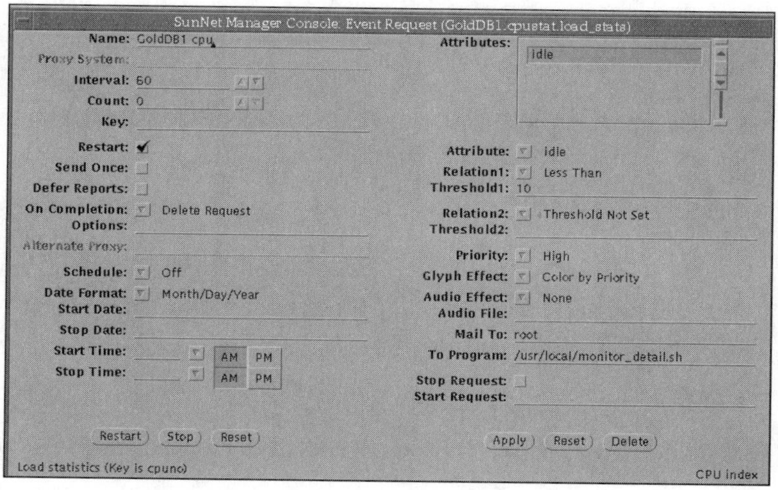

Figure 14.2 The versatile nature of the event management software features a variety of options to cater to all configurations.

In Figure 14.2, an event request is being submitted to monitor the CPU idle time on a database server, GoldDB1. It checks the system every 60 seconds to see if the idle attribute is less than 10%—that is, to see if the CPU is more than 90% busy. If this is true, then a mail message is sent to the root user, the icon for GoldDB1 will turn red (as defined by the attributes Glyph Effect and Priority), and the script /usr/local/monitor_detail.sh will be executed. By default, the priority colors are yellow for low priority, amber for medium priority, and red for high priority, although these can easily be changed. My own personal preference is to always create the managed objects with a color of green, symbolizing "go—no problems." The icon will change from its initial color only if an event is triggered.

Another useful feature is the "pending" state. When an event criteria is met, the icon is changed to a specified color (different from the three priorities); further event notifications for this device are suspended so that the administrator does not continually receive event alarms for the same device. When the problem has been rectified, the administrator can manually change the Glyph State to normal, and the events automatically start monitoring the device again.

Proxy Agents

One of the best features of the product is the proxy agents. Here, the Site Manager console delegates event requests to designated proxy systems. The result is that the proxy system polls the managed object (instead of the management console) and reports back to the console only when a threshold is exceeded or a test condition is met. This reduces the amount of network traffic that passes between the console and the managed objects. Proxy agents are normally local to the managed objects to reduce traffic further. Figure 14.3 demonstrates this kind of configuration.

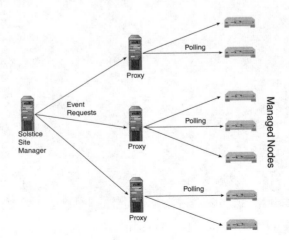

Figure 14.3 The delegation of requests to proxy agents greatly reduces the load and traffic that a management console must deal with.

Browser and Grapher Tools

The Browser tool provides access to the data that has been collected via data requests. The information is organized into individual streams, which contain the output from each data or event request for a specific device. Data that has been gathered can be viewed using this tool or can be selected for display using the Grapher tool.

The Grapher tool provides the administrator with the facility to view data graphically, either in 2D or 3D graphs. When a data request is submitted, the option exists to have the results sent straight to the Grapher tool. In this case, a cumulative graph will be created and updated as new data is received. The Grapher tool also accepts data that has been stored by the Browser tool. Figure 14.4 shows a cumulative graph from a data request monitoring CPU usage over a period of time.

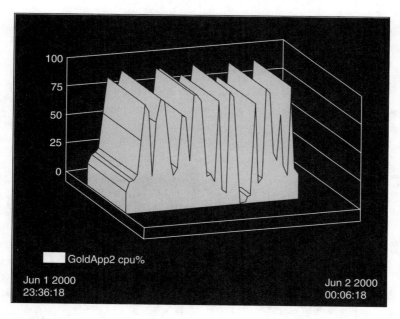

Figure 14.4   The data request graph shows clearly where usage peaks and troughs occur.

When a graph has been created, it is managed by the Grapher tool and can be merged easily with other graphs to create new graphs containing the composite data from the original graphs. Figure 14.5 shows the Grapher tool display.

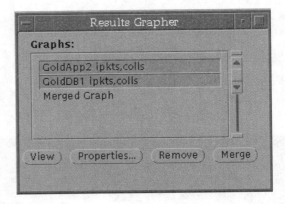

Figure 14.5   Select the graphs to be merged and click Merge.

This feature is useful because it allows graphical comparisons between multiple systems. Figure 14.6 displays the merged graph created from the data in Figure 14.5.

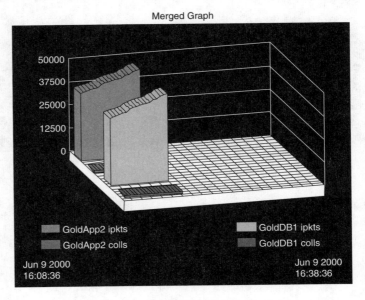

Figure 14.6   The merged graph enables attributes from several different data requests to be displayed as a single graph.

Novell NetWare Support (IPX Discover)

Solstice Site Manager can centralize network management by using the NetWare Management Agent (NMA), an SNMP agent sold by Novell that resides on NetWare servers running TCP/IP. This agent allows Site Manager to manage the NetWare server's file system, print queues, and users. Site Manager also can import the topology details from a Novell ManageWise network management console and can use this to view the PCs on the NetWare LAN as a separate view from the systems it is already managing.

Solstice Domain Manager

Solstice Domain Manager is the tool to use for large or multisite network management of Solaris systems, although it also manages multivendor environments. The software is designed to manage up to 10,000 separate nodes.

The Domain Manager software includes all the tools present in Solstice Site Manager, but there is no restriction on the number of managed nodes. In addition, it comprises the full version of Solstice Cooperative Consoles so that it can send and receive information to other consoles. Solstice Domain Manager is designed for use in large installations so that multiple Solstice Site Manager consoles can feed information into a Solstice Domain Manager, or even multiple Solstice Domain Manager systems. These can be configured as peer-to-peer devices, enabling shared administration capabilities, if required. Figure 14.7 shows how a typical configuration might connect multiple Solstice Site Manager consoles.

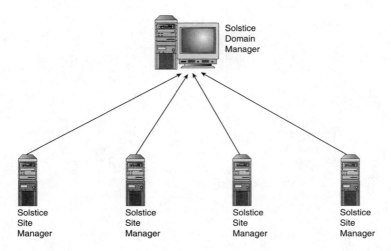

Figure 14.7 The Domain Manager console provides a further level of hierarchy and manages all the attached Site Manager Consoles, which, in turn, can still delegate requests to proxy servers.

A significant benefit of using a product such as Solstice Domain Manager is that multiple sites can be managed from a central console. This feature can be utilized to good effect, particularly during out-of-business hours, when there might not be any staff present at any of the remote sites.

Solstice Domain Manager meets the majority of the requirements for network management. However, more than 300 applications run on Solstice Site Manager and Domain Manager, providing additional network management capabilities and data analysis.

Solstice Cooperative Consoles

The Cooperative Consoles product is provided as part of Solstice Site Manager and Solstice Domain Manager. The Site Manager version is restricted in that it can send information only to another management console; it cannot receive information and act as a domain manager. The Solstice Domain Manager version contains a full release of Cooperative Consoles, allowing it to both send and receive information from other management consoles.

The real power of Solstice Domain Manager is that multiple domain managers can be flexibly configured to share information. Each console can be configured as a peer-to-peer console, allowing each to have equal access to the other so that they can monitor and control each other's resources, such as multiple Solstice Site Manager consoles. Alternatively, a Domain Manager console can be configured to receive from multiple management consoles but not to send information to them, making it a super network management console, as demonstrated in Figure 14.8.

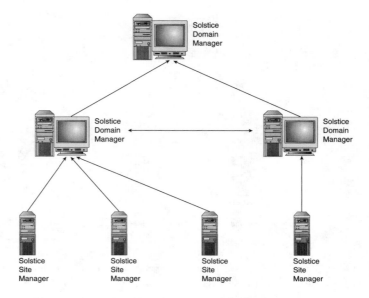

Figure 14.8   The super network management console provides overall corporate network management from a central location.

This facility is used particularly where sites might manage their own network during business hours but pass to a central network management console for out-of-hours monitoring and management. The out-of-hours console might act as the master for multiple sites but would not return information about its own activities to any other consoles.

Solstice Enterprise Manager

This is a product for managing large enterprises and complex networks. It is aimed directly at telecommunications and Internet service providers (ISP). It is probably not a product that the Solaris system manager would expect to use, unless working in these specific areas of business.

Enterprise Manager is mentioned here because, using the Cooperative Consoles software, it facilitates connecting Solstice Domain manager and Solstice Site manager consoles to Solstice Enterprise Manager for large-scale network and system management. Enterprise Manager is used to isolate complex system or network problems, resulting in speedier resolution and maintenance of high availability for customers.

Customization of Solstice Site/Domain Manager

Many organizations are happy with the facilities provided by Solstice Site and Domain Manager, but a few customizations can be made to enhance the usefulness of the product and to tailor it more specifically to the needs of the business.

I used SunNet Manager, the foundation of Solstice Domain and Site Manager, to define customized object types. The newly created objects were subsequently treated as a unit so that, for example, a single event and data request could be initiated on every system of this designated type. Also, I added extra functionality to the Tools menu so that housekeeping and administration tasks could be carried out from the same central management position. SunNet Manager was successfully implemented to manage and administer 15 large Sun servers and 300+ workstation clients.

The file in which to make these additions is /opt/SUNWconn/snm/struct/elements.schema, by default. This file defines all the known object types, as well as the commands available from these objects and the icons used to identify them. The elements.schema file can be edited using a standard text editor, such as vi.

To add a new object, you must edit three sections within the file, one to create a new record for the component, one to specify the icon to use, and one to declare the commands that the object type can run.

An abbreviated example of the relevant sections of the elements.schema file is shown in Listing 14.1, demonstrating the changes that need to be made to add a new data object type of DB-server.

Listing 14.1 **Abbreviated Version of the File elements.schema Showing the Values for a Default Type, sun–server, and a New Type, DB–server**

```
###################
# COMPONENTS
#

record component.sun-server (              # generic sun server
        string[64]      Name
        string[40]      IP_Address
        string[40]      User
        string[40]      Location
        string[80]      Description
        string[40]      SNMP_RdCommunity
        string[40]      SNMP_WrCommunity
        string[64]      SNMP_Vendor_Proxy
        int             SNMP_Timeout
        string[256]     SNMP_SysObjectId
        string[40]      Physical_Address
        string[60]      Created_by_cc
        string[64]      _groupId_Layout
)


record component.DB-server (               # Database server
        string[64]      Name
        string[40]      IP_Address
        string[40]      User
        string[40]      Location
        string[80]      Description
        string[40]      SNMP_RdCommunity
        string[40]      SNMP_WrCommunity
        string[64]      SNMP_Vendor_Proxy
        int             SNMP_Timeout
        string[256]     SNMP_SysObjectId
        string[40]      Physical_Address
        string[60]      Created_by_cc
        string[64]      _groupId_Layout
)
        .
        .
        .

instance elementCommand (
(component.sun-server      "Remote login..."  "$SNMHOME/bin/snm_cmdtool rlogin
%Name")
        (component.sun-server      "Telnet to Host..." "$SNMHOME/bin/snm_cmdtool
telnet %Name")
        (component.sun-server          "DB check..."
"$SNMHOME/bin/snm_cmdtool $SCRIPT_DIR/dbcheck %DBINST")
        (component.sun-server          "FS check..."
"$SNMHOME/bin/snm_cmdtool $SCRIPT_DIR/fscheck %Name")
        (component.sun-server          "USER check..."
"$SNMHOME/bin/snm_cmdtool $SCRIPT_DIR/usercheck %Name")
        (component.sun-server          "Start Backup..."
"$SNMHOME/bin/snm_cmdtool $SCRIPT_DIR/start_backup %Name")
        (component.sun-server          "Monitor Backup..."
```

```
"$SNMHOME/bin/snm_cmdtool $SCRIPT_DIR/mon_backup %Name")
(component.DB-server      "Remote login..."  "$SNMHOME/bin/snm_cmdtool rlogin
%Name")
        (component.DB-server      "Telnet to Host..." "$SNMHOME/bin/snm_cmdtool
telnet %Name")
        (component.DB-server          "DB check..."
"$SNMHOME/bin/snm_cmdtool $SCRIPT_DIR/dbcheck %DBINST")
        (component.DB-server          "FS check..."
"$SNMHOME/bin/snm_cmdtool $SCRIPT_DIR/fscheck %Name")
        (component.DB-server          "USER check..."
"$SNMHOME/bin/snm_cmdtool $SCRIPT_DIR/usercheck %Name")
        (component.DB-server          "Start Backup..."
"$SNMHOME/bin/snm_cmdtool $SCRIPT_DIR/start_backup %Name")
        (component.DB-server          "Monitor Backup..."
"$SNMHOME/bin/snm_cmdtool $SCRIPT_DIR/mon_backup %Name")
)
.
.
.
#
# Glyphs for components
#

instance elementGlyph(
( component.sun-server           sunserver2.icon)
( component.DB-server            DBserver.icon)
)
```

Figure 14.9 shows the newly created object being displayed on a Solstice Domain
Manager screen and the commands that are now available to be run.

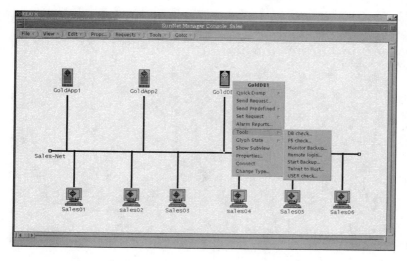

Figure 14.9 The flexible configuration enables administration and
housekeeping tasks to be run directly from the menu.

Solstice Bandwidth Manager

The Bandwidth Manager product is discussed here because it is sometimes necessary for the system manager to guarantee either delivery of information or an acceptable response time. Although the management of the network bandwidth is primarily the responsibility of the network manager, the system manager should identify priority or mission-critical applications that need to be guaranteed a minimum bandwidth to ensure that the high level of service is maintained.

Solstice Bandwidth Manager allows the available network bandwidth to be allocated to either a particular type of service (such as Telnet, FTP, or HTTP) or a specific department or customer. A series of rules dictate how the bandwidth is allocated, but flexibility is allowed, for example, if there is spare capacity when an application has used all its allocation.

This product comes with monitoring and statistics collection so that accurate usage and performance figures can be recorded. These can also be used to help determine whether SLA targets have been achieved or whether the allocation of bandwidth needs to be changed to make better use of the available resource.

Solstice Adminsuite

Solstice Adminsuite is a collection of commands and graphical tools that together enable the system administrator to carry out tasks on remote systems from a central location. Adminsuite is delivered as part of the Server release of the Solaris operating environment; it provides the functionality for managing users, groups, hosts, printers, disks and file systems, system configuration files, terminals, and modems. Admintool is a similar tool that allows basic administration of the local host only, without the host or disk and file system management aspects.

Figure 14.10 shows the initial screen that is displayed when the tool is launched.

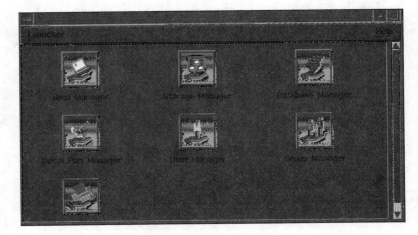

Figure 14.10 The launcher tool is configurable so that other applications can be added or existing ones can be hidden.

Solstice Adminsuite contains a number of applications, briefly described here:

- **Host Manager**—The Host Manager is used to manage clients and hosts on the network. Using this application, an administrator can add or delete operating system services, create AutoClient configurations, and set up remote install servers, such as those used for Jumpstart configurations.

- **Storage Manager**—There are two components of this application, Disk Manager and File System Manager. Together, they allow partitioning and formatting of drives as well as the creation and maintenance of file systems, including making them available via NFS to other remote systems.

- **Database Manager**—This application allows editing and management of the main configuration files, such as the hosts file and others within the /etc/ directory. The facility is available for the local system, remote systems, and an entire NIS domain, if present.

- **User Manager**—This application provides user account management and enables defaults to be set for handling password aging, identifying the user's email server, and setting the login shell.

- **Group Manager**—When a name service is being used, the Group Manager can add, modify, or delete groups for the NIS domain. If no name service is in use, it can be used to edit the /etc/group files on remote systems.

- **Serial Port Manager**—This application is used to install and manage the services for terminals or modems. All necessary files are created by the application, and standard template configurations are also provided to make the setup procedure easier.

- **Printer Manager**—With this application, you can install, modify, and delete printers on a Solaris LP server. The printers can also be centrally managed if a name service, such as NIS, is being used. In this way, printers become available to all clients running the SunSoft print client software.

Other Network Management Products

Multivendor environments that have not previously been managing Solaris-based systems might already be running a network management product. In these instances, it is not always the best solution to install a new product because the existing one might be capable of incorporating any Solaris systems into the current configuration. A number of network management products provide full support for the Solaris operating environment in the form of agents or additional modules. Four of these are listed here, along with the World Wide Web address for each.

- Unicenter from Computer Associates, at `http://www.computerassociates.com`
- Netview from Tivoli, at `http://www.tivoli.com`
- Openview from Hewlett-Packard, at `http://www.openview.hp.com`
- Patrol from BMC software, at `http://www.bmc.com/patrol`

Which Tool(s) Do I Need?

The system manager must decide which network management tools are appropriate for the environment in which the systems reside. In larger companies, some form of network management is essential to be able to monitor and administer the potentially large number of remote nodes.

The Solstice Domain/Site Manager combination is ideal for large companies requiring remote administration and management, particularly where sites are running on a 24×7 basis but may not always have staff on site. In this instance, the network management role can be transferred to be a central support position, where multiple sites can be effectively managed.

For smaller networks and environments, it is often a matter of personal choice whether a network management solution is suitable or justified. The software can be expensive to deploy and obviously needs to be maintained. Some companies leave the network monitoring and management entirely to the network manager, concentrating solely on the systems themselves and relying on the network section for advice and support.

Summary

Network management has become a necessary part of running a busy computing environment to deliver the type of service that the customer expects in a cost-effective way. Sun Microsystems provides products to manage such environments.

Solstice Site Manager and Solstice Domain Manager deliver a fully scalable solution to manage a small single-site operation with fewer than 100 nodes, right up to a large enterprise environment with up to 10,000 nodes. A key benefit of these products is that the application is the same if running on a small SPARCstation or the largest enterprise server.

The Cooperative Consoles product, supplied with Solstice Domain and Site Manager software, enables management consoles to share information and management of the network of Solaris systems. In this way, remote sites can be managed easily on a 24×7 basis, eliminating the need for staff to be present at the sites outside normal business hours.

Mission-critical applications and services can be allocated guaranteed network bandwidth using Solstice Bandwidth Manager, and detailed statistical information can be used to evaluate SLA performance against agreed targets.

Remote system administration of multiple Solaris systems is possible using Solstice Adminsuite, a product that comes as standard with the Server edition of the Solaris operating environment. With centrally managed administration, it is easier to maintain standards of system configurations throughout the organization, making the task of managing the systems much easier.

Resources

Getting Help

The days of wading through countless hard-copy computer manuals are over. A vast amount of information and documentation is available, if you know where to find it and have the necessary access. This section discusses sources of information and help that can answer virtually any Sun- or Solaris-related question and satisfy virtually any requirement—all without you picking up a single book.

Online Manual Pages

A comprehensive set of manual pages is supplied with the Solaris operating environment, but they are installed by default only with the Developer and Entire Distribution configuration options. They contain online help for all the available commands, programming functions, and procedures, as well as a number of configuration files, such as syslog.conf, used for configuring the system-logging daemon, syslogd. The base directory location for the manual pages is normally /usr/share/man or /usr/man. (/usr/man is a symbolic link to /usr/share/man, the physical location of the manual pages.)

The majority of applications installed as Solaris packages also contain manual pages for the specific product. Most of the public domain software installs manual pages by default to the directory /usr/local/man. You can access these extra pages in two ways: by choosing the /usr/share/man location for help files as part of the package installation, or by appending the location of the manual pages (in this example, /usr/local/man) to the variable MANPATH.

Online manual pages can be accessed from the shell (command line) using the man command—or, if you're in a windowing environment such as OpenWindows or CDE, there is also a GUI version called xman. Figure A.1 shows the xman window that appears.

Figure A.1 The small size of the initial window is ideal for keeping it on the desktop for the duration of the session.

xman uses the MANPATH variable to search for valid locations of manual pages. Figure A.2 shows the manual page for the top command, a public domain utility that installs by default into /usr/local.

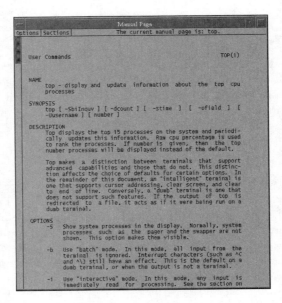

Figure A.2 The scrollbar facility allows easy navigation of the entire manual page.

Answerbook Software

A CD-ROM containing documentation is supplied with the Solaris operating environment. This information contains Solaris manuals, which are fully searchable so that queries can be run against the entire set, showing only the relevant parts of each guide. The Answerbook CD-ROM also contains the manual pages. Figure A.3 shows the initial screen that is displayed when the Answerbook software is started, which is done by selecting the Answerbook2 option from the workspace Help menu.

Figure A.3   The fully searchable documentation collections eliminate the need to look in several different locations for the required information.

Sunsolve

Sunsolve provides important information and resources for Sun customers, including Solaris patches, a comprehensive symptoms and resolution database, white papers, information documents, bug reports, frequently asked questions (FAQ), and an early notification section. These are all available to customers with a SunSpectrum support contract and can be accessed in either of two ways: on the World Wide Web, or using a set of CD-ROMs that are sent to the system manager or administrator on a regular basis.

To use Sunsolve online, go to `http://sunsolve.sun.com` and register. You will need the SunSpectrum contract number to gain full access to all the resources listed previously. Even if you don't have a current SunSpectrum support contract, you can access a limited set of resources, including free patches and descriptions, patch reports, StarOffice support, and Sun security bulletins. Figure A.4 shows the online user interface that is displayed for non-SunSpectrum account holders.

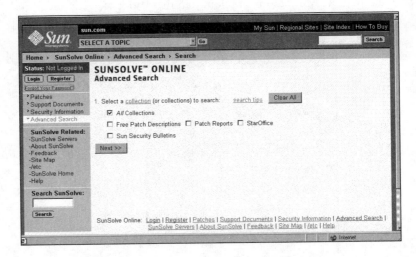

Figure A.4   Sun provides access to important information and resources even if you don't have a current support contract.

The Sunsolve CD-ROMs (currently four per issue) contain the Sunsolve database as well as three CD-ROMs of patches. To use the Sunsolve CD-ROM, simply insert it into the CD drive. If you are using volume management, then the file manager window will appear and the `sunsolve` command can be executed. This starts a Netscape window. Choose the Power Search option to look for specific information. Figure A.5 shows the initial screen where you select the scope of the search.

Figure A.5   The scope of the query can be easily customized to suit user requirements.

Next, enter the required search criteria. As an example, I entered a search for information from all the available collections on "system tuning." Figure A.6 shows this screen.

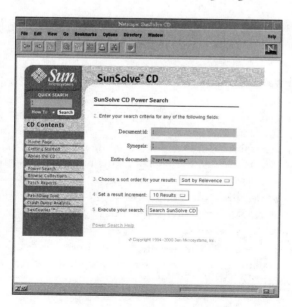

Figure A.6   Sunsolve provides flexibility in searching by using keywords or text strings.

When the criteria has been entered, the search of the Sunsolve database executes. The resulting references to Sunsolve documents are then shown. The results for the example query on "system tuning" are shown in Figure A.7.

Figure A.7 The results can be viewed by clicking on the relevant hyperlink—or, if too many results are shown, the query can be refined.

Sun Documentation Online

Sun Microsystems makes available a vast amount of product documentation on the World Wide Web at `http://docs.sun.com`. The site is fully searchable and contains support for many different languages. A large number of the manuals can be downloaded as PDF files for subsequent reading or printing using Adobe Acrobat Reader.

A useful feature of the site is that it contains a number of contexts through which refined searches can be carried out. Four main categories can be used for searching:

- **Search the entire docs.sun collection**—This searches the whole site without any restriction. Vague search criteria will probably produce unmanageable numbers of results.

- **Browse by subject**—This allows a restricted browse or search by categorizing into system administration, programming, desktop manuals, hardware, or the manual pages.

- **Browse by collection**—A collection is a set of books that might relate to a specific product or suite of products, or that might be aimed at a specific audience. An individual book can be a member of more than one collection, so there might be duplication where the contents of collections overlap.

- **Browse by product**—A refined search can be carried out based on either hardware or software. This option contains information about the Sun product range, such as servers, workstations and storage options, as well as development software products, PC compatibility, resource management software, and clustering. This list is by no means exhaustive, but it provides an initial insight into the type of information available.

The Sun product documentation site contains a comprehensive help facility to aid effective searching and also offers the option to select from the most frequently requested information, such as Solaris 8 or enterprise servers.

Further Reading

Clark, Tom. *Designing Storage Area Networks*. Addison-Wesley, 1999.

Freeland, Curt. *Solaris 8 for Managers and Administrators*. Delmar, 2000.

Kasper, Paul and Alan McClellan. *Automating Solaris Installations—A Custom Jumpstart Guide*. Sunsoft/Prentice Hall, 1995.

Laurie, Ben and Peter Laurie. *Apache—The Definitive Guide*. O'Reilly, 1999.

Lewis, Lundy. *Service Level Management for Enterprise Networks*. Artech House, 1999.

Loshin, Peter. *IPv6 Clearly Explained*. AP Professional, 1998.

Salus, Peter. *A Quarter Century of Unix*. Addison Wesley, 1994. (This is an excellent book if you want to know the real history of the operating system and how Sun Microsystems came into existence.)

Siever, Spainhour, and Patwardhan. *Perl in a Nutshell*. O'Reilly, 1999.

Sturm, Rick. *Foundations of Service Level Management*. Sams Publishing, 2000.

Useful References on the World Wide Web

http://www.cerias.purdue.edu/coast: Computer Operations, Audit, and Security Technology (COAST)—the computer sciences department at Purdue University—carries out computer security research. You can find lots of useful security information here.

http://www.cert.org: Formerly known as the Computer Emergency Response Team, CERT is a center of Internet security expertise. From here, you can subscribe to a regular mailing list.

http://www.gocsi.com: The Computer Security Institute maintains this site.

http://www.ipv6.org: This site dedicated to IPv6 contains information and useful links as well as a FAQ.

`http://www.latech.edu/sunman.html`: The Sun manager's searchable archive. This site contains summaries of the popular mailing lists going back to 1991.

`http://playground.sun.com/pub/ipng/html/ipng-main.html`: This site provides an excellent introduction to IPv6.

`http://www.sans.org`: This is the site of the SANS research and education organization. Subscribe here to receive regular news and security alerts. The biggest Unix system admin salary survey can be downloaded from here as well.

`http://www.searchsolaris.com`: A more recent Solaris site, full of news, reviews, events, recommended links, and tips. The site has a system management section containing useful links to articles and documents.

`http://www.solarisguide.com`: An unofficial guide to the Solaris operating environment, full of news, man pages, reviews, and RFCs. This site was founded by John Mulligan, author of *Solaris Essential Reference*.

`http://www.sun.com`: The main Sun Microsystems Web presence.

`http://www.sunfreeware.com`: The place to download public domain software for use with Solaris. The site offers versions for virtually all versions of SPARC- and INTEL-based systems.

`http://sunsolve.sun.com/`: Support information, patches, bug reports, security reports, and white papers—free areas and contract-only areas.

`http://www.unixinsider.com`: Formerly www.sunworld.com, This is an online magazine designed for the Sun community.

`http://www.e-recovery.com`: Web site for disaster recovery options offered by Sungard.

`http://www.survive.com`: A business continuity group for management professionals.

`http://www.perl.com/perl/`: The home page for Perl, for news, source code, documentation and more on the subject of Perl.

`http://www.apache.org`: Home of the Apache Software Foundation.

`http://www.cio.com`: An excellent resource for IT managers.

`http://www.securityportal.com`: Extensive security information. This site also has a great article on "Firewalling with IPF."

Index

Q-R

HOW TO CONTACT US

VISIT OUR WEB SITE

WWW.NEWRIDERS.COM

On our Web site, you'll find information about our other books, authors, tables of contents, and book errata. You will also find information about book registration and how to purchase our books, both domestically and internationally.

EMAIL US

Contact us at: **nrfeedback@newriders.com**

- If you have comments or questions about this book
- To report errors that you have found in this book
- If you have a book proposal to submit or are interested in writing for New Riders
- If you are an expert in a computer topic or technology and are interested in being a technical editor who reviews manuscripts for technical accuracy

Contact us at: **nreducation@newriders.com**

- If you are an instructor from an educational institution who wants to preview New Riders books for classroom use. Email should include your name, title, school, department, address, phone number, office days/hours, text in use, and enrollment, along with your request for desk/examination copies and/or additional information.

Contact us at: **nrmedia@newriders.com**

- If you are a member of the media who is interested in reviewing copies of New Riders books. Send your name, mailing address, and email address, along with the name of the publication or Web site you work for.

BULK PURCHASES/CORPORATE SALES

If you are interested in buying 10 or more copies of a title or want to set up an account for your company to purchase directly from the publisher at a substantial discount, contact us at 800-382-3419 or email your contact information to corpsales@pearsontechgroup.com. A sales representative will contact you with more information.

WRITE TO US

New Riders Publishing
201 W. 103rd St.
Indianapolis, IN 46290-1097

CALL/FAX US

Toll-free (800) 571-5840
If outside U.S. (317) 581-3500
Ask for New Riders
FAX: (317) 581-4663

New Riders

W I N D O W S   2 0 0 0

ISBN: 0735709211
800 pages
US $49.99

MySQL

Paul DuBois

MySQL teaches readers how to use the tools provided by the MySQL distribution, by covering installation, setup, daily use, security, optimization, maintenance, and troubleshooting. It also discusses important third-party tools, such as the Perl DBI and Apache/PHP interfaces that provide access to MySQL.

ISBN: 0735710074
400 pages
US $34.99

Solaris 8 Essential Reference

John Mulligan

A great companion to the solarisguide.com website, *So 8 Essential Reference* assumes readers are well-versed in general UNIX skills and simp need some pointers on how get the most out of Solaris. book provides clear and con instruction on how to perfor important administration and management tasks.

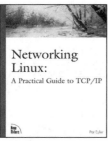

ISBN: 0735710317
400 pages
US$39.99

Networking Linux: A Practical Guide to TCP/IP

Pat Eyler

This book goes beyond the conceptual and shows step-by-step the necessary know-how to Linux TCP/IP implementation. Ideal for programmers and networking administrators in need of a platform-specific guide in order to increase their knowledge and overall efficiency.

ISBN: 0735708770
672 pages
US$39.99

CLP Fast Track: Lotus Notes/Domino 5 Application Developme

Tim Bankes and Dave Hatter

After honing our skills with coverage of the Release 4 ex New Riders has approached R5 exams by offering CLP candidates just what they ne know to pass the exams. We again partnered with Lotus professionals to bring exam candidates the most accurate information for exam preparation.

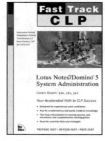

ISBN: 0735709920
960 pages
US $39.99

CLP Fast Track: Lotus Notes/Domino 5 System Administration

Tony Aveyard, Jay Forlini, Karen Fishwick

This *Fast Track* is intended fo networking professionals wh familiar with the intricacies o Lotus Notes and provides th best way for more-advanced candidates to learn how to p the Lotus certification exam upgrades. Lotus has restructu the exam process so that all required exams are geared directly toward skills that an administrator will need to us